READER'S DIGEST

BEGINNER'S GUIDE TO HOME

COMPUTING

Microsoft® Windows®
vista™
edition

Reader's
Digest

PUBLISHED BY THE READER'S DIGEST ASSOCIATION LIMITED
LONDON • NEW YORK • SYDNEY • MONTREAL

A READER'S DIGEST BOOK

Published by The Reader's Digest Association Limited
11 Westferry Circus
Canary Wharf
London E14 4HE
www.readersdigest.co.uk

We are committed to both the quality of our products and the service we
provide to our customers. We value your comments so please feel free to
call us on 08705 113366, or via our website at www.readersdigest.co.uk.
If you have any comments about the content of any of our books, you can
contact us at gbeditorial@readersdigest.co.uk

Based on *Beginner's Guide to Home Computing* (first published 1997)
and subsequently updated editions
This paperback edition Copyright © VNU Business Publications 2007

A CIP data record for this book is available from the British Library

This book was designed, edited and produced by Eaglemoss Publications Ltd
in association with VNU Business Publications Ltd,
based on the partwork *Easy PC*

Printed in Singapore

® Reader's Digest, The Digest and the Pegasus logo are registered trademarks
of The Reader's Digest Association, Inc., of Pleasantville, New York, USA

ISBN 978 0 276 44302 2
Book code 410-710 UP0000-1
Oracle code 250011366S

10 9 8 7 6 5 4 3 2 1

Croydon Libraries

You are welcome to borrow this book for up to 28 days.
If you do not return or renew it by the latest date stamped
below you will be asked to pay overdue charges. You may
renew books in person, by phoning 0208 726 6900 or via the
Council's website www.croydon.gov.uk

CROYDON COUNCIL
www.croydon.gov.uk

Contents

GETTING STARTED

Welcome!

This is the essential guide to everything you need to know about computing for the home, the small office and, most important of all, the family. PCs are no longer a luxury. We all use them in one way or another – at work, in school or college and at home. Computers have become an important means of storing and using information, as well as for playing games. They have even opened up totally new ways of learning.

With a computer you can do some everyday things with more flair and ease. You can write letters, monitor your bank accounts and keep track of names and addresses. But, on top of that, there are a number of new things you can do with the more modern multimedia computers. These allow you to find information easily, show pictures and play sounds and movies.

Then there's the Internet, which allows you to search the world's computers for information on any topic you can think of, from aardvarks to zephyrs. You can also get in touch with other computer users worldwide and exchange information. And that's all for little more than the cost of a local phone call.

For many of us, computers still seem complicated and frightening. Yet anyone who has watched children using computers will know that this can't really be true. Once you've broken through the barriers of jargon that surround using a computer, you'll find this box of electronics is no more difficult to work than a CD or a DVD player. And it can do a whole lot more for you.

This beginner's book on home computing is here to guide you through the jargon. We'll explain in plain English what all the components do. We'll guide you towards the products you can buy. And we'll suggest useful and fun projects you can try out. Each section concentrates on specific topics, from using basic software to going on-line. This is a complete reference work for anyone new to the world of personal computers.

You'll soon find that a CD-ROM is no more a mystery than an audio CD player, and computer memory is something you will understand and not have to think about. Computers are changing all the time, and here you'll find information on what is worth looking for and why. If you own a multimedia computer running Microsoft Windows Vista, this book will help you get the most out of your PC. ●

Green PCs

Your PC

A PC has two main elements: the hardware and the software. The hardware consists of the parts of your PC that you can hold, touch and see. The computer itself, the monitor, the printer, the mouse, the modem, the add-on boards that plug into the PC, even the cables, are all examples of hardware.

The *system box* contains the computer's main electronics and additional parts, such as the hard disk, memory and display cards.

The *monitor* displays everything you are working on, usually in full colour. It uses LCD, or Liquid Crystal Display, and can handle high resolutions while using less electricity than the old TV-type monitor (known as CRT or Cathode Ray Tube).

The *mouse* is used to control the software and move around the screen. You need a mouse pad or mat with an even but slightly rough surface to allow the mouse to move smoothly. This will also help it stay clean.

Your PC may have internal or external *speakers,* which you can use for stereo-quality sound when playing CDs and games.

The *keyboard* is used to enter text and numbers, control the software and move around the screen.

Why a PC?

Most people will buy a desktop PC, which is one that sits permanently on your desk, as opposed to a portable one that you carry around with you. In addition to the PC itself, you will probably buy extra pieces of hardware called peripherals, such as a printer or a scanner.

The *printer* prints out your documents. There are black-and-white and colour printers, mains and portable printers, and low-cost good-quality and more expensive high-quality printers.

The computer may also have a *modem* that connects to your telephone line. This lets you join the worldwide community of computer users on the Internet. Most new computers have modems built in but external modems are also available such as the one here. A broadband or cable modem gives you 'always on' high-speed access to the Internet.

The computer we know as the PC is built around an original design created by IBM. Because IBM didn't mind if other people used its basic concepts, many other manufacturers started producing personal computers that copied the way the IBM PC functioned. As more of these copies of IBM PCs – called clones – came on the market, more software companies decided to start writing programs for them. In turn, that encouraged more manufacturers to make IBM PC-type computers.

The situation has snowballed to the point where the PC, PC components and software for the PC are now produced by hundreds of thousands of different organisations, making the PC the world's most successful type of computer. This is why we will be concentrating on PC products. Whether your PC is made by Hewlett Packard or Viglen, it will work in much the same way and it will run the same PC software.

Apple Macintosh

Apple started making its own type of personal computer at around the same time that the PC was born. Its system was incompatible with PC hardware and software. But Apple had a big advantage that made it successful. It was the first company to use pictures and windows – years before Microsoft Windows became popular. It also made plug-and-play machines. This meant people did not have to buy so many extra bits and pieces to do the things they wanted to do. For example, Apple machines already had a sound capability included, which made them easy and fun to use compared to the early PCs.

The Mac, as it is now affectionately called, became the preferred computer for people in the more creative fields, such as architects, musicians and designers, who needed a powerful and easy-to-use computer. The Mac is still the main alternative to the PC, and Windows Vista can run on the latest machines alongside the Apple operating system. However, Macs are not universally used, because unlike IBM, Apple has been reluctant to let anyone copy the design of its computers.

The rest

While many manufacturers followed the IBM PC design, others developed their own computer systems. These were incompatible with the PC, so hardware and software developed for one system won't work on the other. But, freed from IBM's way of doing things, these manufacturers could make home computers that were better in other respects. They may be much cheaper, better at playing games, or better at handling sound and pictures. Many of these computer systems are excellent but tend to be used mainly by people with an interest in a specific function.

Inside your

Processors

The microprocessor, or processor – aka the CPU (central processing unit) – is the brain of the computer. It's the main chip on the motherboard and works almost like a supercalculator that does the calculations it is told to do by the computer programs.

To look at, the processor resembles an After Eight mint with small pins attached. You can identify a processor by the number on its top, which tells you how powerful it is.

One of the first PCs built used a processor designed by Intel. Intel gave it the reference number 8086. After that, Intel gave each new generation of processors a new number: 80286, 80386 and 80486, which was shortened to 486. Intel has broken away from this tradition with its latest generation of processors, called Pentiums, although they are still referred to by some as the 586.

Processors are also measured by how fast they perform. This value is given in megahertz, abbreviated to MHz. The bigger the MHz number, the faster the processor.

Some software programs, like word processors, do not need much in the way of mathematical calculation power. Others, like spreadsheets or programs that display complex computer-created images, need lots of additional calculation power. The latest PCs now feature dual-core processors – that is two processors using the same chip. As a result, your PC can handle several things at once – such as browsing the Internet while listening to your favourite radio station – without affecting other tasks.

ook inside any PC and you will see similar items of hardware. They all have motherboards, processors, disk drives, power supplies and memory chips. Many of these items are built to a fixed set of standards. This means that these parts are interchangeable and that computers can be fairly easily upgraded with additional items of hardware, which just plug into the main system.

It's worth getting to know your way around the insides of your PC. There may come a time when you want to add more memory or an expansion card for a special purpose, such as a fax/modem or wireless networking. But remember, never open your PC when it's connected to mains power.

The *CD-ROM/DVD-ROM drive* has become an important part of the multimedia PC. Each CD-ROM disc can hold a vast amount of data, pictures, video and sound. But the standard CD-ROM discs are what is called 'read only'. You cannot store your own data on them. Most new PCs have a DVD drive. DVD, originally 'digital video disc', now stands for 'digital versatile disc'. DVD-ROM is a faster and more sophisticated multimedia tool than the CD-ROM. Many PCs also come with a CD or DVD rewriter drive that enables you to record over a disc many times.

USB ports allow you to connect external devices, such as a scanner, to your PC.

The *on/off button* switches power to the computer and its power outlets.

Integrated sound ports allow you to connect a microphone, headphones and speakers to your PC.

PC

The *motherboard* contains all the main electronics of your computer, including the main chip that does all the processing. The *BIOS chip* also lives on the motherboard. BIOS stands for 'basic input/output system' and is pronounced 'bye-oss'. This chip is responsible for making sure that all parts of the computer communicate with one another. It is permanently programmed with the instructions your computer needs to follow when it is switched on and loads the operating system from the disk. It also translates complex instructions from the CPU into information understood by devices such as the keyboard.

Additional memory chips can be plugged into the *spare slots* to increase your PC's internal memory capacity.

The *power supply* turns the mains power into the 5V and 12V low voltage power feeds needed by the motherboard, disk drives and additional cards plugged into the expansion slots.

Random access memory (RAM) chips are used by the computer for temporary storage of the program you are using and all the data you are working on. RAM is measured in megabytes (MB).

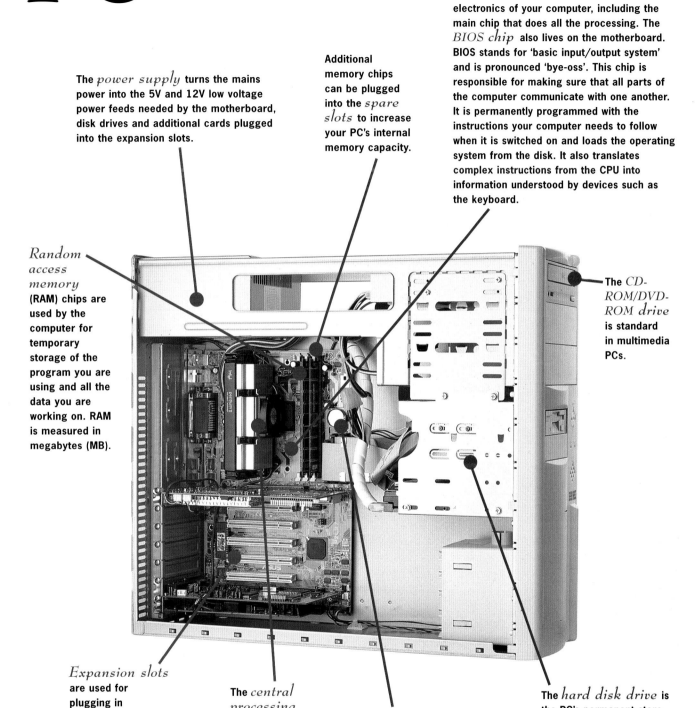

The *CD-ROM/DVD-ROM drive* is standard in multimedia PCs.

Expansion slots are used for plugging in additional cards with special functions, such as a fax/modem, and to enable wireless networking.

The *central processing unit* (CPU) chip is the heart of your computer. All the real computing work is done by the CPU.

The PC uses a small *battery* to supply power to several special memory chips when the computer is switched off. These chips store such information as the computer's setup details and the time and date.

The *hard disk drive* is the PC's permanent store of programs and data. The data is recorded on a small disk covered in a magnetic material that is similar to the surface of a cassette tape. Hard disk size is measured in gigabytes (GB), and most new PCs have disks of 80GB–320GB or more.

Input

The computing process breaks down into three areas: input, processing and output. Inputting to the PC gets information into the system and gives you control over the instructions you send to the computer. Processing, which is carried out by the software and the computer processor, follows your instructions to do all the things you want to do with the information. Finally, output hands the results back to you.

It's just like a washing machine. You input water, dirty clothes and washing powder; the machine washes, or processes, the clothes by going through various wash, rinse and spin cycles; and the output is clean clothes.

There is a whole range of devices that will feed your computer information. The mouse and keyboard are the most obvious, but microphones, image scanners and digital cameras are all input devices that you may use. An input device can be anything that takes information from the outside world and turns it into data that the computer can understand. Every piece of information, whether it is being entered at that moment or has been taken from something prepared earlier and stored on disk, has first of all to go through an input device of some sort.

At a glance

- Keyboard
- Mouse
- Scanner
- Digital camera
- Webcam
- TV card
- Modem

Keyboard and mouse

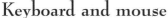

The input devices that everyone recognises are the keyboard and the mouse. The PC's keyboard is essential. It has a typewriter keyboard, a calculator number pad, a set of function keys that allow you to do specific tasks, and a set of direction keys with arrows for moving around the screen. The mouse is much better at the job of navigating around the screen and is particularly useful for software that calls for drawing and retouching pictures.

Sound

Sound cards turn sound into digital information. They take the sound from a CD, hi-fi or microphone and convert it into digital audio in the same way that sound is digitally recorded in a studio for a CD. The sound card can take in real sound and the special MIDI ('musical instrument digital interface') information used by music synthesisers and electronic keyboards. So a PC can be used as the heart of a home music studio. With the right sound card, you can plug a MIDI box into your computer. Then plug the MIDI cables from your musical instruments into the box and you'll have your very own orchestra.

Scanners

What sound cards do for sound, scanners do for pictures. The scanner uses sensors to pick up different colours and areas of light and dark on a printed picture or slide. This produces a digital version of the image, which is passed to the PC. The scanner scans the image into the PC in much the same way that a photocopier does. Then you will be able to see the image on the screen. You can buy cheaper hand scanners, which you pass over the picture yourself.

Digital camera

Digital cameras do away with the film you would normally use in a camera. They turn the image directly into a digital picture that your computer can use. You can take a picture with a digital camera, then connect it to your PC and download the image so you can see it on your computer screen.

Webcams

Add a mini camera – called a webcam – to your PC and with a microphone for the sound you've got a ready-made video-phone. Some webcams have a built-in microphone, but for others you'll need to plug a separate microphone into your PC. To video call someone else who has a webcam attached to their PC you can use Windows Live Messenger. To install it, go to the All Programs menu on the Start button and select Windows Live Messenger Download.

TV

There are TV input cards that allow you to use your PC to watch, or even record, TV programmes on your computer.

Joysticks

As well as general input devices, like the keyboard and mouse, there are those designed for specific applications. There are joysticks and pilot controls for games and flight simulators, which are programs that imitate piloting an aeroplane.

Other computers

It's not only you who can communicate with your computer. Other computers can input information, too. In many offices, computers are connected electronically to form what's called a network. Once connected, you can take information from any of the other computers on the network and use it on your own PC.

The computers do not all have to be in the same building. By using a modem, which connects your computer to the telephone line, you can link up with a computer anywhere in the world and receive information from it in the form of messages and files. This is the whole basis of the Internet, which uses the national and international phone system to create a worldwide network of computers large and small. The Internet contains every type of information you could possibly want to access on your PC at home.

Output

At a glance

● **Monitor**
● **Inkjet/laser printer**
● **Sound card**
● **Headphones/speakers**

Being able to input information and process it would be a pointless exercise if you couldn't get it back out of your PC. As with input systems, there are some very common output devices. You obviously can't live without something as vital as a monitor, but when it comes to printers or headphones, you might decide to buy these later. However, if you want to buy them from the start, you may find that you can get a good deal from the vendor.

Monitors

No PC can be without a monitor, or display. For PCs the display is a colour monitor, with more than a passing resemblance to a small colour TV. First, the computer sends the display information to the display card inside your PC. That turns it into a video signal that your monitor can display as a picture. Over the years, the quality of images produced by a PC has increased enormously. The first PCs could show only single-colour text, while today's display cards and monitors can produce more detail than a good TV and show over 16 million colours.

Laptop computers have a flat-screen display that uses technology similar to that used in calculators. The difference is that these computer screens can show pictures and not just numbers – and they're also in colour.

Printers

The printer does the same job as the monitor, except the words and pictures are printed on paper rather than shown on a screen. The process is much the same. The computer sends the information to be printed to the printer card inside your PC. That turns it into an image of the page that your printer can reproduce on paper.

There are two common types of printer for the home user: inkjet (some are called bubblejets) and laser. The best can produce copies of almost magazine quality – quietly, quickly and in full colour.

Inkjet printers work by spraying tiny dots of ink on to the paper. Inkjets are virtually silent in operation. They can print to a high quality, and most print reasonably well in colour. They are not that expensive and are the most popular type of printer for home computer users.

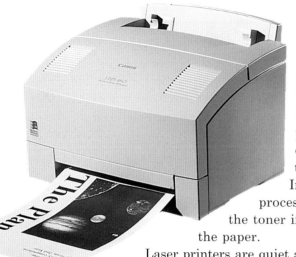

Laser printers work in much the same way as photocopiers. An image is beamed on to a metal drum by a small laser. Toner powder is transferred via the drum on to a sheet of paper, thus transferring the image. In the final stage of the process, the paper is heated and the toner image bonds to the paper.

Laser printers are quiet and can produce the highest print quality – ideal for graphics and desktop publishing, although they are more expensive to buy than inkjet printers. The speed varies from one model to another, and is measured in pages per minute, abbreviated to ppm. Basic models can print at up to 12ppm while the more advanced home laser printers can generally print at up to 24 or 48ppm or more. Colour laser printers are also available. Once very expensive, they are becoming more affordable.

Sound cards

The sound card that records sound and music can also be used for play-back. When connected to speakers, a PC's stereo sound can be as good as CD quality. PC sound is used for music and effects in games, as well as educational and reference software. It can add small audio cues to everyday programs to tell you that the right or wrong keys have been pressed. However, one of the most common uses for sound on the PC is simply to play audio CDs or music you have downloaded while you are working!

Headphones and speakers

There's no point in having a sound card if you can't hear what it is outputting. For that you need headphones or a set of speakers. You will probably have to buy these separately. You may find that you already have a set of headphones for a personal stereo system that will fit the audio output jack on the back of your PC. You can choose from all kinds of speakers, depending on the sound quality you want.

Processing

Processing is the job of the software and the computer's central processor. It takes the information you have entered and processes it the way you want. There is a huge range of software to handle different sorts of data in different ways, from word processing and painting to playing music on a synthesiser via your PC. The section on software on page 16 will give you a better idea of the range of software available. But, whatever the process, every software program produces a result that has to be sent to your PC's output so you can see or hear it.

Software

Software is the collective name for all types of computer programs. Software programs are simply a huge set of instructions that make your PC do something useful. They tell your PC what to do with the information you are feeding into it, what to show on screen and what to print.

Software is usually supplied as a digital download if bought on-line, or on CD-ROM discs from which you transfer the program to your PC's hard disk. When you buy a PC, the important software items, such as Windows, should already be loaded on to the hard disk.

When you want to run a particular software program, such as a word processor or a spreadsheet program, you turn your PC on and choose the program you need. Programs are represented by a small picture, or icon, on the screen. The PC finds the program on the hard disk, loads it into the PC's memory bank and gets it ready for you to use.

In this book we concentrate on software that works with Microsoft Windows Vista, which is the latest operating system available for most PCs today. Windows Vista presents you with graphics, images, icons and lists of choices called menus, which make it easy to use. This type of software is called a graphical user interface or GUI (pronounced 'gooey'). When you look at the screen, 'what you see is what you get' when you start printing, so Windows is an example of what's become known as a WYSIWYG (pronounced 'wizzywig') program.

If you buy Windows-compatible programs, they will work with Windows. Once you have mastered the way Windows works, you can often work your way around any Windows-compatible program, no matter how new it is to you.

There is a software program for every conceivable job. Each main category of software will be covered in depth later in the book. Here we give you an introductory overview of the more important types of software.

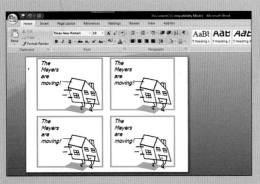

Desktop publishing
If you want to produce a newsletter, magazine or even a CD label, you will need a desktop publishing program – usually called DTP. These programs can handle graphics and fancy lettering.

Word processors
This is software for creating letters and documents like these 'Moving House' postcards. You can type in text and make it look the way you want it to on paper. Word processors often include a spell checker. If you are not sure of your spelling, the computer will check it for you and give you the correct spelling.

Spreadsheets and accounting software
These are used mainly in business. They make manipulating rows of figures quick and simple. As well as doing calculations, they have excellent report-printing facilities that can extract essential information and present it neatly. There are also accounting programs to help you keep track of your personal finances.

Graphics

Graphics software offers almost limitless possibilities, from creating your own pictures to retouching photographs, as above with Windows Photo Gallery. There are also computer-aided drawing, or CAD, programs, which are ideal for creating highly accurate plans and drawings. CAD programs are usually very sophisticated. They often have the ability to draw in two or three dimensions and are generally used by architects and product designers.

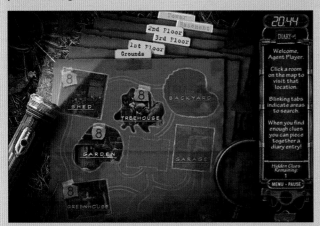

Games

For some, games are the best excuse to buy a computer. Many titles that are available for games consoles also have PC versions, and there are many specially developed PC games with stunning visuals and sound, such as MCF: Ravenhearst.

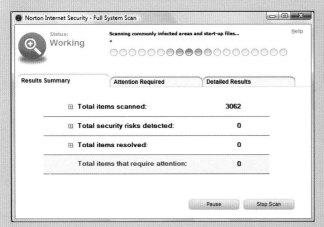

Utilities

Like most pieces of equipment, your computer needs to be maintained. Most of the maintenance work is done not with a screwdriver but with utility software. Utilities help check that everything is working well. They can organise your hard disk and clear out unwanted programs. They will back up files for safety and check for viruses.

Databases

These are filing-cabinet programs that enable you to store all kinds of lists and then instantly find the data you want. You can load as much information as you like and then ask the program to sort the entries.

Communications

Increasingly, people want to use their computers to talk with others. There is a huge range of communications software to do this. This software can hunt out computers around the world on the Internet that contain information you might be interested in. You can also use the Internet to find out information on almost anything you can think of.

Edutainment

This software merges education with entertainment. It covers topics from architecture and animals to robots and reference works. Many programs mix text, graphics, sound, music, animation and movie clips, all in one program.

Will it work?

How do I keep up?

Software is likely to be replaced much more frequently than hardware. This is not because it wears out but because the makers keep thinking of new things you can do with a program. When you buy a software program from one of the larger software companies, such as Microsoft or Corel, you can usually buy the upgraded version at a reduced price.

Some programs will run on very basic PCs. Others need lots of power and memory and several different extras, such as sound cards. Check out whether the software will work on your PC by looking on the panel at the back of the box. This tells you how powerful your computer must be and what facilities it needs to run the program. If the word *recommended* is used, beware! For example, it may say the software requires 64MB of RAM, but 128MB is recommended. Usually this means you need 128MB or the program won't perform up to expectations.

One question you should ask yourself if you are buying a games program is does it support a controller and joystick? For the committed gamer, a controller or joystick gives better results than using a keyboard or mouse. Also check whether the game can be played on-line. If so, you'll need Internet access. How much hard drive space does the program need? While the game featured below takes little space, some, such as Microsoft Flight Simulator X, take up a massive 14GB! Always make sure you have sufficient space free on your PC or the game won't run properly.

When you buy a PC, it will normally be loaded with *Windows*. Make sure, though, that your version of the operating system is advanced enough to cope with the demands of the game.

It needs a *3-D display card* to capture all the graphical richness of the game.

To use Lego Star Wars® II, you need:

- Multimedia PC with a Pentium 3 1.0GHz or AMD Athlon 1000MHz processor or higher
- Microsoft® Windows® Windows XP (Service Pack 2) or Windows Vista
- 256MB of RAM
- 64MB 3-D Graphics Card with Vortex and Pixel Shader (VS/PS) capability
- Keyboard and Microsoft Mouse or compatible pointing device
- Quad speed or faster CD-ROM drive

It needs a computer with a *Pentium 3 processor* as a minimum. A faster processor will make the program run more smoothly.

It needs at least 256MB of *internal memory* to work.

If your *mouse* works with Windows, it will work with this program too.

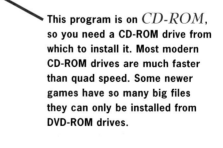

This program is on *CD-ROM*, so you need a CD-ROM drive from which to install it. Most modern CD-ROM drives are much faster than quad speed. Some newer games have so many big files they can only be installed from DVD-ROM drives.

What to look for

When looking at adverts for computers, remember to read the fine print. You will save yourself disappointment if you learn what to look out for before you place an order. Remember to check what is included in the price. If you are careful, you may get yourself a bargain.

The type of *processor* inside the PC. If you need speed, go for an Intel Core 2 Duo or AMD Athlon Dual-Core chip.

The amount of *memory* included. 512MB is the absolute minimum for running Windows Vista, but 1GB or 2GB will make things run more smoothly.

How big is the *hard disk*? The minimum should be 80GB. Buy as big a hard disk as you can – you'll always find ways to fill it up.

The computer can be in a standard *desktop case*, which sits on your desk, or more commonly a vertical tower.

The more *memory* on the display card, the better the image quality. 128MB is the minimum but to play PC games, you need 256MB or 512MB.

The *inputs* and *outputs* that connect the PC to the mouse, printer and other external devices.

The computer will come with a *mouse* and a *keyboard*.

The spare slots to plug in peripherals, such as *printers*.

The electronics have been manufactured with minimum risk to the environment and have a *power-management* feature.

Joe's Bargain PCs

Check out our prices on PCs!

This month's best buy

~~£750~~
£629

- AMD® Athlon™ Dual-Core processor
- 2GB RAM
- 320GB hard disk
- Desktop case
- 256MB ATI Radeon PCI Express graphics card
- USB 2.0/ Firewire ports
- 102-key keyboard
- Mouse
- 3 PCI expansion slots
- Green motherboard

MasterCard or Visa accepted

- 9 in 1 memory card reader
- 20in flat panel monitor
- Sound Blaster Music card
- 16x DVD+/- RW

INCLUDES FREE SOFTWARE!
Windows Vista™ Home Premium Edition loaded
Microsoft Works

Plus 12-month on-site warranty

Call our hotline now
0200 123456
Fax 0100 123456

JOE'S BARGAIN PCS
NORTH STREET
ANYTOWN AB1 2CD

NEXT-DAY DELIVERY

Make sure that the items advertised are *in stock*.

Make sure that the *price* advertised is what you will have to pay.

The *card reader* enables you to download pictures direct from the flash card in your digital camera.

This tells you how big the *monitor* is. 20 inch is a good size for everyday use.

A good *sound card* is essential for multimedia and games, as well as listening to downloaded music.

A *DVD rewriter* is useful if you want to back up a lot of photos and videos.

Most computers come with *Windows* already up and running these days. Many dealers also add in other software, which is a cheap way of getting the basic word-processing, database and other software that you need.

You may be able to pick up the computer yourself and save on *delivery charges*.

It's safest to buy with a *credit card*, although many companies charge extra for this. Check if this is the case, and that the company will not debit your credit card until the item is sent.

Warranties vary greatly, so ask the salesperson to specify the terms of the warranty. The computer here is guaranteed for a year. On-site means the firm will repair it where you live, but check the response time.

Check when the computer can be *delivered* and whether this will cost extra.

What to buy

You should regard your computer as the machine you need to run your software. First decide on the sort of things you want to do with your home computer. You must decide what sort of software is going to be needed. Then you can choose a computer that is going to run that software properly.

The newest version of the Windows operating system is Windows Vista. This should be your first purchase, as virtually everything you are going to do will run from within Windows. Both Windows Vista and its predecessor XP are easy-to-use software systems that control everything you do on your PC. But the downside of this ease of use is that Windows eats up a lot of power and memory before you even start running application software, such as a word processor or a spreadsheet. If you don't have enough power or memory in your computer, then Windows and programs running under Windows may not work.

The most obvious way to tell if your computer is running slowly is whenever new images are shown on screen. You press a key and instead of an instant reaction, the computer busily whirs away for seconds – which can seem like minutes – before anything new happens. When playing games, the animations and video footage may have slow or staggering action, and there may be breaks in the sound tracks as well.

To avoid this, you will need a computer that has at least a 1GHz processor and 512MB of RAM to run the Home Basic edition of Vista. For Vista Home Premium, you'll need at least 1GB of system memory. The more powerful the processor, the more efficiently the system will run, and the better equipped it will be to handle new software packages.

What size computer is for you?

Computers come in many shapes and sizes, and what you buy will depend on what you need it for as much as what you can afford.

Laptops

These are portable computers light enough and small enough to fit into a briefcase. Many are as powerful as desktop computers and have a standard keyboard. They tend to be more expensive than their desktop computer equivalents.

Palmtops

Palmtop computers are more like electronic organisers. They are pocket-size and some come with a miniature keyboard. They are suitable for taking memos or for use as an address book rather than for heavy-duty computing work.

Most people are amazed that more RAM memory can make as big a performance difference as buying a faster processor. To keep the price down many computers are sold with only 512MB of RAM as standard, but in order to run programs under Windows properly, it is much better to have 1GB. If you can afford it, buy a machine that has 1GB of RAM from the start. You can add extra memory by buying the chips to insert into your PC.

The other main item to look out for is the size of the hard disk, which is where your computer will store all your programs. Since some collections of programs, or suites, can use up more than 1.5GB of your hard disk, you will need a lot of hard disk space – at least 80GB. If you have the option, it is worth spending a little extra to get a bigger hard disk from the outset. You'll soon find ways to fill it up.

All computers should come with a keyboard and mouse, a Super Video Graphics Array – abbreviated to SVGA – display card, and monitor. SVGA is the current standard for colour monitors and allows you to have a monitor that displays a wide range of colours at an affordable price.

You may also want to buy some extras. If you have a library of images or videos stored on your computer, you may choose a DVD rewriter instead of the standard CD-ROM or DVD-ROM drive. That way, you can easily back up the files. If you want to use the Internet or receive faxes on your PC, you will need a modem that will connect your PC to the phone line.

It is also worth comparing the bundled software that different companies supply along with a computer. It's called bundled software because it comes with the computer, and it is often a very cheap way of buying hundreds or sometimes thousands of pounds worth of quality software.

Desktop

The most common form of PC is the desktop computer. This sits on your desk and has one box that contains the main electronics, along with a separate monitor, keyboard and mouse. Computer manufacturers are gradually packing more and more into one box. Over the next few years, people will increasingly buy their multimedia PC, TV, telephone and modem as an all-in-one item.

Desktops are the best value for money because it is easier to upgrade them to take advantage of the technological advances expected in the future. They are also very versatile and can be used in the office as well as the home, and for games as well as finance. The good thing about choosing a desktop that is IBM-compatible is that they all adhere to the same standards. You can run a lot of software, and it is easy to buy extra RAM memory, expansion cards and peripherals, such as printers and CD-ROM drives.

Where to buy

N ow that you have decided that your home will not be complete without a PC, where is the best place to buy one? There are several different types of computer suppliers. None of them has a monopoly on being the best or the worst, so look for the type of dealer that meets your needs.

COMPUTER DEALERS

Computer shops vary from small local dealers, which normally advertise in the local press, to computer superstores such as PC World. Smaller local shops will have a limited range of brands but can make up a system to match your needs exactly. They will test it all out and show you how it works. Although the price of the hardware is likely to be very attractive, they are less likely to be able to offer the bundled software packages that the bigger dealers can add in.

GOOD POINTS	**Local; will tailor a system to meet your needs exactly; good advice**
BAD POINTS	**Limited range of hardware; unlikely to be able to offer software bundles; can be variable in quality and reliability**

ADVICE 😃 😃 😃 😃 😃　　PRICES 😃 😃 😃 😃 😃
RANGE 😃 😃 😃 😃 😃　FLEXIBILITY 😃 😃 😃 😃 😃
CONFIDENCE 😃 😃 😃 😃 😃

HIGH STREET STORES

The most convenient source of computers may be the computer department of a major high street electrical chain or one of the large department stores. You can see and use the computer, and you have the confidence that you are buying from a well-established retailer that is likely to be there next year should you have any problems. A high street store will sell you a complete package and credit deals may be available. But if you want a variation on the theme with a different printer, more memory or a larger hard disk, you may be out of luck.

GOOD POINTS	**Local; supply ready-made systems; you've probably bought other electrical goods from them before**
BAD POINTS	**Little flexibility in altering parts of a system; knowledge not quite up to that of the specialist dealers**

ADVICE 😃 😃 😃 😃 😃　　　PRICES 😃 😃 😃 😃 😃
RANGE 😃 😃 😃 😃 😃　FLEXIBILITY 😃 😃 😃 😃 😃
CONFIDENCE 😃 😃 😃 😃 😃

COMPUTER SUPERSTORES

The superstores are often located out of town, so you may have to travel. You are not going to get the same personal service as you will at your local shop, but they do offer a huge range of packages and systems.

GOOD POINTS	Supply ready-made systems and made-to-order systems; reasonable advice
BAD POINTS	You are lucky if they are local; like any superstore, professional but impersonal

ADVICE	☺☺☺☺☺
PRICES	☺☺☺☺☺
RANGE	☺☺☺☺☺
FLEXIBILITY	☺☺☺☺☺
CONFIDENCE	☺☺☺☺☺

MAIL ORDER

Choosing a mail-order supplier is no different from choosing a high street shop. Browse through the ads, and call the companies to ask them what they offer. Don't be afraid to ask for advice, and see who impresses you most. Always shop around.

GOOD POINTS	Specialist knowledge; can often make to your specification; lower prices
BAD POINTS	You need to know what you want; more difficult to return for repair; dealing with an unknown supplier you can't see face to face

ADVICE	☺☺☺☺☺
PRICES	☺☺☺☺☺
RANGE	☺☺☺☺☺
FLEXIBILITY	☺☺☺☺☺
CONFIDENCE	☺☺☺☺☺

Stores

● Don't be afraid to ask questions and get a feel for the salespeople. Do they seem knowledgeable? Does the company give you confidence?

● State what you want the machine to do. Can they show you a PC running the software you will need?

● Pay by credit card because this gives you extra protection.

SECONDHAND

Secondhand computers are cheap and normally reliable. But because they are generally a few years old, they are not likely to be powerful enough for today's needs, let alone for the future. At present, it is unlikely that the secondhand market will offer a really useful computer. You may save money in the short term, but don't think of it as a long-term investment. Plus, there won't be a warranty if something goes wrong, and you will have no redress, just as if you had bought a secondhand car. Take along a friend who can ask the right questions, and never buy one without seeing it working.

GOOD POINTS	Cheap; you can buy something with all the right parts so you don't have to buy extras yourself
BAD POINTS	No warranty, no backup, often no track record to rely on, and could be out of date

ADVICE	☺☺☺☺☺
PRICES	☺☺☺☺☺
RANGE	☺☺☺☺☺
FLEXIBILITY	☺☺☺☺☺
CONFIDENCE	☺☺☺☺☺

THE INTERNET

There is no shortage of virtual PC shops on-line. You can also buy new or second-hand PCs on on-line auction sites, such as Ebay (www.ebay.co.uk), or have them custom-made to your order by Dell (www.dell.co.uk) or other manufacturers. It's easy to find what you want, and usually at a good price. On several price comparison sites – Kelkoo.co.uk for instance – you can enter what you want and a list comes back with the on-line stores that have it, plus prices. However, many of the difficulties that apply to mail order also apply on-line. You can't see the PC beforehand and advice may be limited. While some have on-line buyers' guides these will be fairly general. A few provide telephone numbers that you can call for specific advice.

GOOD POINTS	Generally lower prices; PCs can be made to order; fantastic range
BAD POINTS	Specific advice hard to come by; you are often dealing with unknown suppliers; returns can be difficult

ADVICE	☺☺☺☺☺
PRICES	☺☺☺☺☺
RANGE	☺☺☺☺☺
FLEXIBILITY	☺☺☺☺☺
CONFIDENCE	☺☺☺☺☺

Mail order

● Confirm the exact prices you are going to have to pay. You may find that once you've added delivery charges and VAT, the final price can be a shock.

● Check all the details by phone and find out how long delivery will take.

● Keep a copy of the order and any other correspondence. If you talk to anyone on the phone, keep a note of what was said and the person's name.

● Pay by credit card because this gives you extra protection.

Internet

● Pay by PayPal or similar on-line bank. This enables you to pay by credit card, or funds you have stored with them, so you don't have to give your financial details to the seller.

Key

☺☺☺☺☺	Watch out!
☺☺☺☺☺	OK
☺☺☺☺☺	Good
☺☺☺☺☺	Very good
☺☺☺☺☺	Excellent

Shopping list

Make it easy to select the type of PC that will match your needs. Check the boxes for the facilities and functions you want, and fill in the shopping list with an idea of your requirements and the minimum and maximum specifications you think are realistic. You can then take it with you or copy it and use it when you talk to computer dealers. It will give them a clearer idea of what you want your PC for, and help them to advise you.

Steps to buying

1. Decide what you want your PC to be able to do, and make a shopping list of all the items this will require.

2. Choose a brand and a model.

3. Set a price. You may adjust this in light of your research. Initially, it will be what you can afford.

4. Choose where to buy, whether from a mail-order supplier or retail store.

5. Check prices by studying advertisements in newspapers and computer magazines, and adjust your budget if necessary.

6. Make your purchase.

Your easy checklist

Hardware

	MINIMUM	RECOMMENDED	HIGH-PERFORMANCE
PROCESSOR	☐ Intel Celeron or AMD Scorpion	☐ Intel Pentium or AMD Athlon Dual-Core 4	☐ Intel Core 2 Duo 2.13GHz
RAM	☐ 512MB	☐ 1GB	☐ 2GB
HARD DISK	☐ 80GB	☐ 160GB	☐ 320GB
MONITOR	☐ 17in	☐ 19in	☐ 20in
GRAPHICS CARD	☐ 16MB Video	☐ 256MB	☐ 256MB
PRINTER	☐ Colour inkjet	☐ Laser	☐ Laser
CD-ROM/DVD-ROM DRIVE	☐ 16x DVD-ROM	☐ DVD rewriter	☐ DVD and CD rewriter with DVD player combined drive
FAX/MODEM	☐ 56K	☐ 56K/ADSL	☐ 56K/ADSL
OPERATING SYSTEM	☐ Vista Basic	☐ Vista Home Premium	☐ Vista Home Premium
SCANNER	☐ Handheld colour	☐ Document colour	☐ Flatbed colour
WARRANTY PERIOD	☐ 6 months	☐ 12 months	☐ 3 years

Extras

GAMES JOYSTICK	☐ No	☐ Yes
SPEAKERS	☐ No	☐ Yes
COMPUTER ACCESSORIES	☐ Disks	☐ Disk boxes
	☐ Manuals	☐ Mouse mat
PRINTER ACCESSORIES	☐ Connecting cable	☐ Spare ink/toner

Software

INTEGRATED PACKAGE	☐ Yes	☐ No
WORD PROCESSING	☐ Yes	☐ No
DESKTOP PUBLISHING	☐ Yes	☐ No
GAMES	☐ Yes	☐ No
EDUTAINMENT	☐ Yes	☐ No
PHOTO EDITING	☐ Yes	☐ No
ACCOUNTING	☐ Yes	☐ No
SPREADSHEETS	☐ Yes	☐ No
DATABASES	☐ Yes	☐ No
COMMUNICATIONS	☐ Yes	☐ No

PRICE   £ _____

DELIVERY   £ _____

VAT   £ _____

TOTAL   £ _____

NAME OF SUPPLIER _____

TELEPHONE NO _____

2 UP AND RUNNING

Get Set!

In the first chapter, we took you through the basics of what a PC is and what it can do for you. In this chapter we explain how to get your computer up and running. We take you through the basics of unpacking your PC, connecting it and getting it working. We explain simply and clearly what all those plugs and cables do – and where they go. We also show you what you have to do to connect all the accessories, such as speakers and a printer, and what the expansion slots inside your PC are for.

We will help you find your way around each of the important parts of your computer system, including the keyboard, the mouse, the monitor, the printer, the disks and the disk drives. You'll find out how they work and, more importantly, how you are going to get the most out of them. Plus, we give hints and tips on how to keep your computer in tip-top condition and how to look after the information you put on disk.

But it's not only your computer you have to take care of. Where you put your PC and how you operate it can affect your comfort. Placing the monitor at the correct height, getting the lighting right and making sure that you are sitting correctly all help to ensure that using your PC is a rewarding experience.

Finally, we cover what to do if setting up your PC doesn't go as smoothly as you had hoped. Our troubleshooting tips will give you a clearer picture of how to turn a collection of electronic components and packaged software into a working computer system. ●

Unpacking

O nce you get your PC home, you have some work to do before you can start using it. This is a good time to learn a little about how your computer system fits together. If you have to move it or change anything later, you'll need some idea about what all the leads and cables do.

Usually there will be three boxes to unpack, unless you buy an all-in-one PC with the monitor attached. Generally, the box containing the computer is also likely to have the mouse, keyboard and cables packed with it. The monitor and the printer will come in separate boxes, which should also contain all the necessary cables, accessories and manuals. Clear enough space to work in and remove each unit from its packing, and make sure all the documents and accessories are kept with each unit.

At this point, it is worth pausing to look through all the manuals. These will usually tell you where all the connectors are to be found and give advice on how to put your computer system together. While you are setting up the system, it will be easier to place the PC with its back to you so that you can see where all the wires go.

Tower PCs are generally placed to one side of the monitor or under the desk. If you are right-handed, it is better to position the computer to the right of the monitor. This makes it easier to load CDs and DVDs into the PC and also means you don't have to trail the mouse cable across the back of the desk. The most common place to put the monitor for an older desktop computer is on top of it. This will save desk space and leave the monitor at about the right height.

Wherever you are going to use your computer you will need convenient mains sockets and enough space for the computer, keyboard, mouse mat and any paperwork. The computer and

Box clever
It is always a good idea to keep your box and packing if you have somewhere to store it – like the loft. If you ever need to transport the computer anywhere or return it for repair, the packing it came in is going to be the safest way of protecting it in transit.

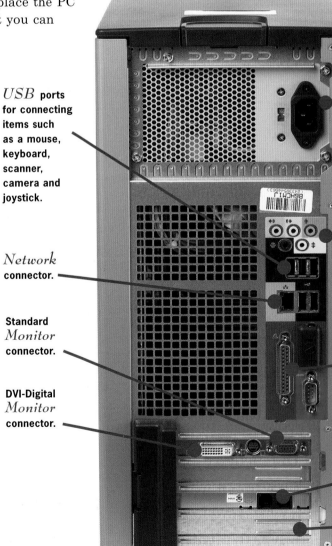

USB **ports for connecting items such as a mouse, keyboard, scanner, camera and joystick.**

Network **connector.**

Standard *Monitor* **connector.**

DVI-Digital *Monitor* **connector.**

& connecting

peripherals, such as printers and monitors, use only moderate amounts of power, so you can use a multiway mains adapter on a single wall socket. However, it is better to use a power strip, which will fit under the desk and make it easier and safer to plug in additional items. If you are going to use a modem, you will also need a telephone socket nearby.

There should be two leads coming from the monitor. One is for the mains (1); the other feeds the monitor with data from the PC. Plug the power cable into the mains outlet and the D-shaped (5) cable into the monitor port at the back of the PC. Then connect the mouse (2) and keyboard (4) to the marked ports on the PC. Connect the printer cable to a USB port and the printer power lead to the mains. Finally, connect the computer's power cable to the mains socket.

Mouse and keyboard cables
Your new PC may have dedicated ports for mouse and keyboard. Installing them is simply a question of plugging the small round PS/2 connector (2 and 4) for each one into the corresponding socket. To make it easy there will usually be an icon of the mouse or keyboard beside the relevant port. The cable plugs may be colour coded. Alternatively, your mouse and keyboard may connect via a USB connector (3) to a USB port. Certainly, if you have a laptop and want to add an external mouse and keyboard – to make it easier to type and navigate around the screen – you will need to use USB connections.

Mains power supply to the *PC*.

Monitor cables
The monitor gets its power from the mains outlet at the back of your PC or from the wall outlet. For a standard monitor, a small D-plug with up to 15 pins (5) feeds it data from the PC. The socket your monitor's D-plug goes into should be marked either SVGA, Monitor or Video. As LCD monitors are digital display devices, they can be connected directly to the PC (whereas older displays used analogue signals).

Multimedia PCs have extra ports for *headphones, microphones* **and** *audio in and out*.

Printer
Most printers are now connected via a USB connection, rather than the dedicated printer port used previously. Increasingly, they will also have a wireless adapter so you can print to them from different PCs in the home – such as your laptop or desktop PC – without the printer being physically connected to a specific computer.

Printer **port.**

Ports
The outlets for the monitor, printer, mouse and keyboard are called ports. While many peripherals are connected by the USB ports, some users prefer wireless connections to remove the 'cable clutter'. In particular, a wireless keyboard and mouse are popular. All that's needed is a wireless connector – normally Bluetooth (6) – that plugs into a spare USB port to receive the signals from the mouse and keyboard.

Modem.

Holes to insert *expansion cards*.

Keyboard

Every computer needs a keyboard to get information into it and to control the software. Some of the keys are there to enter text and numbers, and others are there to control what happens within the software or to move around the screen. Many keys can be used to do both, so the computer keyboard is a little more complicated than the one you find on a typewriter.

Keyboards can differ in layout, but they all have the same features. Most obvious are the main letters and numbers that are in the standard QWERTY layout (read the top five letters on the first row of letter keys) which has been used on keyboards since the invention of the typewriter. Numbers are laid out on the top line of the typewriter section and are repeated on full-size keyboards as a numeric pad on the right. The numeric pad is easier to use if you are entering a lot of numbers.

Across the top of the keyboard are the function keys, which software programs use as a quick way of accessing specific functions, such as printing a document or saving a file. The action each of these function keys performs varies from program to program, with the exception of the F1 key, which is nearly always used to summon the on-screen help feature. So if you get stuck in a program, you can usually just hit F1 for guidance.

Two-fingered exercise?

Most computer users manage to get by with the trusty two-fingered typing technique. But if you are likely to be using the computer a lot, it is worth learning to type properly, as this speeds up everything you do and makes it that much easier to use. It also means that you are less likely to suffer from any health problems, as you will learn how to hold your hands correctly.

One option is to use a teach-yourself typewriting software package. These help you learn to type with all fingers and get more experience with the computer at the same time. They take you through different exercises and often let you know how you are doing by giving you speed tests. You can buy learn-to-type programs for children, too.

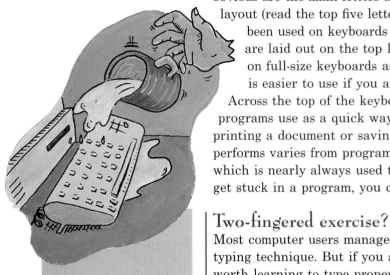

Clean up!

Keyboards will accumulate dust and a surprising amount of general debris over a period of time. To clean the keyboard, you should use a keyboard cleaning kit. This has a brush and a canister of compressed air to blow the dust out from underneath the keys. The key caps will also get grubby over a period of time. Use a barely damp cloth to clean them.

If your keyboard stops working or works erratically, clean it and check the connections. While it may be worth asking a computer engineer to look at it, you may find that it is cheaper simply to buy a new one.

Try not to spill drinks on your keyboard. If you do, switch off the computer as quickly as you can and then unplug the keyboard and shake any excess liquid out of it. Leave it somewhere warm (not hot!) to dry off.

The *Escape key* is the one key to help get you out of trouble. If you call up a function or menu box by mistake, pressing Esc should cancel it.

For upper case, or capital letters, you have to hold down the *Shift key* while you type. Pressing the *Caps Lock key* switches the whole typewriter keyboard over to capitals until you press it again to switch Caps Lock off.

The *Tab key* has the same function as the typewriter Tab key. It is also used to move across columns in tables and the cells – boxes where you enter in figures or words – in spreadsheets, as well as to move around in some Windows dialog boxes.

In most Windows programs, pressing the *F1 key* will call up the help information to guide you through the program.

Twelve *function keys,* which the software uses to give you instant access to particular functions, such as printing and saving.

On many keyboards there are three *LED lights* to remind you whether the Num Lock, Caps Lock or Scroll Lock keys are currently depressed or not.

The *Print Screen* key can be used with the Ctrl + Alt keys for taking pictures of what's on screen. However, the *Scroll Lock* and *Pause keys* are rarely needed now in Windows.

Standard *typewriter keys* for letters, numbers and other characters.

Press *Backspace* and the cursor – the line or arrow on the screen that tells you where you are – will go back one space, deleting whatever letter is in the way. *Delete* moves the cursor forward one space, deleting whatever letter is in the way. If you switch *Insert* on when you type, you will then automatically type over any letters that are already on a line.

The *Cursor Control keys* let you move the cursor vertically and horizontally around the screen without using the mouse. You can jump up or down a page using *Page Up* and *Page Down* or to the beginning or the end of the line with *Home* and *End.*

The *Control* and *Alt keys* are used together with the typewriter and function keys to give you access to more of the software's functions. The menus in any Windows program menu bar can be opened by pressing Ctrl and its underlined letter.

The *Calculator* or *Number keys* are laid out calculator-style to form a numeric pad with divide (/), multiply (*), add (+) and subtract (-) keys. These are activated by pressing the *Num Lock key*. When Num Lock is off, these keys duplicate the functions of the Cursor Control keys.

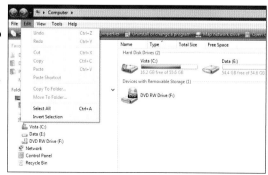

Mouse

Dangermouse

If you use a computer intensively, some muscles in the hand, wrist or arm can suffer strain from constantly repeating the mouse actions. Reduce the possibility of repetitive strain injury (RSI) by making certain you are using your mouse correctly and using keyboard shortcuts instead of the mouse when possible. Switching to a tracker ball can help. RSI usually hits those like designers and journalists, who use their computers intensively for long periods. Nevertheless, it is a good idea to be careful.

The mouse is what makes moving through Windows so easy. You use your mouse to move around the screen and select Windows menus and commands. The mouse is always used in the same way, and you will find that the manuals that come with your software will tend to use the same words for the four basic mouse functions. *Point* is when you use the mouse to move the cursor over a particular item on the screen. *Click* is when you press the button once, either to fix the cursor at that position on the screen or to select a menu. *Double-click* is when you press the mouse button twice quickly to start a menu function or a program. *Drag* is when you hold the button down while moving the mouse.

Mouse hold

It is worth learning how to hold your mouse correctly. Hold it with your first and middle fingers resting gently on the left and right buttons and your arm more or less horizontal. Make sure the mouse mat is close to your keyboard so you don't have to stretch your arm out too far to operate the mouse.

Now gently move the mouse around the mat. In many older models, the action of the ball inside the mouse running over the mat made the cursor move. However, in the latest mice, a laser or optical light tracks movement. Whichever type you have, lifting up the mouse and moving it – a mistake often made by those new to computers – will have no effect. It takes a little practice to master the point, click and drag techniques, but it will soon become automatic. When you feel expert at it, run Paint in Windows, or any other drawing or painting program, and see how you can use the mouse to draw straight lines and circles freehand!

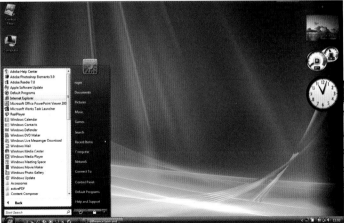

The mouse can be used both to *control* **Windows functions and to move around the program's screen and** *select* **things.**

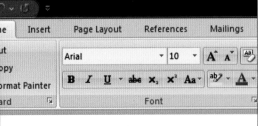

How to spot a hoax virus warning

Difficult as it is to detect real viruses, there are also virus hoaxes Internet. They may have come from a source you know – a friend forwarded a warning about a particularly nasty new virus doing the hoax viruses spread – such as the Family Pictures virus. The emai Intel, the manufacturer of PC processors. In the email you are enc warning to as many people as you know. In fact it is a hoax.

Mousework

Most standard mice work by detecting the movements of the mouse ball. Two rollers, connected to sensors, press against the ball. One turns when you slide the mouse backwards and forwards, the other when the mouse moves from side to side. The information from the sensors is turned into electronic instructions for the movement of the on-screen cursor or arrow. There are other types of mouse that don't have a ball but work through an optical sensor. A laser mouse provides the best resolution but is expensive, while an optical mouse uses a red flashing light to track movements. Such mice may have trouble picking up detail if used on black or shiny surfaces.

Mice of all kinds

The standard mouse uses a cable to connect it to one of the USB ports on your computer. Some are designed to sit comfortably in your hand and others are designed just for fun. There are cordless mice that use an infrared beam instead of a cable. The alternative to a mouse is a tracker ball. This has the ball on the top rather than underneath, and you use your hand to roll the ball. Tracker balls are sometimes built into laptop PCs. As an alternative, many laptops have a trackpad that follows your finger movements to move the cursor on screen.

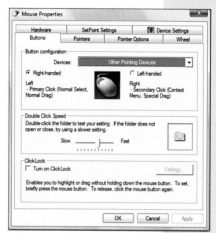

Mouse mats

Every mouse deserves a mat to play on. The mat has the right sort of surface, and provides just enough friction, to let the ball run without slipping or jumping. Mouse mats also reserve a space on your desk on which to operate your mouse. They come in all shapes and sizes.

Adjusting your mouse

Some users like a mouse to respond very quickly to their movements and clicks. Others find that they like the action to be a bit slower so that they don't accidentally overshoot. By clicking on the Mouse icon in the Windows Control Panel, Windows lets you choose the right tracking and double-click speed for you and even lets you swap the functions of left and right buttons if you are left-handed.

Ickey mouse?

If you are using a standard mouse with a ball, the inside of the mouse can get dirty over a period of a few months. If the cursor loses its smooth action around the screen and jumps, then it is likely your mouse needs cleaning.

So, with the computer off, turn the mouse upside down. You will see a ring surrounding the mouse ball. The ring is released by either twisting or sliding it.

With the ring removed, take the ball out and then use adhesive tape to pick up any dust or lint on the surface of the ball. Wipe away dirt or lint inside the mouse socket. You can also blow gently to remove any dust. If anything is trapped inside the socket or on the rollers, use a cotton swab dipped in isopropryl alcohol to loosen it. Allow the surfaces to dry completely before cleaning. Replace the ball and secure the ring and you will have a smooth-running mouse again.

Monitor

Acceleration

The big difference in display performance between different monitors is not so much the image quality but how fast the screen is updated.

The display card and PC have to work out the exact colour combination of half a million groups of red, green and blue dots for each image. This takes up a lot of processing power and a lot of memory. Without the processing speed and adequate memory, each time you change something on the screen, there will be a delay as the display adapter calculates the information for all of the pixels.

This is even more of a problem when you want to use your PC to watch video or animations, which can play very jerkily. For fast graphics display and good video playback, you should have an accelerator/ video display card, which has additional processors and at least 256MB of its own video memory to take over a lot of the PC's display work.

A monitor is essentially a TV screen that takes its information from your computer and displays it for you in full colour. The instructions for what is to be shown on the monitor are created by the computer and the software and are then passed to the display card inside the PC. It is this card that turns that information into the red, blue and green signals that make up the screen images for the monitor to display.

The image you see is in fact made up from just three beams of electrons that fly across the screen, making groups of red, green and blue phosphor dots on the inside surface of the monitor's glass glow. Because the dots are grouped closely together, the eye does not see the individual dots, but a single spot, or pixel, of the colour that is made up from the three glowing dots. If all three guns are firing at full strength, the effect is of a single white pixel spot. If they are all firing at absolute minimum strength, you will see what looks like a black pixel spot on the screen. By changing the relative powers of each of the three beams, it is possible to create pixels in millions of different colours.

Controls

Your monitor has its own controls to adjust the look of the display on the screen. It is best to set up the monitor using a screen of black text on a white background. Turn the controls and you will feel a slight click at their centre point. Set all the controls to their centre point first and then make adjustments to suit your own needs.

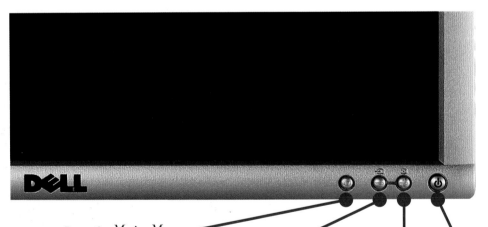

Press the *Main Menu* **button to select options for Brightness, Positioning, Image Settings, Color Settings and so on. Use this button to confirm an option after you have altered the setting.**

Press the *Minus* **button to move down the options in the Main Menu. Use this button to reduce a value when altering a setting.**

Press the *Plus* **button to move up the options in the Main Menu. Use this button to increase a value when altering a setting.**

The *On-Off* **button switches power to the screen.**

Screen size

When a monitor is described as being 19 inches, this measurement indicates the physical size of the screen measured diagonally from the top corner to the bottom. The amount of information you can display on a monitor depends on the screen resolution as well as the size of the screen. Typically, the maximum resolution for a 17 to 19-inch monitor is 1280 pixels horizontally by 1024 pixels vertically (usually written as 1280 x 1024). However, the resolution is easily changed in Windows Vista. Right-click on the Desktop and select Personalize, then Display Settings. Under Resolution, move the slider to a new setting, such as 1024 x 768 pixels and click OK. With this lower resolution, you'll find that fewer items will fit on the screen, but they will be larger in size.

Size and shape

For most home PC users, a 17 to 19-inch monitor will be just right. It is big enough to show all the detail needed for normal work and not too big to fit on the desk. Larger 20 to 30-inch monitors are used for professional desktop publishing and technical drawing, for which a large screen is essential, but also consider buying a monitor of this size if you want to turn your PC into a home cinema.

Keep it clean

If your desktop monitor starts to get dusty or finger-marked, and does not have a mesh anti-glare coating, buy some screen wipes to clean the surface. If you can't find any, turn off the power to the system and the monitor. Then, with a soft cloth and window cleaner, clean the screen by squirting a little cleaner on to a damp cloth and applying it to the screen. Avoid using abrasives or solvents, as they will permanently damage the finish.

Flat panels and laptops use an entirely different display technology called *Liquid Crystal Display (LCD)*, where small electrical currents make small squares in the screen go dark. The colour may not be quite as bright as a traditional PC monitor.

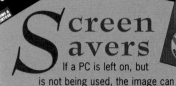

Screen Savers

If a PC is left on, but is not being used, the image can burn itself into the phosphor surface of older monitors, leaving a permanent shadow. To get around this, software developers came up with the idea of screen savers, which replace the display with a moving image after a few minutes. As soon as you press a key or touch the mouse, the screen saver disappears.

While no longer needed for protection, screen savers have turned into an art form. As well as being a fun way to personalise your PC, they can hide your on-screen information from prying eyes. You can set them so that you need to type in a password before the screen returns to normal. Windows comes with its own set of screen savers, but you can buy additional ones that display everything from the famous Flying Toasters to *Star Trek* images. To open the screen savers available with Windows Vista, right-click on your Desktop and select Personalize. In the window that opens select Screen Saver and try out the different options offered.

Printer

There are two main types of printer: the inkjet and the laser. Although they print on to paper in different ways, they all use the same information from your PC and they connect to the same USB ports. When you unpack your printer, make sure you read the instructions carefully before connecting it, since there may well be several parts, such as the paper feeder, that have to be fitted before it is ready for action.

When the printer is assembled, it will usually connect directly to the USB port. On some older computers you may need to connect the printer to a dedicated printer port, normally marked LPT1 or Printer. Make sure the mains lead is plugged into the printer and connected to the mains socket on the wall, or a power strip.

Windows uses software called drivers to translate the image you see on your monitor screen into information your printer can understand. Before you start printing, you have to ensure that Windows has the right Driver installed for your printer. Selecting the Printer icon in the Control Panel will show you which Printer Drivers are installed and that the print information is being sent through the right port. The printer will then work with any Windows program you have now or will have in the future, without your having to do anything else.

Pick your printer

● Inkjet printers (below) fire tiny bubbles of ink on to the paper to create the image. Although inexpensive to buy – and cheaper than a laser – the cost of replacement ink cartridges does need to be taken into account.

● Laser printers (below right) will produce the best-quality printing, but are more expensive to buy.

Printer controls

While some printers are controlled entirely by on-screen software, most have some controls built into them with indicators to tell you more about the printer's current settings. Try out each of the controls to see what they do. The power switch is usually found at the back of the printer. If you don't switch off at the wall socket when you finish working, switch off the printer using its own mains power button.

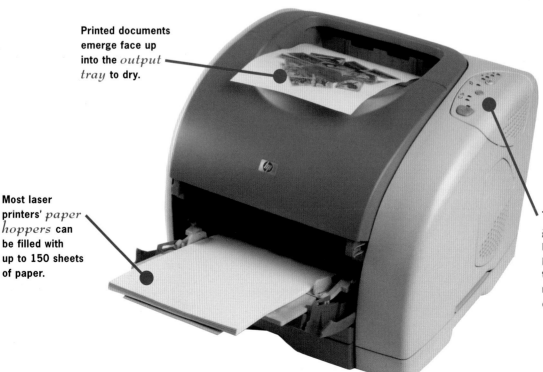

Printed documents emerge face up into the *output tray* to dry.

Most laser printers' *paper hoppers* can be filled with up to 150 sheets of paper.

The *control panel* of many printers is positioned at the top of the machine for easy access.

Printer drivers

When you send a job to a printer, the printer must have some way of knowing what you want it to put on the paper. It has to recognise italics, special fonts, bullets, pictures, graphs and all the other things that people want to print. To do this, it uses a piece of software called a printer driver. Each model of printer has its own driver, provided by the manufacturer. The driver contains all the information needed for the printer to interpret what you put into your documents so that the printed output looks exactly as you intended.

While each printer driver is particular to one printer, if you can't find exactly the right one, it is worth experimenting with the nearest you can get. A Hewlett-Packard LaserJet 4 driver may work well with other HP LaserJet models for instance; but you cannot expect a Canon driver to work well with a Fujitsu printer. Up-to-date drivers can usually be downloaded from the manufacturer's website.

If nothing looks suitable in the list of drivers, a default option is often available. This will give a basic output. It is unlikely to produce italics or bold and certainly won't handle graphics or fonts other than Courier, but at least you'll get text on to paper.

*Easy*WINDOWS

PRINTER DRIVERS
Most new printers are plug and play and connect to the USB port on your PC, which is 'hot swappable'. That means you can connect or disconnect a device without having to close Windows and switch off.

To install your plug and play printer, simply plug the cable in and switch the printer on. Windows will automatically detect the device and install the appropriate driver.

Sometimes, though, Windows can't detect your new printer, so you may have to install the printer manually as shown here.

How to take control of your printer driver

STEP 1 Go to the Start button and click on the Control Panel button on the right-hand side. In the Hardware and Sound section, click on the Printer link.

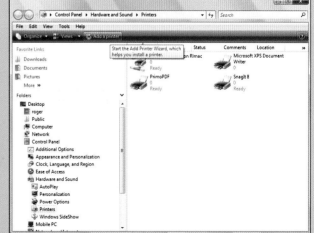

STEP 2 Each installed printer driver has its own icon in the window, and what you see depends on which printers, if any, have been installed. There's also an Add a Printer button in the top toolbar area. Double-click on this ...

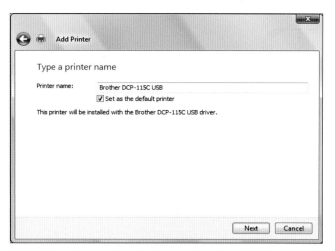

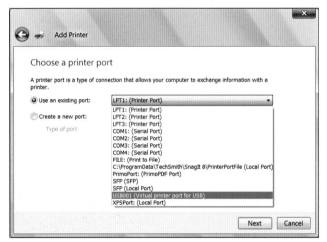

STEP 3 ... and you meet the helpful Add Printer Wizard. You're given two options – to add a printer directly to your PC or through a wireless or network connector. Choose Add a Local Printer unless you are connected to a network, and click on Next.

STEP 6 Your chosen printer is shown and you're asked if you want it to be the default printer. Usually, you'll only have one printer, which will have to be the default, so click the box beside Set as the default printer and click Next. After installing, printing a test page is a good idea, so click on the Print A Test Page button. Then click on Finish.

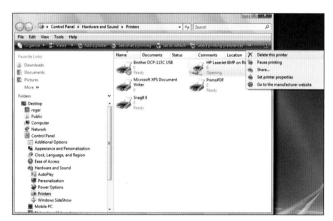

STEP 4 You are then asked about ports, the choice depending on your machine. Although USB printers are normally detected and installed by Windows automatically, if yours is not, you will have to install it manually. Click the dropdown arrow beside Use An Existing Port: and select USB 001 (Virtual printer port for USB), as here. If your printer connects to a different port, select the relevant one from the list.

STEP 7 Delete unused printer drivers by highlighting the icon in the Printers section of the Control Panel and pressing Delete This Printer in the Toolbar at the top. Confirm the action and the driver will disappear.

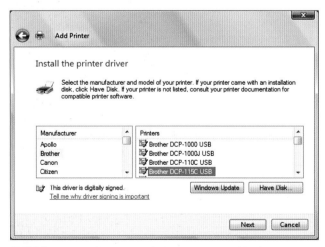

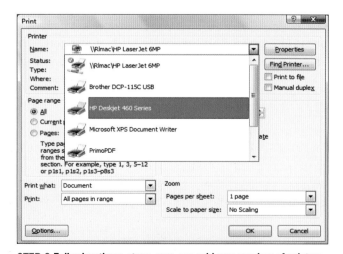

STEP 5 On the left a list of manufacturers appears; on the right, a list of models. Find the make of your printer and the list in the printers column will change to show all the drivers for that brand. For example, if you have a Brother multifunction printer that prints, copies, scans and faxes, your printer would be the DCP-115C USB, so double-click on that. If your printer came with its own driver, put the disk in the drive and click on Have Disk. Select the driver as before. If you can't find your printer, choose Generic and Generic/Text Only.

STEP 8 Following these steps, you can add any number of printers. If a friend comes over with a portable photo-printer such as the HP Deskjet 460, you can have the driver installed and waiting. Unplug your usual printer and plug in the new one. The first time you want to print from, say, Word, click on the Office button in the top left-hand corner and select Print. In the Print dialogue box, scroll down the menu in the Printer Name box, select the relevant driver and print as usual.

Peripherals

Y ou may well have other peripherals to connect to your PC. While some devices, such as scanners and joysticks, will use one of the PC's USB ports, others, such as headphones and sound systems, will use the sockets on the back of special cards that go into the expansion slots of your PC.

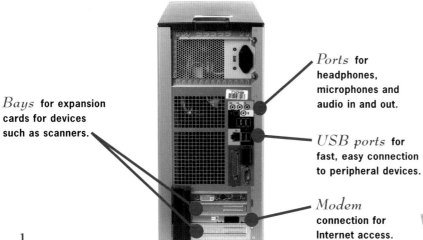

Bays **for expansion cards for devices such as scanners.**

Ports **for headphones, microphones and audio in and out.**

USB ports **for fast, easy connection to peripheral devices.**

Modem **connection for Internet access.**

Sound
A sound card will have an output to feed a pair of speakers. These should be connected by inserting the 3.5mm stereo plug into the speaker or headphone socket of the sound card. Most sound cards have a D-connector, which is a games port. This is where you connect your games joystick if you have one. This port doubles as the MIDI connection for synthesisers and keyboards.

CD-ROM/DVD-ROM or CD-RW/DVD-RW
The CD-ROM drive will be built into your PC; all the connections are done internally. If you want to listen to an audio CD, the CD-ROM drive has a stereo jack socket at the front so you can plug in headphones, bypassing the rest of the computer's sound system. DVD drives can play CD-ROMs, but because of their storage capacity they are good for playing films or holding big programs. As well as the CD or DVD drive, you can add a CD-RW or DVD-RW drive that can copy files to rewritable CDs or DVDs – handy for backing up important data.

Modem
The modem links your computer to the telephone line so you can send and receive files and messages from other computer users around the world using the Internet. Many computers have built-in modems but some modems come as separate boxes (external modems) that connect to the USB port on your computer. These have to be connected to a telephone socket and also need a separate mains power supply. Internal modems are built on an expansion card that slots inside your PC. The only leads needed from these modems are to the phone socket.

Scanners
The other common peripheral is the scanner, used to scan pictures or text into the PC. These usually connect via a spare USB port on the PC.

Sound cards and CD-ROM drives
Sound cards let the computer play real and synthesised CD-quality sounds. All multimedia computers need a sound card and a CD-ROM drive or a DVD-ROM drive. Both drives can hold a huge amount of information. Programs that take up a lot of space, such as multimedia programs, as well as libraries of images and sounds are sold on CD or DVD. A CD-ROM drive can also double as an audio CD player.

Modems
The modem turns computer data into tones that can be sent through phone wires. The PC at the other end of the line also has a modem, which turns the tones back into computer data. Any type of file that you can store on a disk can be sent to another PC this way.

Since the phone system is not very good at handling huge amounts of data this way, modems can transmit data only at relatively low speeds. Most modern modems can transmit data at up to 56K, although ADSL and cable modems are much faster. (See Chapters 9 and 11 for more information.)

Memory

Your PC uses its own internal memory to store programs and files that you are currently working on. This storage area is called Random Access Memory (RAM) and is held on the memory chips inside your PC. Although the programs may still work if you do not have enough RAM, they will run slower. You will notice a big difference in the speed of your system if you increase the amount of RAM in your PC. You need at least 512MB to run the most basic version of Windows Vista smoothly. For the more advanced edition – Windows Vista Home Premium – you need 1GB of memory.

Store it as a file

All the information that your PC uses is stored on its internal hard disk or CD or DVD discs, in individual files. A computer file is just like a real file. You give it a name and file it away. When you want to get the file back, you just look for the file name on the disk and get your PC to open it up. By using the Computer folder or Windows Explorer, you can see all the files on any of the disks in the PC, including the hard disk.

Flash memory

This is most commonly used in the BIOS (basic input/output system) chip, which makes sure that all the different parts of the PC – the other chips, hard drives, ports and processors – communicate with each other. The same sort of memory is used on removable cards, such as USB drives (also known as memory sticks), which simply slot into a USB port to make it easy to transfer files between computers. Flash memory cards are commonly used as the 'electronic film' for storing images taken with your digital camera. Simply slot the memory card into the card reader on your PC and you can transfer the images for editing or storing.

Hard disk drive

At least one, sometimes two, hard disk drives will have been fitted inside your PC. The hard drive is used as the PC's permanent store of programs and data. It is your PC's own library of programs and files. All of the programs that have already been loaded on to your PC are stored on the hard disk, so they are always available at the click of a mouse button. When you buy a new program, the first thing you have to do is transfer it from the CD-ROM or DVD-ROM on to your hard disk.

Software programs are getting bigger, so the hard disk needs to have a large storage capacity. If you have loaded Windows Vista, you will need at least 15GB of available space. With several other programs, such as a word processor, a database, a spreadsheet and a photo-editing program, you should be using at least an 80GB hard disk to leave room for new files and programs. Commonly, you will find that new PCs have two hard drives (or one hard drive divided into two). It's a good idea to load your programs on one drive (normally labelled C:) and your data, or work files, on the other.

Formatting

Formatting magnetically records empty tracks and indexes on to the surface of the disk. When it comes to recording and reading real data, this helps the disk drive know where on the disk particular bits of information have been stored.

When you first put a blank CD-RW or DVD-RW in your PC drive, it needs to be formatted before you can burn (transfer) files on to it. With the DVD-RW shown here, Windows gives you two different formatting options. The Live File System gives you most flexibility, but the Mastered option is more compatible with other PCs.

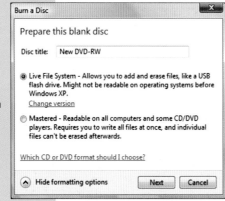

& storage

Bits and bytes

Computers store everything as streams of binary numbers. Binary numbers are simply a string of ones and zeros put together in groups to make up useful numbers. Our normal number system works in the same way, but whereas we work on the basis of multiples of tens, binary works on multiples of twos.

For example, the number 174 is made up of one set of 100, seven sets of 10 and four sets of 1:

100		10		1		
1		7		4		
100	+	70	+	4	=	**174**

The same number in binary is 10101110, made up of one set of 2, one set of 4, one set of 8, one set of 32 and one set of 128.

128	64	32	16	8	4	2	1
1	0	1	0	1	1	1	0

128+0 + 32+ 0 + 8 + 4 + 2 + 0 = **174**

Each of the ones and zeros are called bits and a group of 8 bits is called a byte.

1 or 0	=	**1 bit**
10101110	=	**1 byte**

CD-ROM/DVD-ROM drive

CDs or DVDs are the preferred way of distributing software. For most people the CD-ROM/DVD-ROM is a read-only system (ROM stands for Read-Only Memory). There are also recordable discs (CD-R and DVD-R), which can be written over once and recordable discs (CD-RW and DVD-RW), which can be written over many times.

The main advantage of these discs is the huge amount of data they can hold, which makes them ideal for big software packages. A CD-ROM holds 650MB of information while a DVD-ROM holds several GB.

The software is installed on to the PC's hard disk from the CD or DVD drive. Once loaded, you can store the CD-ROM away, as it won't be needed again unless you need to reinstall the software.

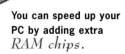

You can speed up your PC by adding extra *RAM chips*.

Kilobytes, megabytes and gigabytes

RAM is always measured by the number of bytes it can store. For Windows work, you need at least 512 megabytes of RAM, but preferably 1GB. Because a byte is such a small unit of storage, files are measured in terms of thousands of bytes (kilobyte or KB) or millions of bytes (megabyte or MB), while hard drives can hold several billion bytes (gigabyte or GB).

What does this mean in real terms? A word processor file of 1,000 words will take up around 15KB, and a half-screen, full-colour picture will be about 150KB. The hard disk needs to be much bigger because it permanently stores all the programs you are going to use on your computer.

	Storage space	Number of bytes	Number of megabytes
CD-ROM	650MB	650,000,000	650
Double-sided DVD-ROM	17GB	17,000,000,000	17,000
Average hard disk	120GB	120,000,000,000	120,000
Large hard disk	320GB	320,000,000,000	320,000

Drives

The data on your hard drive is recorded on a small disk covered in a magnetic material similar to the material on the surface of a cassette tape. The write/read head floats just above the surface of the spinning magnetic disk to read or write data on to it. The drives are intricate devices, which is why they can store so much data on a very small magnetic disk, typically only 3.5in wide.

CD-R, CD-RW and DVD drives

CD-Recordable (CD-R) drives are great for backing up data. They are WORM devices, that is Write Once – Read Many. Once the CD has been written to, it can't be re-recorded. With CD-Rewritable drives, the discs can be written to several times. Rewritable discs are quite expensive and can't be 'read' by conventional CD-ROM drives (although the cheaper CD-R discs can). CD-RW drives work by using several lasers of varying strengths. The most powerful record the data, slightly weaker ones are used to erase it and weaker still are used to read it.

DVD drives are rapidly taking over from CD-ROM drives. Because DVD discs can store a massive amount of data, they can be used for running games, storing several multimedia reference titles or watching the latest Hollywood blockbuster. DVD drives can also play other types of CD. Just as with CDs, there are also DVD rewritable drives that write files to the DVD disc once (DVD-R) or several times (DVD-RW).

Maintaining your hard drive

While your hard drive is remarkably durable and reliable, regular maintenance is important. It is possible for files to get damaged – by a sudden power cut or program crash. Similarly, letting old files that you no longer need clog up your hard drive stops it from working as efficiently as it can. That's why Windows comes with its own utilities to help your hard drive keep functioning smoothly. Disk Defragmenter helps prevent damaged areas of the hard drive being used, while Disk Cleanup removes unwanted files.

CD/DVD drives

On the CD, data is stored as small pits backed by a reflective aluminium surface. A small laser is focused on the CD and light reflected off the pits is registered on a light sensor and then translated back into data. DVD uses a similar optical disc storage technique but is faster, bigger and has much better video and audio quality.

Maintaining your CD/DVD discs and drive

Discs are not indestructible. Scratches and dirt will stop them from working so handle the disks by their edges and put them away after use. Empty CD cases are available at music stores. The lens on the CD or DVD drive's laser can get dirty and should be cleaned using a cleaning kit.

Transportable drives

Removable hard disk drives are just like your PC's hard drive but can be detached from your computer and carried around in a small bag. The REV drive, for example, from Iomega, has the capacity and ease of use of a hard drive but is stored in a removable cartridge that can be ejected and taken away. Able to store 70GB (140GB using the built-in compression), the REV removable disk drive is handy if you want to make a full backup of your system and store it away from your PC.

Expansion

Computer manufacturers know that each person will want to use their PC for different things and will need different peripherals. Some of the PC's basic facilities, such as the display card and the electronics that control the hard disk and floppy disk, can also differ depending on how you want your PC to work. All home PCs need a display card that can instantly deliver Windows screens. Others will also want to play video and animations smoothly. So instead of building these functions into the main PC board, manufacturers give you expansion slots. This also means you can upgrade cards easily. Expansion slots work a bit like ports, except they link straight into the computer's electronics so that the expansion card can communicate directly with the computer's internal processor and memory systems.

These expansion slots can also be used for peripherals that need to be closely linked into the computer's electronics. Typical peripherals that come as plug-in expansion cards are sound cards, display/video cards, modems and network cards.

Fitting an expansion card

You need just a screwdriver to fit a PC card. With the power disconnected, remove the lid of the computer, find a spare slot of the right type, slide the card in and lock it in place with the securing screw. Be careful to hold the card by its edges only. And touch a piece of earthed metal first so that you don't pass static on to the card. Then replace the lid, switch on the computer and run the software that comes with the card. This tells the computer how to communicate with its new electronics.

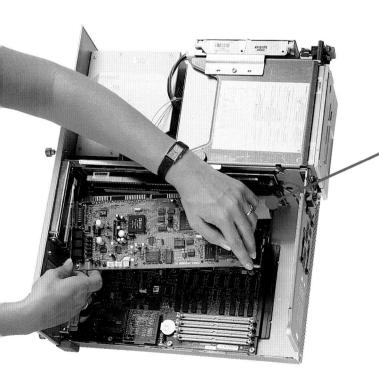

Easy to fit, the *expansion card* **simply slides into the slot.**

8-, 16- & 32-bit

PCs handle data as binary numbers (bits). The early PCs moved around numbers that were made up of eight bits (like 10101011), which cover a range from 0 to 255. Modern computers move around 16-bit (1101010001001010) or 32-bit (110101000100101011010100 01001010) numbers. The bigger the number the computer can handle at any one time, the faster it can operate. The channel that the computer uses to move data around is called a bus and plug-in expansion cards link directly into these buses.

Waiting for the bus

The ISA (Industry Standard Architecture) expansion slots were first used on the early PCs with their 8-bit buses. When computers improved, the ISA connectors were extended to handle 16-bit data buses.

ISA can't handle all the demands of the latest generation of add-on cards, and there are new types of internal slots that are better. The most common is the PCI (peripheral component interconnect). Some new PCs have an AGP slot specifically for graphics cards, leaving the PCI and ISA slots for more general purposes.

Your PC at

Where you put your computer depends on the PC and the people who use it. It is important that there is space between the back of the PC and the wall, to maintain a good air flow. Your monitor also generates heat, so don't cover it up. You should have plenty of mains sockets so each unit can have a plug. Make sure your desk is sturdy enough. Be careful with cups, so that you don't spill anything on the keyboard. Ideally, you should have a drawer to store disks and accessories, and a shelf for manuals.

You need the screen at the right height. A natural position is with the centre of the screen level with your chin and with the monitor angled back a little. Like all TV screens, computer monitors produce ionising and non-ionising radiation. The amounts are minuscule, but you should sit so that your face is at least a couple of feet from the front of the screen.

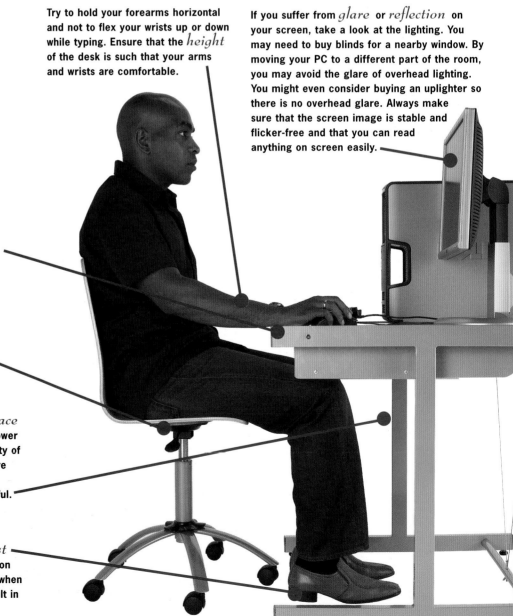

Try to hold your forearms horizontal and not to flex your wrists up or down while typing. Ensure that the *height* of the desk is such that your arms and wrists are comfortable.

If you suffer from *glare* or *reflection* on your screen, take a look at the lighting. You may need to buy blinds for a nearby window. By moving your PC to a different part of the room, you may avoid the glare of overhead lighting. You might even consider buying an uplighter so there is no overhead glare. Always make sure that the screen image is stable and flicker-free and that you can read anything on screen easily.

Allow enough space in front of the *keyboard* to support your hands and wrists during pauses in typing. You can buy separate hand and wrist supports to attach to the work surface if necessary.

Make sure that you can adjust the height and, if possible, the tilt of the *chair* that you will use to provide good lumbar support.

Make sure there is *adequate space* under the desk for thighs, knees, lower legs and feet and that there is plenty of room to allow for changes in posture while using a computer. Prolonged sitting in one position can be harmful.

If your feet do not rest flat on the floor, you can either buy a *footrest* or use an old box to rest your feet on comfortably. Do not use a footrest when it is not necessary, as this can result in poor posture.

home

The room should have good lighting. Try to avoid putting the monitor in a position where it is facing bright lights or a window. These will be reflected in the screen, making it difficult to see.

The right seating position is with elbows level with the keyboard so your arms are horizontal when you type. You should use an adjustable chair, such as a typist's chair, so that you can customise your seating position.

If your children are going to use the computer, make certain that the chair and monitor heights are suitable for them as well as you. If necessary, buy them a desk and chair. Show them how to switch the system on and off and how to insert CDs and DVDs.

Extras shopping list

Once you have your PC system, here are a few things you may need to complete your PC 'office'.

- Furniture: desk, adjustable chair, such as a typist's chair, desk lamp.
- Storage: CD/DVD rack, spare CD/DVD cases.
- Consumables: paper, spare toner or ink cartridge.
- Cleaning: keyboard cleaning kit, CD/DVD cleaner, monitor wipes.
- Others: mouse mat, wrist support, document holder, security tags.

Security

Along with DVD players and TVs, computers are high-tech items loved by housebreakers. You should mark every item with your postcode using a permanent, or invisible ultraviolet, marker. This will at least help you identify the units as yours.

There are computer security systems that attach the computer to the desk with a strong metal cable, which makes it difficult to remove the computer quickly.

You should include your PC in your household contents insurance policy. If you have a laptop, check that your insurance covers it when it is out of the home.

Finally, remember the value of copying important documents on to CDs, DVDs or a removable hard drive. For many people, losing vital information stored on the hard disk is a much more serious problem than losing the computer itself.

On & off

When you switch on your PC, the monitor screen will be black with a few simple lines of text. The PC searches its hardware, checking that everything is working. The hard disk will then whir into action. When it is happy that everything is OK, your PC will beep and launch Windows.

In the meantime, your printer is going through a similar routine. When your PC is ready, the monitor will display the Windows Desktop and play the startup sound clip (provided that you have a sound card).

Switching off

It is not a good idea to switch your PC off without closing down your programs first, as you could lose a file you have been using. Always remove any CDs or DVDs before you shut down.

Now you can shut down Windows. There are two ways you can do this. To put your PC on standby so it temporarily closes down until you need it, click the Start button (with the Windows icon in the bottom left-hand corner). Then click the brown Power button. Windows automatically saves your work, turns off your display and stops the fan. To shut down completely, click the arrow next to the lock button and choose Shut Down.

Computer crashes

The one time you may have to switch off your computer without going through this routine is when the software crashes. A crash is when something happens in the software that confuses your PC. The program stops working, the screen freezes, and pressing the keys or moving the mouse has no effect.

The first thing to do is press the Ctrl, Alt and Delete keys simultaneously. This might let you close down the current program but keep Windows working.

If pressing Ctrl-Alt-Delete does nothing, you have to press the Reset button on your PC. This will put the PC back into its switch-on sequence and should clear any problem. You will, however, lose work that hasn't been saved, so try to save your work regularly. Many programs include an auto-save feature that will save your work to the hard disk every few minutes. The saving is done behind the scenes, as a background operation, so it doesn't stop you from working.

Problems switching on

If there is trouble during powering up, you will normally hear two bleeps and a message will appear on the screen that indicates that your PC has detected a problem with some of the hardware. The computer will then display its own diagnostic screens, which may give you some idea what is wrong. Make a note of all the information on the screen and contact your supplier or the manufacturer, who will be able to tell you what to do.

Operator error

The majority of problems people experience with their PCs are not flaws at all. They are what are called operator errors. Typical examples of operator error are not switching on the monitor or printer, finding that it is not plugged into the mains or is disconnected at the computer end, or finding that the monitor brightness has been turned all the way down.

The message 'keyboard error' may be caused by books resting on the keys. If you have a problem, first make a note of any information the PC is giving you and write down the symptoms.

Then switch off the PC and check absolutely everything. Only when you have done this and the problem still persists is it time to contact your dealer, manufacturer or PC service centre.

3
WINDOWS

View-finder

Windows is a replacement for a system called DOS, which was originally the only way of operating PCs. DOS was controlled via the keyboard and involved learning complicated commands to type in. Windows is a graphical user interface (known as a GUI, pronounced 'gooey') that allows you to operate the PC with a mouse on your desk and images on the screen.

But what does Windows do? It has been described as an 'enabler', an ugly word, but descriptive. Windows, in isolation, doesn't do very much. On its own it doesn't let you write letters, keep track of accounts, or catalogue your record collection. But it does enable you to run the programs – or, as they are sometimes called, applications – that allow you to do these things. So, if you want to write a letter, you use a word processor from within Windows. If you want to keep your business accounts on the PC, you can use an accounting program under Windows.

Think of your computer as a car. The engine (program) does the work, but you drive the car with the steering wheel and pedals (Windows) rather than directly with the engine. We'll be looking at how you can control Windows itself and set it up to suit your way of using your PC. It is worth learning to do that because Windows provides the interface for all the programs that you run (see *Easy Windows* box). Once you understand the Windows interface, you have the basic knowledge to run all Windows programs.

Suppose that you are using a word processor to write a letter to the bank manager, asking for a loan. In another program you have all the figures that justify your request. Windows enables you to pick up the relevant numbers from the second program and drop them into the letter. Even if some of your data is in graphical form (say, a graph of your earnings and expenditures), you can still move it into the letter.

Windows has been regularly updated to make it more powerful and easier to use. We'll be looking at the latest home version, Windows Vista Home Premium Edition. ●

Let's assume that you have just bought a PC with Windows. Having had the fun of unpacking the computer and plugging it in, you turn it on. After hearing some clicking and whirring, you should see a screen that looks like Step 1. Your screen may differ from this, but don't worry. Windows is meant to be configurable – that means it can be changed to suit the PC you have. The supplier of your PC may have configured it for you already. For example, there may be a picture in the background or extra icons (see *Easy Windows* box on page 45).

Step 2 shows all the different things that can appear, but the ones you can probably see on your screen are the desktop (which is essentially the background area on the screen), some icons and the Taskbar.

The best way to learn what these do, and how to use Windows itself, is by doing practical things. Microsoft, the company that makes Windows, supplies several free programs with it, including a word processor – WordPad – and several games. We'll start by opening up the word processor, as an example of a program, and closing it down again.

You'll find the Taskbar at the bottom of the screen. On the left of the task bar is a round button with the Windows icon on it. This is the Start button. Remember that you have real buttons on your mouse and buttons which are part of the interface on the screen. To avoid confusion when referring to these, the usual convention is to say 'Click the Start button.' So click the Start button.

A menu – that's a list of choices – with various buttons and links will appear. This menu stays in place, even if you remove your finger from the button. If there's a small arrow beside the menu, it means a sub-menu will appear if you click on it or allow the mouse cursor to linger over it. The All Programs option on the menu has an arrow, so it has a sub-menu. This is the first of many conventions to remember.

Click on All Programs to view the menu as shown in Step 3, and then click on Accessories. One of the Accessories is a program called WordPad. Another Accessory, Notepad, is a less versatile version of the word processor, so choose WordPad by clicking that option. After a brief

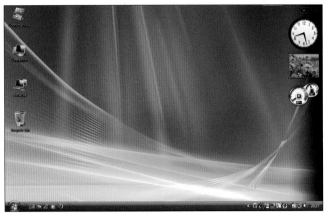
STEP 1 **The desktop in Windows Vista.**

A *window* is a rectangular working area on the screen, normally containing one application and one document.

The *Taskbar* typically appears at the bottom of the screen. But you can move it to any of the other three edges of the screen by clicking on it, holding down the mouse button, and dragging it to the new position.

An *icon* is a small picture that represents something.

A *document* is an icon that represents your data, which could be a picture, a sound clip or a letter. Double-clicking on this will take you to it.

A *shortcut* is a way of navigating rapidly around Windows. A shortcut is marked with a small arrow.

A *folder* is a container for icons and documents.

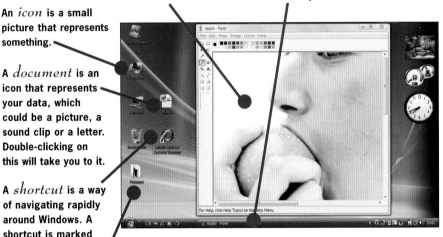
STEP 2 **All of the common items that you are likely to encounter when you use Windows.**

STEP 3 **Click on the Start button on the far left of the Taskbar, and then on All Programs to access the Windows menu.**

pause, the program will appear in a window, ready for you to use it. To close the word processor, find the small button in the top-right corner labelled with an X and click on it. To close Windows entirely, click the Start button again and select the arrow beside the lock and then Shut Down.

Word play

Now you know the very basics of Windows you can begin the task of changing, or configuring, Windows to your liking, for example, by moving the Taskbar from its default position at the bottom of the screen to the top (see *Easy Windows* box below), if that's what you would prefer. Windows usually reads from the top down rather than from the bottom up, so having menus at the top may seem the better option.

First steps

The best way of learning Windows is to use one of the applications, and the easiest one to use is the word processor. So, let's write a thank-you letter to an aunt in New Zealand.

With Windows running, open up WordPad. To access it, click on the Start button and you'll see that the main menu and sub-menus appear. In the main menu, choose All Programs, then Accessories as the first sub-menu and WordPad in the second sub-menu, as in Step 1 (page 48).

After a pause, the duration of which will depend on the speed of your PC, WordPad will appear in a window (see Step 2). The header bar says 'Document – WordPad', and below it is a grey menu bar containing six items. Click on these to see menus of commands for saving, editing and printing your documents. The bulk of the window is filled with plain white space where you'll compose your letter. Type some words to fill up the space, as in Step 3. This is the start of a thank-you letter, with the salutation and some of the body text typed in. As you fill a whole line, you'll see that the next line automatically wraps around without your having to press the Enter key.

If WordPad has opened in a small window, you may find you cannot see a whole line of text at once. You can change the small window to one that occupies a full screen (see Step 4). WordPad is now said to be running in full-screen mode.

We haven't made much progress with our thank-you letter. But we'll save it anyway, accepting the default options for the saving process. Call your document something memorable like Thanks. Now close WordPad.

Easy **WINDOWS**

CONFIGURING WINDOWS

If you decide that you'd prefer the Taskbar to appear across the top of your screen rather than across the bottom, moving it is easy. Put the mouse cursor on the Taskbar somewhere where there is no button, and press and hold down the left mouse button. Drag the cursor up to the top of the screen and you'll see a grey outline indicating the space the Taskbar will take up in its new position. Releasing the mouse button effects the move, and the Taskbar will now stay at the top of the screen. You can also experiment with the Taskbar on the left or right edges of your screen. You're free to choose whichever you prefer and to change it whenever you wish.

ENTER

The Enter key can also be called the Return key, and you'll often find instructions like 'Press Enter' or 'Hit Return'. The naming of this key comes from the days of manual typewriters, which had a lever for returning the carriage to the left-hand side of a document and moving down to the next line. Modern keyboards often have a symbol of an arrow with a tail sticking upwards and a head pointing to the left.

STEP 1 **To open up WordPad, click on the Start button. In the menu that appears, move the mouse cursor to highlight the All Programs item, then click the Accessories folder. Move the cursor down and click on WordPad to open it.**

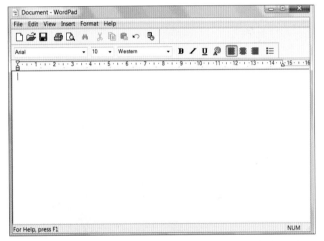

STEP 2 **This is what you'll see on opening the WordPad word-processing application. The white space is like a blank page in a writing pad. A thin line, called a cursor, will blink in the top-left corner. The cursor tells you where the computer's attention is focused; this is where your text will appear.**

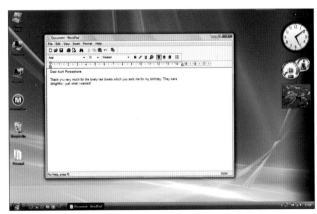

STEP 3 **Type 'Dear Aunt Persephone,'. Press the Enter key twice (see *Easy Windows* page 47). This will give you a line space underneath the salutation and take you to a new line, where you'll begin the letter itself. Write 'Thank you very much for the lovely tea towels' and so on.**

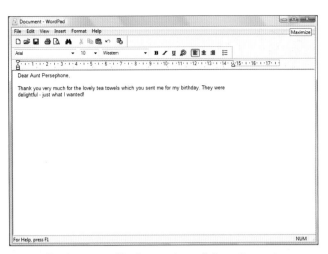

STEP 4 **To give yourself a better view, click on the centre button of the three at the top-right corner of the WordPad window. It shows a rectangle that glows as you hover the mouse over it. Click on this and WordPad now fills all of the available screen.**

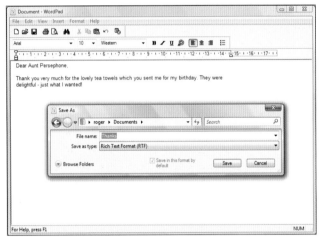

STEP 5 **Click on File in the menu bar at the top of the screen, and then click on Save. The Save As window will appear. Type 'Thanks' into the highlighted File Name box. The rest of the settings can be accepted just as they are for now. To save the letter, click on the Save button at the bottom right.**

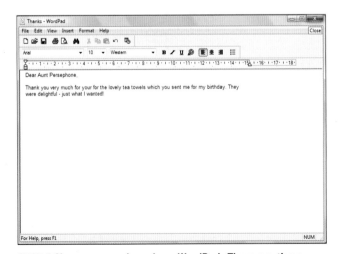

STEP 6 **Now you can close down WordPad. There are three buttons at the top right of the window. The one farthest to the right has an X on it. This button appears on many windows and clicking on it will close the current application. Click on it now.**

Window sizes

By the end of the last pages, we had an unfinished letter that was saved somewhat hurriedly. This time we'll start WordPad and retrieve that letter. So launch WordPad (see *Easy Windows* box) the way you did last time. Click on the File Menu and select Open. Click on the 'Thanks' file.

Now you should have your letter in front of you. Its appearance can be improved by adding your aunt's address and today's date, which can be done automatically using the Insert menu (see Steps 3 and 4, page 50).

Changing windows

You have the ability to move windows around and resize them. Last time, we changed the WordPad window to a full-screen window by clicking on the middle of the three buttons at the top right of the menu bar. There are other options that give even more control over a window's size.

Return to the smaller window by clicking on the same button, which should be showing two overlapping window symbols. To move the whole window, position the mouse cursor over the header bar at the top of the window, click on the left mouse button and keep your finger pressed down while you move the mouse around on the mat. You'll see a grey rectangular outline that moves as you move the mouse. This represents the window, and when that rectangle reaches the place on the screen where you want the window to be, release the mouse button. You can move almost all windows in this manner – it's known as dragging – and you can move them as many times as you like.

It's also possible to change the size of the window by dragging its borders. To make a window wider, place the cursor over the right-hand border of the window. You can tell the cursor is in the correct position when the cursor changes to a double-headed arrow. Click on the mouse button, keep your finger down and move the cursor until the line that represents the edge of the box is where you want it, then release the button.

It's also easy to make windows larger or smaller. To make a window wider and taller in one operation, put the mouse cursor on the bottom-left corner. You can tell you're in the right place when the double-headed arrow appears. This time it will not appear vertically or horizontally (as it does with the sides and the top/bottom) but at an angle. Drag with the mouse and release when the window is the size you want. With your window re-sized, finish your letter. Windows will even show you on screen what it will look like when it's printed (see Step 6, page 50).

Easy WINDOWS

LAUNCHING APPLICATIONS

Launch is a term you'll sometimes come across in computer manuals and magazines and it simply means to start up a program or application.

MOVING UP AND DOWN

To move to the top of a document, you can use the up arrow key on the keyboard, or you can press the Ctrl and Home keys at the same time. This is typical of Windows. It often gives you two or three different ways of doing the same thing. You can also use the mouse and the scroll bar to move around the document. See page 65 for more information on scroll bars.

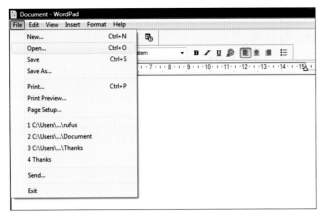

STEP 1 Click on File and then Open, which allows you to open an existing document. A window called Open appears (see below).

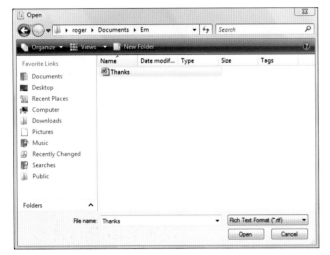

STEP 2 On the right of the window is an icon of a document with a W on it. Next to this is the name you gave your letter. To retrieve this document into WordPad, click on either the icon or the name. The icon will change colour and the name will acquire a darker background. Then click on the Open button at the bottom of the window. You could also double-click on the document icon or its name.

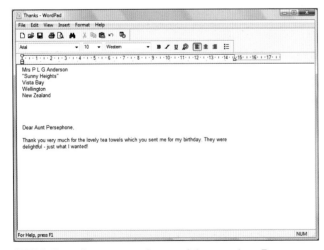

STEP 3 Move the cursor to the top of the page (see *Easy Windows* on page 49). Type in the address. Notice that this time you have to press Enter at the end of each line. This is because each line of an address is very short and the word-wrap feature only works on lines that stretch across the width of the page.

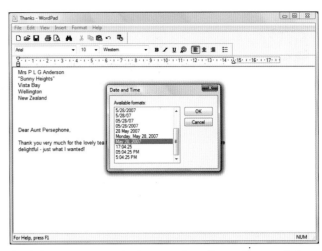

STEP 4 Click on Insert in the menu bar. Choose Date and Time. A window gives you different styling options for the date and time, which will then be introduced automatically into your document. When you click on one you like and click on the OK button, the date instantly appears in your document.

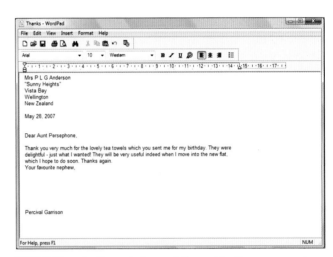

STEP 5 Move to the end of your letter, add a line space and type the closing phrase 'See you soon' or 'Your favourite niece/nephew'. Then leave a few lines of free space, into which you will insert your signature when the letter is printed, before typing your name.

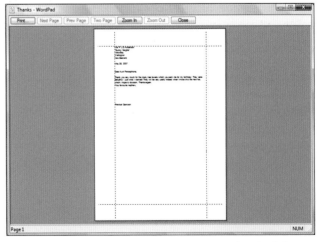

STEP 6 To see how your letter will look when printed, click on Print Preview in the File menu. Here is a preview of the finished letter. It looks OK, but it could be improved by adding a few line spaces at the top of the page. Add those and it's just about perfect.

Saving files

You've already used the word-processor application that comes with Windows to create a document and write a simple letter. The task of saving the letter for future reference was accomplished with little explanation. Now is a good time to look at saving files in more detail.

Windows is described as 'document-centric'. This simply means that, unlike older computer systems, Windows allows you to think mainly about documents, such as your letters, reports, newsletters and so on, and not about the software that was used to create the documents.

Imagine that you have created a report using a word processor for text, a spreadsheet for pie charts, and a drawing package for clip art and logo. If you choose to open this report, Windows will automatically open all the applications used in its creation. All three would be ready and waiting for use with the open report.

So it's perfectly legitimate to click on the icon that represents your thank-you letter. Then WordPad will open and you'll have the text in front of you. It is equally effective to open WordPad and retrieve the document as you did last time. It's another example of the flexibility of Windows, and in time you'll work out your own favourite methods.

Saving a WordPad file

In the screen views on the next page, we return to the process of saving a WordPad file and look at the choices you can make. These cover where you save the file on the computer's hard disk. WordPad gives you the option of saving your file in several formats so that you can edit it with different word processors. Not all word processors save documents in the same format, so this is particularly useful if you need to pass a copy of your document via e-mail to a friend who uses a different word processor. Also, if you are passing files from a PC to a Macintosh computer, or moving files from one kind of application, such as a word processor, to another, such as a desktop-publishing program, you want to make sure they are in a format that can be read. Rich Text Format is supported by most modern word processors, and Text Only provides a lowest common denominator format that can be read by any word processor.

Easy WINDOWS

TEXT BOXES AND DROPDOWN LISTS

On many occasions as you work with Windows you'll see text boxes. They are places where you can make a choice if you wish to. Usually, a text box has a title, describing its function, and a sculpted oblong area where you enter your choice. If you look at the Save As window in Step 4 on page 52, you'll see an example of a text box that is labelled File Name; and the text box itself is where you'd type the name by which your file is to be saved.

Some text boxes have on their right edge a button that shows a downward-pointing arrow. A text box with one of these is called a dropdown-list box. It does exactly the same job, but it's more helpful. If you click on the button, a list pops down, giving all the options available. You simply choose the one you want by clicking on it, rather than racking your brains for something to type in that might fit the bill.

HIGHLIGHTING

To highlight a word, position the pointer to one side of the word. Click the left mouse button and hold it down, then move the mouse to highlight the whole word. Release the button.

If you're highlighting an entry in a text box, it is often easier to start from the right edge of the word and move the mouse to the left. You need to place the pointer more accurately when starting from the left.

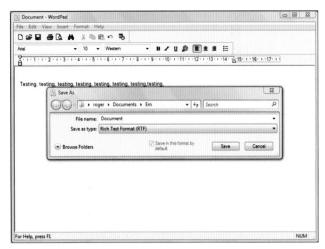

STEP 1 Open WordPad and type a few words into a new document – for example, 'testing, testing'. Click on the File menu and on Save. A Save As window opens in which you enter details of a file to be saved for the first time. Above the File name you'll see the address bar. It shows the current location, where the file will be saved, as a series of navigation links separated by arrows.

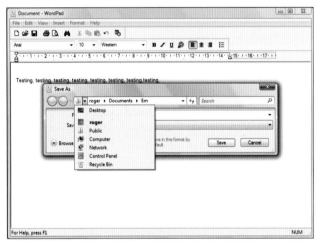

STEP 2 These navigation links are what Vista calls breadcrumbs. You can follow the navigation trail that got you to the current location, right back to the entry point of your computer, by clicking on the arrows in the breadcrumb trail.

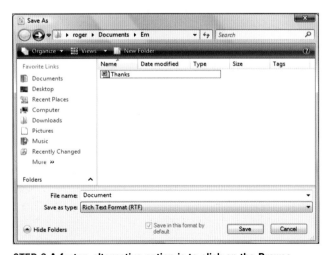

STEP 3 A faster, alternative option is to click on the Browse Folders button. The Save As box extends, and on the left-hand side are Favorite Links to places such as your Documents folder or Desktop, where you might often save your files. Click on a link to select one.

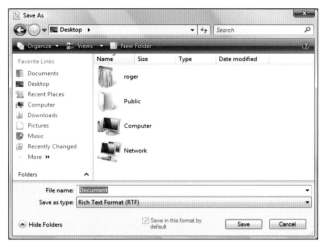

STEP 4 Here, the Desktop has been chosen as the location. The next thing is to give your file a name. When the Save As window first opened, the default name Document was highlighted. If you'd wanted to accept the default location for your file, you could have just typed a file name and it would replace the default. Changing a file's destination or making other choices means the default file name will no longer be highlighted. Highlight the word and type in a name (see *Easy Windows* on page 51).

STEP 5 You can delete the default entry first, but there's no need to. Simply start typing. There are a few constraints on naming files in Windows, so just call it Test for now.

STEP 6 At the bottom of the screen is a box labelled Save As Type. Rich Text Format (RTF) is already selected. Clicking on the button will show you the other available formats: Text Document, Text Document – MS-DOS Format, and Unicode Text Document. Change the format only if you know your document will be needed by someone who wants it as plain text.

Filing made easy

T he word 'folder' appears in Windows time and time again. The use of folders is one of the main ways in which the latest versions of Windows differ from the previous versions and the even older DOS.

Early versions of Windows used directories and sub-directories for storing files. Very little has actually changed in more recent versions of Windows except that the terminology has changed and the word folder is used instead of directories.

Windows uses a filing system that stores files in folders rather like paperwork stored in a filing cabinet. Think of your hard disk, drive C:, as a filing cabinet. This filing cabinet is represented by a folder in which everything on your hard disk is stored. The filing cabinet has three drawers, labelled Correspondence, Reports and Personal, which equate to sub-folders. In each drawer live many manila folders, which represent the files. On screen a folder is represented by an icon that depicts a typical thin, cardboard folder.

Remember the thank-you letter that you wrote using the WordPad word processor? Suppose that you have decided that it would be a good idea to keep all such personal correspondence together, and that you would like to create a new folder for it. You can do this when you save a document, and you can also move documents that already exist into a folder. We will take you through the procedure on the next page.

Easy WINDOWS

BUTTON LABELS

Icons on buttons are helpful as long as you can interpret the tiny graphics correctly. Who wouldn't guess, for instance, that the folder is the icon for creating a new empty folder? But they are not always immediately obvious. Windows Vista will help you to identify the buttons that you do not understand. All you have to do is position your mouse pointer over the obscure button and wait for a second. A little label pops out with a brief explanation of that button's role.

FILES

A file is the means of storing all information for use on a computer, and there are many different types of files. In Windows Vista, each type of file is represented by a different icon.

Files are divided broadly into two categories: the files that you or other people have created using such applications as word processors, spreadsheets, graphics packages and the like (these are known as documents), and the files created by programmers, which are for use by the computer itself.

As you have already seen, files created by WordPad have icons that look like sheets of paper from a notepad with blue lines and a blue W on them. Files such as these can be opened up and the contents can be inspected and edited. Files for the computer's internal consumption are not really meant to be read by people and their file names are not usually listed when you're within an application, such as a word processor. If you want to see them, you can – and marvel at the completely indecipherable icons used to represent the different types of computer file.

If you are opening a file from WordPad, for instance, you can see the different types of files by clicking the downward pointing arrow beside the default Rich Text Format (*.rtf) and selecting All Documents (*.*). Then take a look at the root directory of drive C:. Several files with strange icons appear. When you have finished looking at them, simply change the option back to Rich Text Format files.

If you make a mistake and try to load one of these files into WordPad, nothing worse than an error message transpires, saying that a file of that type cannot be loaded. Just click on the OK button to continue as if nothing had happened. Even if the file does open, the contents will just appear as gibberish – a random collection of letters and characters.

STEP 1 **Open WordPad and create a document of a personal nature – a list or whatever. Click on File and on Save, as you did on page 52.**

STEP 2 **Your old friend the Save As window opens. Look at the collection of buttons in the Toolbar. There is a folder with what appears to be an orange rosette at its icon's top right-hand corner. Next to it are the words New Folder. Rest your mouse on it for a second and a help label appears, saying 'Create a new, empty folder' (see *Easy Windows* on page 53).**

STEP 3 **Click on it and a folder icon labelled New Folder will be added to the list of places where you can already store files. The folder icon and the name are both highlighted, and now is your chance to change the name to something more relevant to you. Type Personal (or any name you wish) and press Enter.**

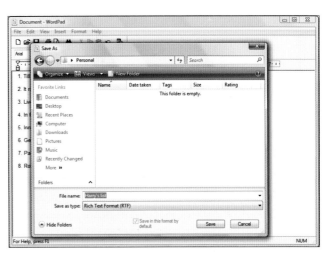

STEP 4 **Double-click on your new folder to select it as the destination for the file you are saving. You can see that Personal is now the location in the address bar. Fill in a name for your new file, just as you did last time. Clicking on the Save button completes the operation.**

STEP 5 **Return to the Desktop by clicking on the Minimize button in WordPad, which is on the top right – the one showing a small, single bar. You'll see the icon for your new folder floating there, as well as the icon for your WordPad document called Thanks. To move the Thanks file into the Personal folder, click on the file icon and, keeping the button down, slide the icon over the folder icon until that icon is highlighted.**

STEP 6 **Release the button and the file is magically transferred. Return to WordPad and click on File, then Open. Select your Personal folder (using the same technique as you did when telling Windows where to save your files) and there you will find your list and your thank-you letter both filed neatly.**

Lost files

Inevitably, when you are using a PC, you'll lose a file or a folder at some stage. You know it exists, you're almost sure you remember what it was called, but now that you want to retrieve it, it's not where you thought it was.

Usefully, Windows Vista has a special tool for searching for these errant files that is both flexible and easy to use. You can search for a name or part of a name. You can search for files created on the date you modified or last used them, or by the file type. And you can search through a specific part of your hard disk or all of it, and search a CD or a DVD as well.

This wonderfully useful tool is called, simply, Search. To launch Search, access the Search box at the top of each folder, open the Search folder by clicking the right-hand side of the Start menu and selecting Search, or use the Search box on the Start menu itself.

How to find a missing file or folder

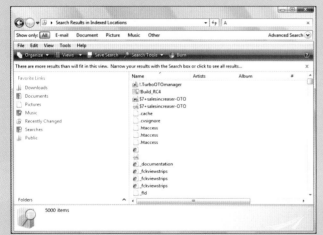

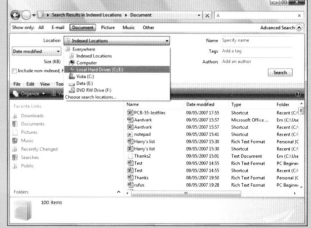

STEP 1 Go to the Start menu by clicking on the round button with the Windows icon on it in the bottom left-hand corner of the Taskbar. Then click on the Search button to open the Search folder. You'll see that the program will, by default, look for all types of file. If, however, you are looking for a specific picture or piece of music, you can limit the search to that type of file. To start the search you simply need to type a few letters in the Search box at the top right-hand side. As you'll see, the search starts with the first letter you enter, then refines the results as more letters are entered. Let's say the missing file is called 'Aardvark' but you can't remember how to spell it. Typing in A gives you too many results to wade through. The number of items found – 5000 – is shown in the bottom pane. Instead, use the Advanced Search option to filter out irrelevant results.

STEP 2 Click on the arrow beside Advanced Search to refine your search. First you need to make sure you're looking in the right place. By default, Windows will search certain specific locations that it regularly indexes in order to speed up the searches. It may be, however, that your file isn't in one of these indexed locations. To have Windows search elsewhere – such as on your CD or DVD drive – you need to change the location it uses. Click on the dropdown arrow beside Location and you can choose various options. You can search Everywhere, select the different drives on your computer, or indeed any drives that are attached. As the most common place to lose files is on the hard disk, select the Local Hard Drives (C:;E:) option. If you know who wrote the document you could add their name to the Author's box, and you can filter out file types that don't apply by selecting Document from the Show Only Toolbar. Click Search and a list of results appears in the main navigation pane.

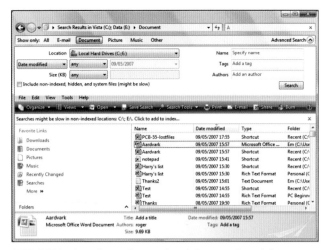

STEP 3 This view shows the results of the search and, in among them, is the Aardvark file that you are looking for. Notice that Windows asks you if you want to add the search location C:\; E:\ to your index for faster searching in the future.

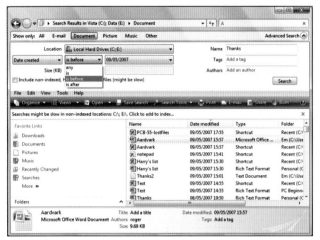

STEP 4 Another way to refine the search results is by the date a file was last modified or created. For example, click the arrow beside Date Modified and change it to Date Created. To restrict the search to a certain date, click the arrow beside Any and select Is. Then select the date from the dropdown calendar in the next box. Alternatively, you can select only files modified or created before or after a certain date. Here we are searching for a thank-you letter written before today. If you're using the modification date to locate files, beware of your computer's clock. It stamps the current time and date on to any new file or updates that information on an existing file if it is re-edited and saved again. If your computer's clock is not set correctly, it will stamp the wrong time and date on all your files, thus making it impossible to search for them by date.

*Easy***WINDOWS**

WILD CARDS

These are symbols that are used to represent 'anything' when you're working with file names. An asterisk represents any number of characters, while a question mark represents a single unknown character. Typing A*.* will find any file beginning with A, from a Word file called Alice.doc to a program file called Alligator.exe. Typing Aardvark.* will find the document file called Aardvark.doc, the picture file Aardvark.jpg, and any other type of file called Aardvark. Typing Aardvar?.doc will find any document called Aardvara.doc to Aardvarz.doc or other variations on the aardvark theme.

STEP 5 To check the date and time, click on Start, Control Panel, Clock, Language and Region, then on the Set the time and date link in the Date and Time section.

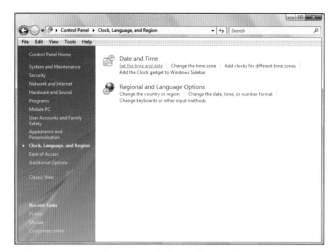

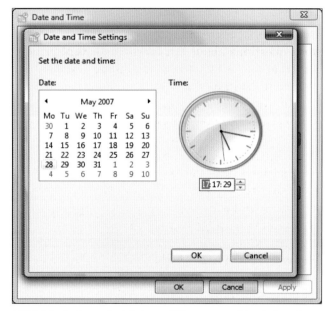

STEP 6 A window called Date and Time opens. Check that the year, month and day are correct and adjust them if necessary. To change the hour, click on the hour, then use the arrow buttons. Change the minutes and seconds in the same way. When everything is correct, click on OK, and OK to finish.

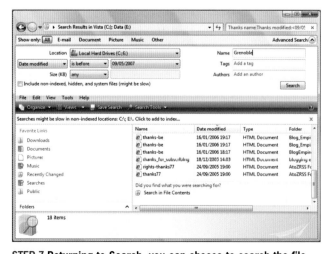

STEP 7 Returning to Search, you can choose to search the file contents for any text you know is contained there. Searching for files containing 'the' will call up many files, but searching for an unusual word such as 'Grenoble' will result in a smaller list. To run the search, enter the word in the Name box and click on the Search in File Contents at the end of the results box.

A helping hand

What should I do if I get confused about what to do? How can I easily remember the steps needed to do a certain job? Help is at hand. The Help system can also tell you more about your computer. For example, you can use Help to teach you about wallpaper, a selection of different styles of background for your desktop that you can access in the Windows system, which enable you to enhance the appearance of your screen (see Steps 1–6, page 58).

Windows Help and Support is a context-sensitive help system (see *Easy Windows* box) that is always available to you on your PC, whatever you happen to be doing. It contains all the information you need to answer your questions about Windows. Instead of printing millions of copies of a paperback of monstrous proportions, and destroying thousands of trees, the text is all contained in documents held in your computer.

This way help is always at your fingertips. No longer will you reach for the manual, only to discover someone has borrowed it – and without asking first. Help systems usually have an index, so you can look things up, just as you would in the index of a book. They also usually have a way of showing you the various topics that are covered, just like the table of contents in the front of a book. There is often a way of printing out sections of the Help system, so you can print out the information on adjusting the rate at which your cursor blinks, for example, and study it at your leisure.

To get assistance from the Help and Support system, click on Start and then on Help and Support. Another way of accessing Help is simply to press the F1 button (see *Easy Windows* box). If you are already using an application such as WordPad, pressing F1 will take you to the Index section and show you a list of all the help topics appertaining to WordPad.

The Help system not only gives you information on making the most of Windows Vista, it also links you to troubleshooters and tutorials, and other Internet-based help resources. You can, for example, use Windows Remote Assistance to get help from a friend, post a question or search for an answer to a problem in the on-line Windows Vista Community discussion group.

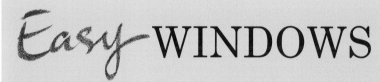

Easy WINDOWS

INSTANT HELP

This means that help is always there waiting for your call. You don't have to do anything except tell it you need it by pressing F1 or selecting Help and Support from the Start menu.

CONTEXT-SENSITIVE HELP

This means that Windows is aware of what you're doing at the time you call for help. For example, if you're in the Paint application, it will offer you Paint-oriented help.

THE F1 KEY

At the top of your keyboard is a row of keys marked F1 to F12. The F stands for function, and these keys are known as function keys. In Windows Vista they are used as part of shortcut keystrokes. For instance, pressing Alt-F4 will usually close an application. Function keys are occasionally used alone, as with the F1 key for calling up Help. It has become a convention that F1 accesses Help, and most software publishers adhere to this.

HYPERTEXT HELP

This term is used to describe the layers of information in the Help system. In the initial chunk of information, certain words or phrases are highlighted to make them stand out from the rest of the text. Clicking on these words pulls out another layer of explanation of the topic in question. That explanation can also contain highlighted words from which you can see further information. This could go on indefinitely, but as it's easy to become confused after more than a couple of layers, most Help systems stop at one or two.

STEP 1 Click on Start and Help and Support, and this is the window you'll see. Notice how it automatically opens to cover only about a third of the desktop, so you can keep it open to refer to while using Windows. If you know what you need help with, just enter the topic in the Search box. Below it, the Find an answer section has links to the on-line help, troubleshooters and, ideal for getting started, Windows Basics. Click on this.

STEP 4 If you find it easier to refer to printed instructions at this point, click on the Printer icon at the top of the Help and Support window, which will bring up the Print box, and print the page. You'll see there are three steps to changing the wallpaper, and the first step is carried out for you automatically by selecting the Click to Open Desktop Background link. This opens the Desktop Background folder.

STEP 2 Browse through the Windows basic topics to get a comprehensive view of Windows Vista and all that you can do with the operating system. Then click on The Desktop (overview) for a more complete explanation of the different ways in which you can customise and personalise it to suit you – say, for example, by changing the desktop background, also called the wallpaper.

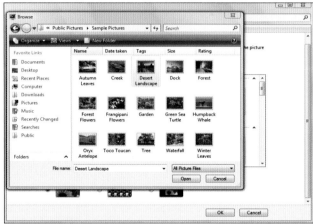

STEP 5 Scroll through the list of photos available in the Windows Wallpapers and simply click on the photo that you want to make your new background. If you want to use your own photo, click on the Browse button, navigate to the folder where your pictures are stored and double-click on the one you want to make your wallpaper.

STEP 3 Scroll down through the various sections until you get to Picking a Desktop Background. Here, there is an explanation of the various sources you can use for the wallpaper – your own digital pictures, or photos from the Internet, as well as those provided with Windows. If you want to go back for any reason, for example to look at a different topic, click the left-pointing blue arrow at the top. To return, click the right-pointing arrow. For now, click on Change Your Desktop Background (Wallpaper).

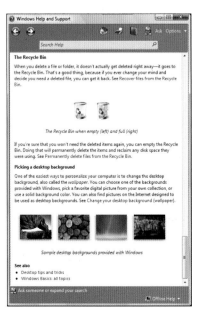

STEP 6 Finally, Windows asks you how the picture should be positioned, and gives you three options. If the picture is big enough to fill the whole screen, click beside the left-hand image. The second option repeats the picture to fill the space, so there may be one or several join lines. The right-hand option shows the image in its actual size surrounded by a coloured border. You can change the border by clicking on the Change Background Color link. Click OK to save the changes.

Playing it safe

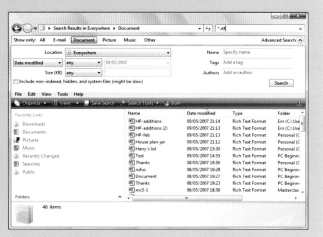

Backup is a computer term that makes some people feel smug while the rest of us suffer feelings of unease, guilt and anxiety. A backup is a copy of the files on your PC, made for the day that your hard disk fails or your computer decides it's had enough and won't boot. There are several different kinds of backup. You can keep a copy of the entire contents of your hard disk, or just some important files. Backups are usually of data files only. You should keep the original disks or CD-ROMs for the applications you use in a safe place anyway. You can also back up only the file or files from a single project if it is especially important.

Many options

The easiest way to back up your complete system is to have an external hard drive that you can link to your PC. Alternatively, there are removable hard drives such as the Iomega REV. This is a hard drive contained within a cartridge, which you can eject and take with you when the backup is finished. To help speed up regular backups, use special software called backup software, which only backs up the files that have changed since the last time you used them. If you have a recordable or rewritable CD or DVD drive, you can also use them to back up your files. Whichever method you choose, if the worst happens and you have to replace your hard disk, you can copy the files back on to the new hard disk and everything from the last backup you made will be transferred.

If your data is really important – the complete files of your small business, for example – your backups should be stored off-site, in a fire-proof safe. Even a dry place in a garage would be better than on the desk alongside your PC.

It is up to you to decide how often to back up. Hard disks have become more reliable, and the temptation to trust them is strong. You have to weigh the hassle of backing up against the potential misery if the worst should happen. If you decide that regular backing up will help you to sleep better, develop a routine, rotating your backup between at least two different sets of disks, or CDs or DVDs. They are handy for easily backing up important files and folders. External or removable hard drives are useful if you work with the larger files produced by sound, video or multimedia software programs.

Easy WINDOWS

BACKUP
A backup is a copy of a file or files from your hard disk.

BOOT
A term meaning to turn on the computer and have it reach a stage where it's ready and able to do your bidding.

How to back up word-processor documents

STEP 1 When it comes to backing up your files you have two choices – you can do it manually or you can let Windows Vista handle it for you. If you only need to back up a small number of files – for example, all the letters relating to a plan to build an extension to your house – then it might be easier to burn them to a CD or DVD manually. To do so, you need to make sure you have all the files together. The best way is to do a search. Launch Search by going to the Start menu and clicking on the Search button. In the Search box that opens, click the arrow beside Advanced Search. In Location, select Everywhere. You can use wild cards to pick out all the word-processor files (see *Easy Windows* page 57). If you're using WordPad, the default file extension is .rtf. So type *.rtf in the Search box.

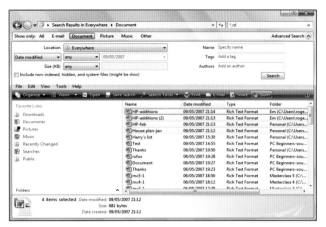

STEP 2 All the word processor files are displayed in the Search Results, regardless of where they are actually located. Although the top four documents all relate to the house plan, you can see from the folder column that they are located in different places. Select them all, then copy the files to a backup CD or DVD by simply clicking the Burn button on the Toolbar.

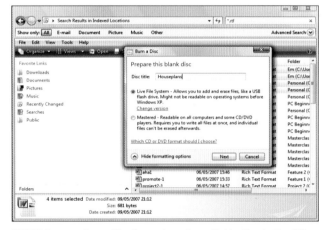

STEP 3 A popup box will ask you to put a writable disc in the CD or DVD drive. In the Autoplay box, select the Burn Files to Disc using Windows option. Give the disc a name when prompted – here it's Houseplans – then choose between the two format options. Live File System enables you to write over the disc many times, whereas Mastered means the files can be written to the disc once only.

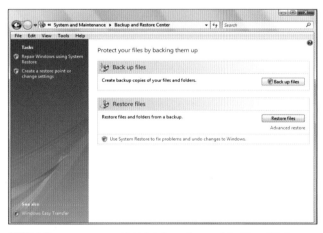

STEP 4 For a more complete backup of your data files, Windows Vista comes with its own Back Up Files Wizard. This backs up most file types apart from program files and Windows system files. To run the Wizard, go to the Start menu, select the Control Panel and in the System and Maintenance section click on Back up your computer, then click on the Back up files button. As a security measure, to stop unauthorised changes being made to your computer, the User Account Control will pop up. To go ahead, enter your administrator's password or click the Continue button.

STEP 5 Select where you want to back up the files. Here, it's a second hard drive, Data E. Click Next. Now select the various types of file you want to back up. Some may not be relevant but leave all options ticked for the moment and click the Next button.

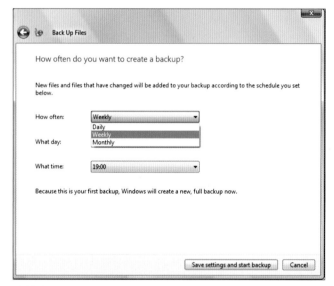

STEP 6 The next screen enables you to schedule when – and how often – you want to create a backup. Select the Frequency from the first dropdown list, then the Day and finally the Time. The first time you run the Back Up Files Wizard, it will do a complete backup of your files, which may take time. Subsequently, it should be much faster as it will only back up files that have changed – or have been added – since the previous backup. Once you've chosen your settings, click on the Save settings and Start Backup button to begin.

File managers

Once you've built up a number of applications, folders and files that you use regularly, you will probably feel the need for some method of navigating around them all. You will need an easy way of carrying out everday tasks such as finding, copying, moving and generally keeping house. Windows provides you with several ways of doing just this.

Tools that perform the tasks described above are called file managers because that's exactly what they let you do: manage your files. The main file managers for Windows are Computer and Explorer. The Computer folder is more visual, while Explorer makes it easier to navigate between your different files and folders. The Computer folder gives you direct access to your hard drives, CD or DVD drives, removable media such as flash drives, and any network drives linked to your PC. Its icon is on the desktop and you can change its name to whatever you like. Click the right-hand button of the mouse on the icon, click on Rename and type in your preferred name.

*Easy*WINDOWS

ROOT

This is the name given to the first level of storage possible on a disk. The path for any file held in the root of drive C: will be C:\Filename. There is no folder containing the file; it's just sitting there on drive C:. The same is true for other drives – such as a second hard drive or a CD or DVD drive. They will have different drive letters starting from D:\ and going down through the alphabet.

FILE MANAGERS

Explorer

With Explorer you can also view folders on other PCs in a network. To start Explorer, double-click on any folder or click on the Start button, then choose All Programs/Accessories/Windows Explorer.

Computer

If your PC has other disk drives and removable drives, you can open them using the Computer file manager by double-clicking on the icon that represents them. On the left are links to Favorite items, such as your documents, pictures or music.

How to find your way around using Computer

STEP 1 Double-click the Computer icon on your desktop and a window opens. In the window are several icons representing different drives. Each drive is represented by its own icon. Typically, there will be one for any hard drives (C:) and one for CD-ROM drives (D:). If you have other drives as well, such as a CD-RW or DVD-RW drive, as in this picture, the drive letters may be different.

STEP 2 Here, a USB drive – CleverStuff – has been plugged into a spare USB slot with some party photos to upload to the PC. Double-click on the icon for the drive and then on the folder containing the pictures. Select one and, holding the left mouse button down, drag it to the Pictures folder under Favorite Links on the left.

STEP 3 Now look through the contents of your hard disk: if you have two drives, as here, select one and double-click on its icon. You'll see its icons and file names. Use the scroll bars to get a feel for how many there are. If there are many of them, this is not a good method of searching for a particular file.

STEP 4 Click on the dropdown arrow beside Views in the Toolbar across the top. You'll see that there is a bullet against the entry Tiles, indicating that this is the view you're currently seeing. There are six other options: Extra Large, Large, Medium and Small Icons, List and Details. Try Medium icons...

STEP 5 ... That's better. You still get the icons to help identify the types of file, but you can see more of them. If you still cannot see them all, use the scroll bar. When you have a lot of files, even clicking the Maximise button to enlarge the window may not show them all. Let's try the other options.

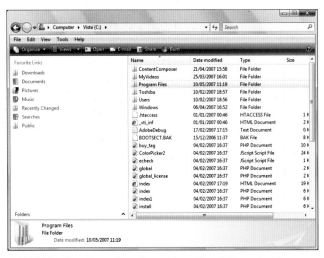

STEP 6 The Details option gives a long list of files, showing their names, size, type and the date and time they were last modified.

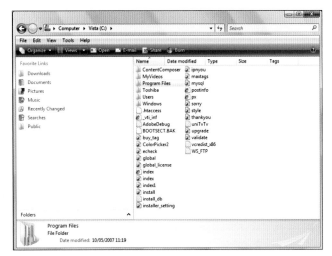

STEP 7 The List view is the most helpful and compact view. Looking at the contents of drive C: you're looking at everything stored directly in the root of drive C: (see *Easy Windows*, page 61). The first files to be listed are folders and they're listed alphabetically. To see the contents of a folder, double-click on it; another window of icons will open. If there are folders in this window, you can double-click on the icon to see what's in them. In this way, you can move through your folders until you find what you want. If you get confused, check the name of the folder you're inspecting. It's shown at the top of the window in the address bar.

WORD PROCESSING

Take note!

Y ou've seen how your PC fits together and how it works. Now it's time to look at the most important software package of them all: the word processor. A word processor is the one piece of software that has universal appeal. Not everyone needs a database or a spreadsheet. Not everyone wants to play games on their PC. But it is almost impossible to use a PC without typing a letter or a note.

When word processors first appeared it was easy to see what they could be used for, and people soon realised the advantages they had over a typewriter. This made word processing the driving force behind the PC's popularity in offices around the world. And, with Windows, word processors show you on screen exactly what you are going to get on the page, which makes it simple for even the most inexperienced user to create attractive documents.

In this chapter, we'll take you through word-processing techniques. We'll cover the basics of how to enter text and edit it. And we'll show you how to create all sorts of documents, from letters and envelopes to newsletters. If you are planning to buy a PC, this will give you some idea of what you can do with a word processor. It will help you decide what sort of word-processing software is right for you. Is it worth spending money on one of the larger packages? Or should you stick with the simple WordPad and Notepad word processors that come with Windows Vista?

If you already have a PC, you will know how to use a word processor for entering and editing text. We will guide you through the other functions your software offers. You will discover how to use your word processor to set up document styles that keep your work looking good, and how it can check your spelling and grammar.

In dealing with businesses, correctly spelled and well-presented letters are always a help. But using a word processor doesn't always have to be serious. There's a lot of fun to be had making your own newsletters, badges, bookmarks, labels, stickers, cards and invitations. The list is practically endless. If it can be printed, you can do it yourself with your PC and a word processor. ●

What is a

Word-processor software turns your PC into a computerised typewriter. But when you use a typewriter you put your words straight on to paper. If you make a mistake or want to change things, you have to start again. The most important difference with a word processor is that you see everything on screen first, so you can make all the changes you like. Only when you are happy with the result do you go ahead and print it.

And whereas a typewriter can only deal with letters and numbers, a word processor can do a great deal more. You can use any type of lettering style. You can make the letters bigger or smaller. And you can add pictures and lay the pages out any way you like. You are not restricted to producing pages of print, either. You can create images that are used for slides, for overhead projection, or just to be viewed on a computer screen.

Which word processor?

Word-processing software comes in all shapes and sizes, from the modest WordPad that comes free with Windows, to more sophisticated processors, such as Microsoft Word, WordPerfect and the more business-oriented Lotus Word Pro.

You can buy your word processor on its own or as part of an integrated suite. Suites put together a bundle of commonly used software, such as a word processor, a spreadsheet and a database. Microsoft Works and Microsoft Office, Corel WordPerfect Office and OpenOffice, which is free, are good examples of integrated suites. A good time to buy your word processor is when you buy your PC because many companies offer special deals.

What do I need?

Sophisticated word processors give you more in the way of layout features, so you can do more interesting things with your text. They also have extras, such as spelling and grammar checkers, the ability to speed up functions using macros, better help facilities, and even simple drawing tools.

If you are only going to write a few letters, you need go no further than the WordPad or Notepad word processors that come with Windows Vista. But as soon as you think you want to do more, consider buying a more powerful word processor.

If you are working in a specialist area, you may need a specialised word processor. For example, not every word processor can show formulas, so, if you are working in science or mathematics, you will need to look for a word processor that includes an equation editor. Translators may also find a specialised word processor useful. A word processor designed for international languages will automatically reset the keyboard settings so that the keys equate to the right letters and symbols for each language.

Getting started

The first time you launch your word processor, you can simply open a blank new document and start typing or you can open a template. This is a professionally designed outline of a pre-styled document – such as a letter – that you can re-use again and again. A wider range of templates is often available on-line. To open a template in Word click on the Microsoft Office button in the top left-hand corner and select New.

Easy Word Processing Examples

While the groupings of the different instructions in the Ribbon bar in Microsoft Word may not be the same as other word processors, most of the same commands will exist. So, every processor will have a command to cut and paste letters, to underline a word, or change the colour of the font. It's just that Word groups all these together under the Ribbon bar. They may appear under different menus in other word processors. The Ribbon is also context-sensitive. So, for example, the Picture Tools tab appears only when an image is selected.

word processor?

The *Office button* replaces some of the commands that used to be on the File menu and includes the basic commands to open, save and print your file.

The *Quick Access Toolbar* contains the Save, Undo and Redo buttons by default. To customise which buttons are shown, click on the arrow beside the Toolbar.

Information boxes tell you about text and document styles. You can change the size and style of a font here, using the arrow buttons.

Word processing *work area.* **This** is where you type in text and where you can insert pictures and graphics.

Scroll bars **are used to** move around the page. Imagine you have a sheet of paper on a roller – the scroll bar will move the paper up and down the roll.

The *Ribbon* bar replaces what used to be the Menu and Toolbars. Commands that perform similar tasks are grouped together under different tabs.

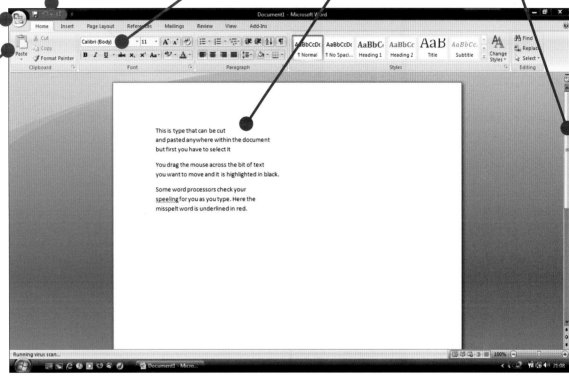

Find your way around Word 2007

The layout of most word-processing programs was much the same until Word 2007 became available. There was a Menu bar across the top from where you could access all the different functions of the software, and below that, at least one, probably more, Toolbars. In Word 2007, there is no Menu bar. (If you can't do without it, go to the on-line Office Marketplace on the Microsoft site where you will find an add-in – mini-program – that you can download to restore the classic menu). Instead of the Menu bar, the Toolbars have been upgraded to the Ribbon bar. This groups various commands together under separate tabs. So, for example, under the Home tab you will find all the commands needed for writing a letter, say – such as the type and size of lettering to be used, how a paragraph is to be aligned and any special styles to be applied. To make it less cluttered, not all the options are displayed under the various tabs. For example, you can change styles – which are a pre-set combination of fonts, text sizes, line spacing and other formatting features for everything from headings to quotes – by clicking on the downward pointing arrow under the Change Styles button. Similarly, some tabs are displayed only when they are needed, such as the Picture Tools tab, which will appear only when you click on an image in your document. You can then use this to edit the image.

What sort of PC?

Once word processors used little computer power, but as they continue to offer more, bigger and better features, they keep growing in size.

The latest version of Microsoft Word takes up more than 1.5GB of hard-disk space, and needs at least 1GB of memory if you want the Grammar and contextual spelling features to work (256MB if not). You will also need more space to store your documents. What you create on your word processor could be anything from an envelope to a newsletter, so we use *document* to mean any type of file that you are working on. Word-processor files are generally quite small unless you include a lot of pictures.

Starting off

You can start your word processor by going to the Start menu, selecting All Programs then Microsoft Office and clicking on the Word icon that represents it on the screen (see page 46). You will be faced with the word-processor window, with a blank space to type into. If you want to continue working on an existing document, go to the Office button and choose the Open command – or select it from the list of Recent Documents on the right. Alternatively, use Windows Explorer to look through your folders for the document you want, or hunt for it using the Search box at the top of every folder. When you double-click on the document, Windows will automatically start your word processor and open the document. You don't have to finish with one document before starting another. Word processors can have several files open at once, and you can switch between them and transfer information from one document to another.

Typing

What you see in the work area is often not the whole document. Use the scroll bars to move around the pages. For typing text, just key in the words and they appear on the screen. You do not have to tell the word processor when you come to the end of a line. It will automatically start a new line when you have run out of space. Pressing the Return key will start a new line because the word processor perceives this as starting a new paragraph.

Moving around

The cursor that tells you where your typing is going to appear on the screen – called the Insert Point – is a flashing vertical line. When it is in the typing area, your mouse pointer appears as a vertical 'I' and reverts to being the normal mouse arrow when it is in the Toolbars.

If you want to insert an extra word in a sentence, you can use the mouse to go to the spot and a single click will put the cursor where you have placed your mouse's 'I' pointer. Alternatively, you can use the keyboard arrow keys to move around the screen to get the cursor in the right position.

Selecting text

Before you can change anything on screen, you've got to tell your word processor what it is you want to change by selecting, or highlighting, it. Say you want to get rid of a sentence. You select it by using the mouse to put the cursor by the first letter, then dragging the mouse across the whole sentence. Hold the left mouse button down while you move the mouse to the right. Anything you select is turned into black text on a light blue background.

Now click on Cut in the Ribbon bar (under the Home tab) and the sentence disappears. If you decide you liked the sentence after all, don't worry. Your word processor keeps track of what you've been doing and if you click on the Undo button (the semi-circular curved arrowhead) in the Quick Access Toolbar at the top of the screen, it will undo your last action or command. To restore the sentence, click on the Redo button next to it and the sentence reappears. Selecting and Undoing applies to virtually every editing and formatting function that your word processor offers.

Saving for others

When you save a document, everything it contains (text, pictures and formatting) is stored together in a format that is particular to your word-processing package. If you are using only one word processor, this is no problem. But you may want to send your document on disk to someone else, or you may want to use your text in another type of software system, such as a desktop publishing (DTP) package. Then you have to save your text in a format that the other software package can understand.

Some word processor and DTP packages can translate files created by other packages. But if you want to be sure, save your words as a text file. Doing so saves each letter and symbol as an internationally agreed code number called ASCII (pronounced 'askey'), which every word processor can read. You can be sure all the letters and numbers are handled properly, but ASCII text files cannot contain any formatting information. Also watch out for some symbols, such as the £ sign, which may not be correctly translated and could appear as a ú in someone else's package.

Copy, paste and cut

Once you have selected a piece of text, click the Copy icon on the Ribbon bar to put a copy of it into your PC's Clipboard, which is your PC's temporary storage area. This text can then be pasted somewhere else in your document by moving the cursor to where you want the text to go and pressing the Paste button – the icon is a piece of paper on a clipboard. A copy of the text you have selected remains in the Clipboard. Some word processors, such as Word, can store several items in the Clipboard. If you have something you want to repeat many times, just keep pasting copies of it into your document.

Cut simply lifts the selected text so you can put it somewhere else and rearrange what you have written. Remember, if you have several documents open at once, you can Copy, Cut and Paste text between documents as well as within a single document.

Easy searching

Your word processor can search out words in your text for you, using the Find command on the right-hand side of the Ribbon bar. This is handy if you spelt someone's name wrongly, like McTavish rather than Mactavish, and it appears several times in your text. Instead of searching for the misspellings yourself, you can use the Find and Replace function to do all that work for you. You tell your word processor which word is wrong and what to replace it with, and it will hunt through the entire written file, delete the wrong word and insert the right one.

Saving

Saving in Word can be done in two ways. One is to click the Office button in the top left corner and select Save. The other is to click the small disk icon on the Quick Access Toolbar at the top.

Over a period of a few months you can easily create hundreds of word-processor files, so it is a good idea to create separate folders and sub-folders (using Computer or Windows Explorer) so that you can easily find your work again. Some people find it easier to file items by month, with folders for January, February and so on. Others like to file by the type of documents they are: Letters, Faxes, Notes and so on. Before you start filing your documents, think of a folder structure that will suit the way you work.

FonTs

All Windows word processors are WYSIWYG (pronounced 'wizzywig'), which stands for 'What You See Is What You Get'. In other words, what appears on screen is what your printed page is going to look like. Make your text bigger and bolder, and it will appear bigger and bolder on screen, just as it will when you print it out. This may seem obvious, but all the early word processors could only show you typewriter-like text on screen, which gave you no idea of exactly how it would look when you printed it out.

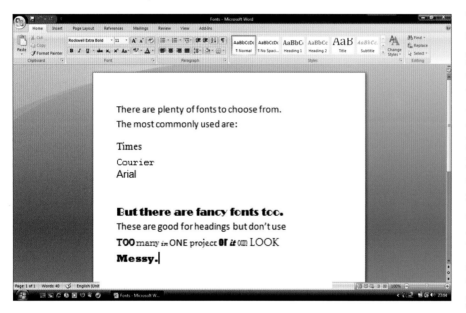

Many different *fonts* – also known as typefaces – are available.

Typefaces

The shape of the letters you see on screen is determined by the typeface, or font, that you choose. Windows stores these as font files on your PC's hard disk. Your word processor will come with a set of fonts, which will include Times, Courier and Helvetica. These are already available for Windows. For letters and documents, it is usual to use a single font, but you can liven up a presentation by using several different ones.

Sizes

The size of your text is always measured in points (pt). This is a typesetting term, and one point is equal to 0.35mm ($^1/_{72}$in). As a guide, the text used for the words you are reading now on this page is in 10pt. The heading at the top of this page is 80pt. Remember that your text has to be big enough to be readable. If it is likely to be used by someone with less than perfect eyesight, why not use a bigger type, so that it is easier to read?

Making it stand out

When you want to highlight a particular word or sentence, you can do it by using *italic* or **bold** text or <u>underlining certain words</u>. Select which of these you want before you start typing by clicking on the relevant button from the B, I, U buttons in the Ribbon under the Home tab. Now when you type, everything will come out as *italic*, **bold** or <u>underlined</u>. The alternative is to type everything normally, highlight the text you want changed and apply the Italic, Bold or Underline formatting.

Buying more fonts

There are many collections of shareware and freeware typefaces that you can buy very cheaply on CD-ROM. These disks usually come with software to view and load your choices on to your hard disk. Fonts take up a significant amount of disk space and memory, so only load the ones that you are going to be using.

99% Wysiwyg

Windows Wysiwyg is not quite 100% perfect. The problem is that your PC has to use special display font files to display your text on the monitor and separate printer font files to send the text to the printer. While font developers do their best to make sure the screen and printer versions of the font match perfectly, sometimes there are tiny differences, which usually go unnoticed. However, very occasionally the layout can be affected minimally, so always check any complex layout by printing it. Getting it perfect on paper may mean having to alter the layout slightly so it doesn't look quite right on screen.

Other languages

Most fonts include all the letters of the English language. They also have the numbers and symbols you find on the keyboard, and most, if not all, of the special letters used in other European languages. Fonts are available for most of the non-European languages, although you would need a matching keyboard to make these useful for regular work.

Not every font is pure lettering. Go to the Font section of the Ribbon bar and select the dropdown arrow beside the font names. Select Wingdings. Now, type on the page. This is a font file with no letters or numbers but a lot of neat symbols, for which you can always find a use.

Page layout

Your word processor can show you your work in several ways. You enter text in Draft View, which gives you some idea of the layout. But when you want to start putting in pictures and multiple columns, you also need to use the Print Layout view, which shows an image of the page as it will be printed. For a quick check before printing, you may also want a Print Preview. This puts pages on screen in the layout that will appear on the printed page.

Margins

First go to the Page Layout tab and click on the downward arrow under Margins. This offers several pre-set sizes for choosing how far in from the sides and the top and bottom edges of the page you want your text. Typically, you'll stay with the Normal setting, which starts the text the same distance, 2.54cm (1in), from all sides of the paper. The Mirrored option is useful if you're writing a document, such as a newsletter, that's going to be printed on two facing pages. If you want to set your own margins, select Custom Margins. Once you have set the margins, your word processor will keep that space clear on every page.

Aligning the text

Most letters have the paragraphs aligned to the left, so the first letter of each line starts on the edge of the margin. With Align Text Left you get a ragged look at the right of the paragraph, which is good for letter writing because it makes what you have written look a little more personal.

Now look at a newspaper. In each column, the text is aligned on both the left and right. This is called justification. When you justify a paragraph, the word processor works out how many words it can fit on the line and then stretches the spaces between the letters and words so that they fit.

You can also Align Text Right. This puts it on the right of the page, ending at the right margin, which is good for some headings. A more useful effect is to Centre your text. The word processor places the text so that it is centred on the page. This is excellent for headings and titles. To apply the alignment you want, highlight the text and click the relevant icon in the Paragraph section of the Home tab.

Tabs and indents

Use tabs to indent the start of the line. When you press Tab, the cursor jumps to the first Tab position on the line, marked on the on-screen ruler. You can clear the default settings and put in your own.

Indent each paragraph you type by pressing the Tab key. You can alter the tab stop positions manually by clicking on View and checking the box beside Ruler in the Show/Hide section. Tabs are useful for putting your text into columns. Set Tabs to 50.8mm (2in), 101.6mm (4in) and 152.4mm (6in) and type in

See your page as it will be printed using *View, Print Layout* **(above).**

Different *paragraph alignments* **suit different sections (right).**

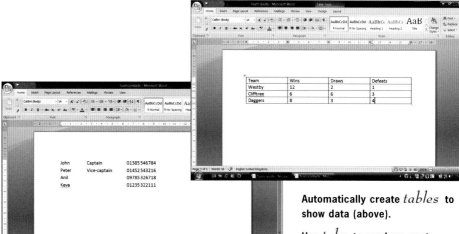

a list of names, job titles and telephone numbers, pressing Tab after each. You will end up with a nicely aligned set of columns.

Automatically create *tables* to show data (above).

Use *tabs* to produce neat columns (left).

Give yourself space

If the page is cramped, your word processor can allow more space between the lines or words. On the Home tab, click the icon at the bottom right of the Paragraph section on the Ribbon bar to open the Paragraph dialogue box. In the Spacing section, set line spacing at 1.5 and click OK. Type a couple of short paragraphs and you'll see how they have opened up.

How many columns?

Letters are usually typed in one column with the text going right across the page, but newsletters and magazines run text into several columns. You can easily do the same by choosing multiple columns. To do so in Microsoft Word, click the Page Layout tab on the Ribbon bar and then select from the dropdown list under the Columns icon. If you select a two-column layout, the word processor will fill the left and then the right column, automatically moving on to the columns on the next page.

Make a break

When a page is full, your word processor moves on to the next. Sometimes you might want to choose where to start the next page – maybe at the end of a paragraph. You can do this by inserting a Page Break (from the Insert tab), which tells the word processor to move on to the next page.

Fields

You will often find it useful to put in standard text, such as the date or the page number, on your page. Your word processor puts these into the page as Fields, which it will automatically update. A Date Field in a letter will always insert the current date, for example. Go to the Insert tab and select Date and Time and choose the format you want. Select Update Automatically to keep it current, then click OK.

Tables

Most word processors include a Tables function, which you can use to make tables of any size you like. Each box in a Table is called a cell, and if there is a Table function then there is usually a calculator function, too, so the word processor can do all the adding up of lines and columns. Tables can be boxed in with grid lines or left open.

Headers and footers

These are special areas that fit at the top or the bottom of the page that can be used to repeat the document, section or chapter title on every page and include the page number (using the Page Number Field).

Store your style sheets

Every element of your paragraph — the type of foNt used, the font size, whether it is *italics* or **bold**, the tabs and the s p a c i n g – can all be grouped as a Style.

If you work on the same type of document regularly, you will want to get the same look each time. You can store this information and instantly apply it to the text in a new document.

To do this, go to the Home tab where you can select a pre-set style from the boxes on the Ribbon. There's one for your normal text, with different size headings, titles and so on. Scroll down to see more. To change a style, click on the icon in the bottom right-hand corner and, in the Styles box, click on the one you want to alter. Hover your mouse over the dropdown arrow, click and select Modify, make your changes in the Formatting section and click OK to save. If you give your modified style a different name, you'll create a new style. Alternatively, click on the New Style button at the bottom left-hand corner of the Styles box. The Create New Style from Formatting box is similar to that for modifying styles. Give the style a name and choose an existing style on which to base it. Then alter the parts you want, such as the font size. Make sure there is a check mark beside Add to Quick Style List so it will show in the Styles section of the Ribbon bar, and click OK to save.

Letters

Here is a letter and envelope layout that uses a lot of the word-processing tools you have read about so far. The letter uses an A4 page, and your word processor will have several standard envelope-sized pages as options in the Page Setup menu. To access them in Word, for example, click the Page Layout tab on the Ribbon bar, then select the dropdown menu under the Size icon in the Page Setup section (known as a group).

This envelope makes clever use of the Margins and Paragraph Indents, which is possible to do with many, although not all, word-processing packages. The envelope's left margin is set to 89mm (3¹/₂in) so that when you type in the address, it is placed where it should be, half-way across the envelope. But to get the message to appear near the left edge of the envelope, we have given it an indent of –76.2mm (–3in), so it moves to the left of the margin by that amount. It is now positioned 12.7mm (¹/₂in) from the edge of the envelope.

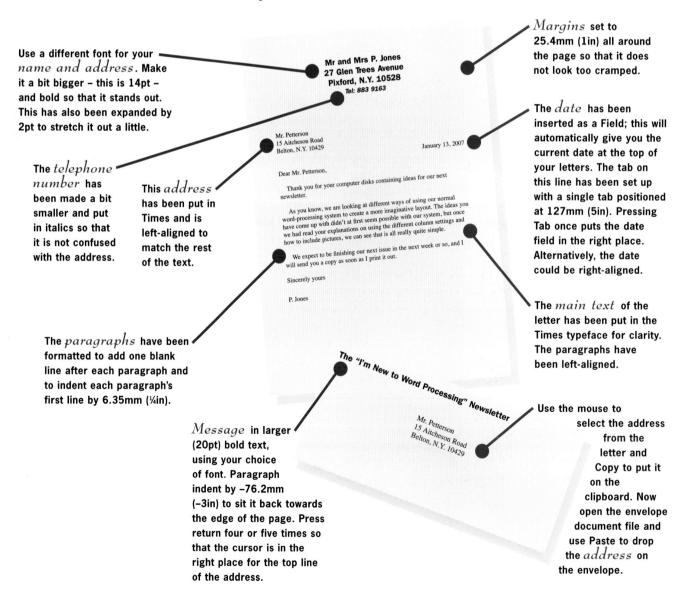

Use a different font for your *name and address*. Make it a bit bigger – this is 14pt – and bold so that it stands out. This has also been expanded by 2pt to stretch it out a little.

The *telephone number* has been made a bit smaller and put in italics so that it is not confused with the address.

This *address* has been put in Times and is left-aligned to match the rest of the text.

The *paragraphs* have been formatted to add one blank line after each paragraph and to indent each paragraph's first line by 6.35mm (¼in).

Message in larger (20pt) bold text, using your choice of font. Paragraph indent by –76.2mm (–3in) to sit it back towards the edge of the page. Press return four or five times so that the cursor is in the right place for the top line of the address.

Margins set to 25.4mm (1in) all around the page so that it does not look too cramped.

The *date* has been inserted as a Field; this will automatically give you the current date at the top of your letters. The tab on this line has been set up with a single tab positioned at 127mm (5in). Pressing Tab once puts the date field in the right place. Alternatively, the date could be right-aligned.

The *main text* of the letter has been put in the Times typeface for clarity. The paragraphs have been left-aligned.

Use the mouse to select the address from the letter and Copy to put it on the clipboard. Now open the envelope document file and use Paste to drop the *address* on the envelope.

Mr and Mrs P. Jones
27 Glen Trees Avenue
Pixford, N.Y. 10528
Tel: 883 9163

Mr. Petterson
15 Aitcheson Road
Belton, N.Y. 10429

January 13, 2007

Dear Mr. Petterson,

Thank you for your computer disks containing ideas for our next newsletter.

As you know, we are looking at different ways of using our normal word-processing system to create a more imaginative layout. The ideas you have come up with didn't at first seem possible with our system, but once we had read your explanations on using the different column settings and how to include pictures, we can see that is all really quite simple.

We expect to be finishing our next issue in the next week or so, and I will send you a copy as soon as I print it out.

Sincerely yours

P. Jones

The "I'm New to Word Processing" Newsletter

Mr. Petterson
15 Aitcheson Road
Belton, N.Y. 10429

Fancy features

All the best word processors build in a whole host of additional features that take you way beyond simply typing in and laying out a document. Many are there to make life easier for you and to guarantee that your documents are presented at their best.

How's your spelling?

Whether you trip up on really unusual words or just tend to put your *e* before your *i* when it's not after *c*, your word processor can come to the rescue. Once you've finished your work, press F7 or go to the Review tab and click on the Spelling and Grammar button and your word processor will go through your text. It will compare every word you have written against a large dictionary with hundreds of thousands of words. This dictionary is stored on your hard disk as part of the word-processor software. If it finds a word you have typed that doesn't match anything it has to offer, it will highlight it and offer some alternatives. Because the misspelling is nearly always a matter of only a letter or two, nine times out of ten it has a pretty good guess at which word you really wanted. More sophisticated spelling checkers monitor your typing. If you regularly make the same mistake, they will automatically replace the wrong spellings as you go along.

Ain't no good at grammar?

One of the more helpful features of a good word processor is its grammar checker. This works just like the spelling checker, but instead of looking for words that are misspelled, it looks for sentences that break the rules. You may think your English is quite good until the grammar check goes to work on your split infinitives, misplaced modifiers and vague quantifiers.

The grammar checker will not only show you where you have gone wrong but also give you explanations and suggestions on how to make corrections and improvements. As a final help, you can ask the word processor to give you a readability report on your efforts. This will tell you the average length of each sentence and how easy it is to read.

Stuck for a word?

Then call up your word processor's Thesaurus. This lists all the alternatives you could use for a given word and also the word's antonyms (words with the opposite meaning). If you choose one of the alternatives offered, you don't even have to type it, as your word processor will instantly insert it in place of your original word.

The neat hyphen

Ragged paragraphs can be made to look neater by telling your word processor to hyphenate the big words so that they are split over two lines. This keeps them from causing a big gap at the end of a line or making justified text too spread out.

Hyphenation **helps to neaten your pages.**

Desktop Publishing

H ere we have put together a newsletter using most of the word processor's important functions. The general explanation of what has been done is in the Newsletter itself. We have also given the formatting details of each element, which may give you some tips for your own work. Come back to these when you have tried out some of the ideas yourself.

Newsletter title or *masthead* using large (30pt) font in black. The paragraph is Centre-Aligned and set for one Column. The background is dark blue (called cyan by printers).

THE 'I'M NEW TO WORD PROCESSING' NEWSLETTER

Issue 5   June 2007

Issue number and date as small text (10pt) in white. Paragraph is Right-Aligned with a Border Filled in Black.

THE FIRST NEW ISSUE HAS PICTURES!
See how it's done.

Main headline. Same size as Masthead, but now normal black text.

We have at last worked out how to use all this word-processing software that has been sitting on our computer for ages. We thought you could only do letters and the ordinary things in life with it. But no, we can get this newsletter looking pretty fancy without too much effort. We have

been reading a lot about columns and have decided to run this bit in three columns across the page.

It will automatically put our text into the three columns. But we can force it to go to the next column by putting in a Column Break, which is like a page break, just here.

So the rest of this particular item goes on to the end column, making it all look nice and neat.

As you can also see, we have justified this text so it looks much more like a real printed newsletter or magazine. It is these touches that seem to make all the difference!

Heading 24pt Bold. Paragraph is Left-Aligned and set for one Column. This information is saved as a Style called 'Heading 1'.

THE BEACH PICTURE LOOKS NICE!

We said we would add a picture or two, so we've included our vacation beach picture to make the point. This picture has to go in a Frame, which is inserted and sized first and then the picture imported into it. You can set the Frames so the text wraps around it like this. As can be

seen by anyone, this look is quite impressive, considering you are using a word processor

rather than going down to the printers, and having them lay it out for you. You have the option to fix the picture in a permanent position on the page or let it move as you add text above it. These choices are in the Frame, Format Menus. Buy pictures on CD-ROM or scan in your own.

Main text in 12pt. Paragraphs Justified (saved as Normal Style) and put in three Columns with a Line Between Columns (normally in the Column Menus). Column Breaks (look for the Break Menu – in Word it's the Breaks button, which is next to the Columns button on the Ribbon) force the text into three short Columns. The picture is Inserted into the frame. The frame is readjusted to crop and size the picture.

VARY THE FORMAT

Now just because the first stories were put in across three columns does not mean we are stuck with that format throughout the whole newsletter. Although it must be said that it is easier to stick with one format throughout.

But if your want to vary the design, then you can format each set of text differently. For example, this

has been put in two columns to make it stand out as a single section. The headline for this particular item has been put in as a single column paragraph and Left-Aligned. This means it takes up just the room it needs but it still reserves the rest of the line across the page so that the second column of text starts level with the first column of text.

Next headline was formatted by applying the 'Heading 1' Style.

Text same as before, but now in two Columns. Highlight all the text of this item and select Two from the dropdown list accessed by clicking the Columns button under the Page Layout tab.

Title in medium-size (14pt) Bold, Paragraph Left-Aligned, set for single Column and with black Border line.

In Word you can enter a *Table of contents* automatically by clicking the References tab on the Ribbon bar, selecting the Table of Contents button and then clicking on Insert Table of Contents.

Title 24pt Bold, Paragraph Left-Aligned, set for single Column.

This section has been given a simple *Border line.*

The rest of the *main text* is set in two Columns.

These *symbols* have been Inserted from the Wingdings font in Dark Red.

TABLE OF CONTENTS

THE BEACH PICTURE LOOKS NICE!
VARY THE FORMAT

CONTENTS

What is also nice to do is include a Table of Contents or an Index.

The headings of each of these items have been stored as a particular Style, which we have called Heading 1. This Style details the font type and that it is bold and slightly stretched. Some word processors will look out for any text that has been formatted in a particular Heading style and make a list of them in a Table of Contents Field.

All we had to do was to use Insert, Field, Table of Contents, and there it all is.

BORDERS

Borders with shadows are a nice way of making a line of text stand out a little more and look a little neater.

You can also put a border around some text to make it stand out. The border is like a black box around the text, and it can be filled with colour if you want. On the front page we used borders in different ways. The Masthead (the newsletter's title) has been given a border that is filled with colour. This facility normally comes under the Border Menu. The colour of the text has been changed to stand out.

Just under the Masthead is the Issue Number and Date. This has been created in the same way as the Masthead, except the fill colour is black and the text colour is white.

FOOTERS

At the bottom of this page is a footer that the word processor has put in for us automatically.

We have told it what to write and to put a Page Number Field after the words "Page Number". Each following page will have the same text but the page number will change.

The "I'm New to Word Processing" Newsletter

If you look on the front page, the Footer is missing. This is because you don't really need a footer on the front page — you already have the Masthead telling you what the newsletter is.

When you use the Footer function, you are given the option to turn off the first-page footer or print something different in the Footers on the following pages.

SYMBOLS

You can also use the symbols that come in such fonts as Wingdings.

They are good for illustrating a list.

They make things look a little more interesting and, using Insert, only take a second or so to include. Colouring them is a bonus.

Caption: Clip art is cheap and simple to add

The next pages should follow this basic look as we have now set the page style up. It is a straight-forward exercise to fill the page style with text and drop pictures in where you need to.

Page Number 2

This *Footer text* will appear at the bottom of every page.

Clip art imported from a CD-ROM clip art disc.

This is a *Page Number Field* for automatic page numbering by your word processor.

Even though the text is small (10pt Bold), the *caption* stands out because it has been given a border.

School Play Special

HAMILTON HURRICANE

20p

SCHOOL PLAY TRIUMPH!

MOVE TO WEST END OFFERED

This year's school play was rated the best theatrical event of the season by several of the country's leading theatre critics. The juvenile lead Michael Ashfoot, was hailed as the new Macaulie McCalkin. It is rumoured that Hollywood director George Spiegleberg has rushed talent scouts over from the U.S. to sign him up for the next Indiana Smith movie.

The play, performed to packed out audiences of parents, brothers and sisters brought encores and a 15 minute standing ovation for the performers.

FLOYD WEBBER VENTURE LIKELY

The incidental music written for the performance has attracted the attention of Julian Floyd Webber who wants to expand it into a full-length performance piece to premier at next year's Promenade Concerts. 'The finest music I have heard in ages,' he was quoted as saying.

CAROUSEL FOR NEXT YEAR?

Plans for next year's performance are believed to be centring on Carousel, with a complete Merry Go Round as the centrepiece of the stage. A horse has been seen in the woodworking department being used as a model for the carvings. Already the staff are looking for likely candidates for key roles in the performance.

Promising young talent (years 5, 6 and 7) should apply to the English Department before the end of term.

ALSO IN THIS ISSUE

Sports Day -Olympic hopefuls
Year 7 -Sweep the Blooker prizes

● You can make *newsletters* look less formal and more fun.

Printing

The last part of the word-processing job is to print out your document. The quality of your work will depend ultimately on the quality of your printer. The majority of people use an inkjet, which offers reasonable quality and gives you the option of working in colour if you have a colour printer. Colour inkjet printers are just a little more expensive than those that can handle black and white only. The best text quality is delivered by a laser printer. Previously this restricted you to black and white, but laser colour printers are now becoming more affordable.

Colour

A colour inkjet will print colour photographs quite well but by no means to magazine printing standards. It is worth using colour selectively, where it will look best, such as in small blocks and to highlight text. You have the additional expense of the coloured ink cartridges needed for a colour printer, but a small splash of colour added to your printing every now and then can make a big impact on your work.

Paper makes a difference

Quality is also affected by the paper you use. If you are doing a special project and want it to look its best, you should buy paper designed for your particular printer. There are special papers for inkjet and laser printers. These give you sharper images. There is a growing range of fancy papers – some with elegant borders, some that look like blank certificates and awards. You can use these for all sorts of fun projects.

Stick it

Use a blank sheet of self-adhesive labels to create anything from a mailing label to a home-made jam sticker. If you think you are going to make a lot of labels, you can buy special label-making word-processing software that makes the job easier. Always treat sheets of labels with care. If there are any labels lifting off the page, they may get stuck in the printer and be very difficult to remove. If in doubt, use a fresh page of labels.

Fax it

Another use for your word processor is to create and send faxes using a PC fax/modem. The document is created in the usual way, but instead of printing it, you send it to your modem. The fax system creates an image of your page, so what comes out of the fax is exactly what you would have seen from your own printer (see pages 119-26).

Project it

You can use your word processor to create slides. Simply send them on a CD or flash drive to a bureau that will use a special camera system to turn them into full-colour 35mm slides. You do need to check that the bureau can handle your particular word processor's file standard, as it is still uncommon to do this from a word processor rather than a slide-making presentation program.

5

DATABASES

Facts & files

After the word processor, databases are probably the next most important type of software you can run on your computer. But databases have got a terrible reputation for being complex things that are of use only to big businesses that need to keep track of hundreds of customers and thousands of sales. In fact, a database is nothing more than a collection of information on a particular topic.

Databases are nothing new. Look around and you'll find you've already got databases all over the house – the telephone directory, the train timetable, your address book, even your TV listings, are all databases.

The databases on your PC are no different. They, too, are just a collection of facts and information, but organised in a large table of data. The big difference lies in what your PC can do with the information once it has all been loaded. For example, finding a particular name in a telephone directory is fairly simple. Your PC can do it quicker, but it's nothing you couldn't handle without your computer. Now think about trying to list all the people called Jones who live in London and Chicago. That's going to take some time by hand, and you might miss a few, too. But for your PC's database system, this is no more difficult than looking for one name – and it won't miss any. Once it has created the list of the Joneses, the system can then print out those details in a list or, if desired, print out individual envelopes for a mailing.

So the database system lets you do a lot of different things with the sort of data that you use every day. In this chapter, we will be creating a database of your friends and relatives. Then we'll show you how to sort the information, find entries, create useful lists and automatically print out letters to them.

The methods you use to create and use a home database are exactly the same as those companies use for the databases that are essential to running their business. You may find that a database on your home PC will be just as useful. ●

What is a

Look in the databases around your home, such as your address book or TV listings. Each contains lists of information on that subject: your friends' names and addresses, the TV programmes' titles along with the times and days scheduled. These basic categories are set out in the same format for every entry.

A PC database is exactly the same – a long list, or table, of information about anything from a company's stock and the prices of products to a list of the CDs and DVDs that you have at home. The important part of the database software is not so much the list of data itself but the way your PC can search through it to pull out hidden information. Although we call such systems databases, it is more descriptive to call them by their full name, which is database management systems (DBMS), since their advantage is in the way that they let your PC mix and match huge lists of information.

Types of databases

A database is built up of several parts. You may have a separate table of data that relates to a particular topic. So you may want to store the addresses and phone numbers of all your family and friends in one database, while another database may be for your DVD collection. And the kids might want their own database, cataloguing all their books and computer games.

The collection of data on one overall topic can also be arranged as a catalogue of several separate database tables. For example, a business might have separate database tables of its stock, the products' prices and its customers' details. All the sales and invoices may be entered into a separate database. Put together, this catalogue of databases can track every part of the company's activities.

Lists that talk to each other

There are two types of databases: flat-file and relational. With a flat-file database you put the details, such as names and addresses, into a single database. You can then search and sort through this list (for example, to find 'Bloggs, Joe' or 'anyone who lives in London'), but you can't get flat-file databases to merge with other databases.

Relational databases are more flexible. Instead of putting all the information in one file, you create separate database files that contain related information. You could create a list of friends in one file and a separate list of the ones to whom you are sending Christmas cards. The two files have a relationship – something in common – which is the names of your friends. The relational database management system can use the files together. When Christmas comes, it will use the Christmas-card list as a set of instructions to pull out all the relevant names and addresses from the other database and print out address labels for all the Christmas cards.

A *database catalogue* is a drawer full of related information. Each file (or table) contains sets of individual entries. Open the drawer and you can find any single entry or start comparing entries in one file with those in another file.

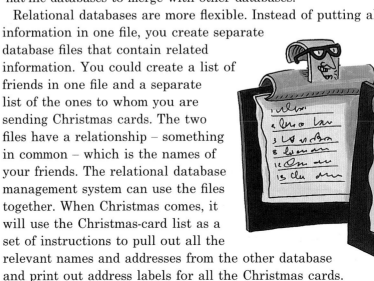

database?

No limits and no hunting

Traditional pen-and-paper databases, such as address books, have a limited amount of space in which to write the information you need, so you tend to include only the more important names and addresses. A database on your PC can be huge, and most give you the ability to put in thousands of entries.

Since the database can sort through even big lists in a fraction of a second, you can put even rarely used entries into your database. Unless you know *a lot* of people, it won't make it any slower to find the important entries, and you'll always know that the name is in there.

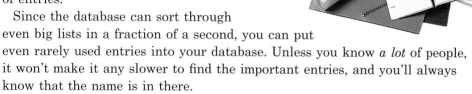

Specialised databases

Using general database software, you can create an infinite range of databases to handle even the most unusual lists. However, a number of database projects are common to many people. Cataloguing any form of collection or building up a family tree are pure database functions and you will find there are ready-made software packages that are fine-tuned for these jobs. Simple database software is included within these programs, and using one of them saves you the effort of having to organise a separate database yourself. Alternatively, your existing database may have formats, or templates, for some of these jobs, ready for you to use.

You can use a database to *catalogue* all kinds of collections and keep lists of everyday items. Microsoft Access comes with its own sample templates.

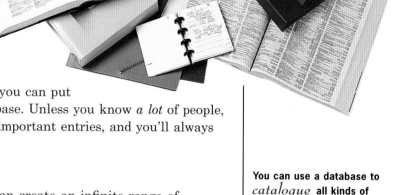

What you need

Databases are not very demanding on your computer and any PC that can handle Windows will be able to handle a database management system. But if you are going to be working with large databases, especially if they include pictures, you'll need plenty of hard-disk space. A fast processor and lots of RAM will help speed up the sorting and finding processes.

Which database?

While you can buy a database on its own, this tends to be costly. Most people will find they already have a database system, which, along with a word processor and a spreadsheet, is provided as part of a suite of "Office"-style programs, such as Microsoft Office 2007 (used here), or Corel's WordPerfect Office. If you have yet to acquire your PC, it is a good idea to buy one with a software suite that includes a database.

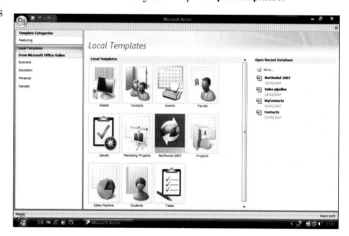

Hidden databases

Word processors and spreadsheets both have simple database facilities. The mail merge function, where you have a list of names and addresses that can be added to personalise a letter, is a basic form of database, as are software address books or the phone and fax directories supplied with modems.

Creating a

Before you can start entering your data in a database, you have to create a form or table to load it into. Each line is called a record and contains all the information about an entry. Each little bit of information, whether it's a first name, a birth date or a product number, is given a little box of its own called a field. Once organised like this, it is easy for your database program to start making lists, sorting entries and finding all sorts of information for you.

Before you begin, you must write down what details you want to put into your database. For a database of friends, you will want first and last name, two to three lines for the road and town details, a field for the county and a field for the postcode. Then there are the other details, such as phone number (make that two if your friends have mobile phones as well), e-mail address and you may want a space for notes, such as birthday and anniversary dates, too.

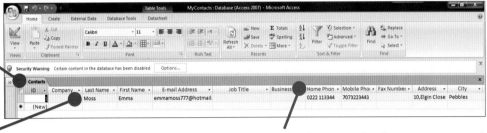

All your information is contained in a single *table*.

Each line contains a complete record, or *entry*.

Each column contains the same category of information with the *field* name at the top.

No place like home

Let's look at creating a database of your friends and relatives by making a new file called MyContacts. Access 2007 comes with a number of ready-made tables that you can either use as standalone databases, or add to others you've already created. There are tables for tasks, for example, as well as one for Contacts, which is used here for your new database. When you open Access, click Local Templates, then Contacts, rename the file and click on the Create button. Select the two chevron arrows to open the shutter bar on the

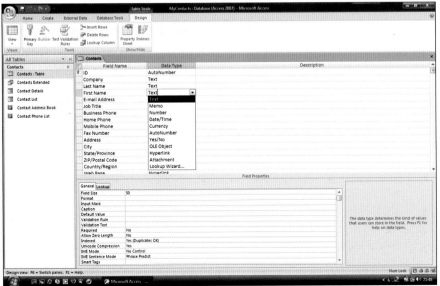

left, and in the Navigation pane below, select Contacts: Table. Click the View button and select Design View. Here you'll see the field information.

As well as the field's name, your database will want to know more about the sort of data that is going to be entered. Click on the First Name row and see that the Data Type is text rather than numbers or a date. You should also tell the system how much space to reserve for the information. Here it is set to 50 letters in the Field Size box on the General tab below.

database

Your PC can do the home/work

If you want to add a few business contacts to your list, you can add a field to distinguish between home and work entries. If most are going to be home entries, instead of typing in 'home' every time you add a friend to the list, you can set up your field to use 'home' as the default, which means the database automatically puts the word *home* in the field for you. On the occasions when the new entry is a work contact, then you just type 'work' into the field instead.

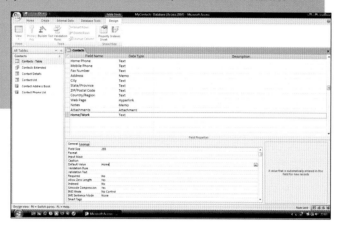

When are numbers not numbers?

The database thinks of numbers as things that it can do calculations with, like the number of products in an order or the price of an item. Numbers like house numbers, postcodes, or telephone numbers are there just to be read, so set these fields as text Fields.

Add more details

When you do need to add an extra field – you may decide to separate home and work data, for instance – it is easy to do. But you will have to remember to change the layout of the entry forms and any reports that use the information.

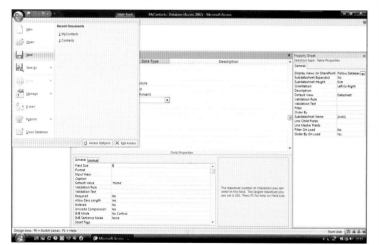

Once you've finished making changes to the database table, you can save it. Click on the Office button in the top left-hand corner and select Save.

57 varieties

Although you can enter everything into the database as words, things like dates, numbers and values really need to be entered in such a way that you can do things with the information later. You may want to use values and quantities for further calculations or move dates around. Your database program has special ways of making the most of numbers, dates and values, so choose the right field type.

● Yes/no boxes

Sometimes you just need to say Yes or No in a box. For example, Christmas card sent? Yes/No. It looks neater and saves typing in more words when you are entering information.

● The open-ended field

Often you need more space in an entry to put in additional comments. Unlike the other fields, which you have set to a fixed length, Memo is an automatically adjusting field. It expands if you are putting in several lines of comments and reduces the field to nothing if the comments field is empty.

● OLE for extras

The OLE Object field can be used to add in information from another software program. This can be anything from a graph to a picture or a sound clip.

What's in a name?

- **Database** A collection of data that you can store in one, or several, files called tables.
- **Tables** These store the data about a topic or part of the database. They contain lots of separate entries, or records.
- **Entries** These contain all the information you are storing on one person or item, just like a card in a card index.
- **Fields** Each separate piece of information in the entry is given its own particular box.

Viewing data

There are two primary ways of viewing or working with your database. You can look at the full table with all the information in columns and rows – the Datasheet View – or you can look at each entry in turn, with the information presented like a form.

Using the table layout to enter your data, you just type the data into the field box, press Tab to go to the next field, and so on. If you make

a mistake, you simply go back to the field and either edit the entry or type over it. The database will also check that you are entering the right type of information. If you try to put letters into a number or date field, it will tell you that you're doing something wrong (see above).

Using forms

Using tables makes it hard to see what you are doing and whether you have filled in all the fields correctly. The best way is to use the on-screen form below (left) that shows you the fields laid out, so you see them all at once.

Even the most *basic layouts* are considerably easier to use than the table, and these can often be created automatically for you by your database program.

After it has been created, you can change the layout by dragging and dropping the *fields* into the best positions.

Getting in and out

If you have already created useful lists of information using your word processor or a spreadsheet, many software systems will let you move, or export, these lists directly into a database program with only a small amount of extra work. Check with your software's Import and Export functions in the File menu because directly transferring the data not only saves a lot of time retyping it all but reduces the possibility of errors creeping in. The Contacts database includes a New Contact form that is considerably easier to use to enter new details than the Datasheet View.

on screen

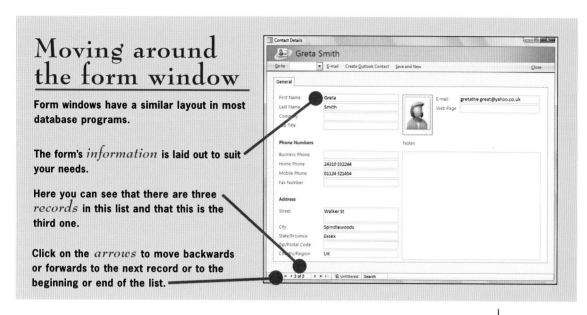

Moving around the form window

Form windows have a similar layout in most database programs.

The form's _information_ is laid out to suit your needs.

Here you can see that there are three _records_ in this list and that this is the third one.

Click on the _arrows_ to move backwards or forwards to the next record or to the beginning or end of the list.

In the picture

It would be very boring if your database could work with text and numbers only. The latest databases support OLE (Object Linking and Embedding), the system Windows uses to let one program access text, graphs, images and even sounds from other unrelated software programs.

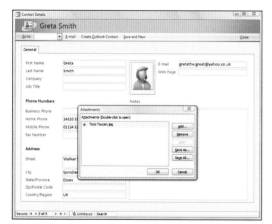

When you create a new table, instead of just putting in text, number and date fields, you can also insert a picture or sound field, or other attachment. To do so in Access 2007, simply click the image on the form and then the paperclip on the toolbar that opens above it. The Attachments box appears. Click the Add button and browse to where your photo – in this case one of a Toucan – is located. Click OK to load the picture in the database. This can be handy not just for pictures of people, but places, drawings, graphs, and all sorts of objects, from the contents of a home to a picture of a prized pet.

Keep a record of your home and its contents

Both for interest and also for insurance purposes, why not make a database of your home contents? Create fields for an item, its purchase price and when it was bought. If you have a scanner, you can add a photo of it, too.

Sort it out

Now you have a database all set up and running, you can start moving, sorting and extracting all sorts of useful information, and print it. It doesn't matter in what order you enter the information into your table; the first job you can do is to organise the data with Sort and Filter. Using Sort and Filter, you can go to the table and look down a specific column and then rearrange the entries so that they appear in alphabetical order. The column, or Field, your database uses for the sorting is called the Key column. Your database will automatically choose the first column as its sorting Key, unless you tell it to use a different one. Note that you can sort your information using any Field as your Key column.

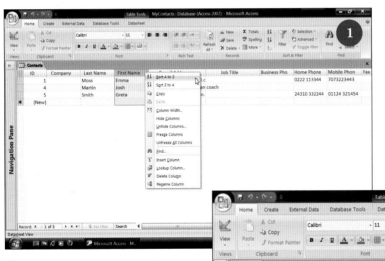

2 You can also instantly *sort* data by selecting the column. On the Home tab on the Ribbon bar go to the Sort & Filter group. Click the AZ icon with the downward pointing arrow to sort in descending order and the ZA icon to put the names in ascending order.

1 Choose the column you want to sort into alphabetical order. Here it's the First Name column. With the names highlighted, right-click and a dropdown menu appears. If you choose the first option, Sort A to Z, the names will be arranged in descending alphabetical order. Select the second option, Sort Z to A, if you want the names in ascending order. Your database program will rearrange all the entries for you instantly.

Super-organise

You can use more than one Key column to sort your database. If you use surnames as the main key and first names as the second, your system will first sort out the entries in alphabetical order of surname. When it finds several entries for the same surname, it will sort them into alphabetical order by first name.

Searching and finding

Once you've got all your friends and contacts listed, you can see them in alphabetical order in the table. If you need to look someone up, you can just run down the table to find them. But why not let the database program do the work for you? It can find things quicker than you can.

Searches can be as simple as looking up someone's address or phone number. Click the Find button on the Ribbon bar and in the box that opens, type the name, word or value you are looking for. Your PC will instantly show the first entry it finds in the database that matches. If there is more than one match, pressing Find Next will display the next record that matches.

Find it even if you can't remember it

While Find is the most basic search function in your database, it is also one of the most commonly used, since you can find an entry even if you can only remember one piece of information. Can't remember the surname but you know the first name is Katy? Then use Find to locate all the Katies.

Filter tips

Finding a single name is handy on a day-to-day basis, but the database system really comes into its own when you want to start making lists. If you are always forgetting birthdays, you can get your database to list them all for you by simply entering the month into the Birthdays field.

Entering a specific requirement for a match in one of the fields is called filtering. The database looks at what you've typed in and uses the information to filter out all the records that match. It then displays them as a table, or you can go through them one by one.

Go wild!

To sort birthdays that match a particular month, you need to use a wild card symbol. You may already be familiar with the asterisk as a wild card when you look for files on your hard disk. In any search, typing in *.txt will locate files with the .txt extension. So if you type */09/* in the Birthdays field, then the program will search for any September birthday (which all have /09/ in the middle of their date entry). The asterisks tell it not to bother checking the day or the year.

Merging mails

Databases are great for producing personalised letters. They print an individual's name and address and other details into a standard letter. This is called mail merging, and the standard mail-merge letter has gaps ready for the details to be loaded automatically.

Printing

There are many ways of printing out database information. If you just want the data you have collected, print out the table, but be sure to set your printer to landscape so it can fit it all in. Alternatively, whatever you can sort, you can print. So, having got your database to produce a sorted list of people, you can then get it to print their names and addresses on labels or envelopes. You can even use it to print out personalised letters.

Wild cards

★ Will stand in for any character or number of characters. So */93 will find 1/93 and 23/08/93.

? Stands in for a single character only, so ?/93 will only find 1/93.

\# Does for numbers what ? does for all characters.

Business

I f you are running a small business, database management systems are essential. You need to keep lists of clients, products, costs, selling prices, stock, and so on. It can all be done in a database: either a general database or one designed specifically for a particular job, such as balancing your accounts.

When you are using database management software for your business, you will be able to create a huge variety of reports from the information you enter. From a single set of database tables, you can create and print reports that keep you updated on what has been sold, to whom, when and for how much. The database reports can mix and match the same information in hundreds of different ways. So you can look at what business has been done with individual customers or look at what has been happening month by month. It all comes from the same set of tables, but the database management software extracts just the information you need and shows it to you in a way that makes it easy to see what is going on.

This *query* is asking the PC to find and display the top ten orders by sales quantity.

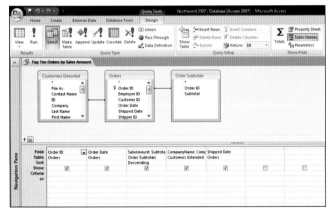

What's your query?

Businesses will want to question the database to find out how sales are going, who has bought what, or what the current stock level is. These sorts of questions are called queries, and you can set up a lot of different regularly used query forms, which you can call up to give you the up-to-date information you need. Each database will have its own way of creating queries, but generally you tell the system which fields are to be used and how they are to sort themselves into a new table that will contain the results of the query.

Automation

Many business database jobs, such as sales reports, need to be done regularly. So instead of going through the whole procedure of opening up the database files, comparing them, choosing reports and then printing them each time, the whole process can be automated using a macro.

A macro is a short computer program that controls the database functions for you. As a security measure, Windows doesn't let them run without your permission. When you open a database with macros, you'll see a Security Warning beneath the Ribbon bar. Click the Options button and click Enable This Content if you trust the source it has come from. Many database programs also supply templates for the more common business databases and reports.

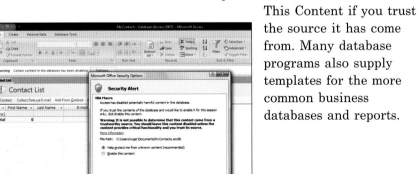

6 SPREADSHEETS

Spread out

The introduction of the spreadsheet was one of the most important developments in PC software. The spreadsheet, and the power it brought to business accounts, prompted the first big burst of PC buying. Remember, this was in the days when there was no Windows and if you wanted to use a computer for letter writing, you bought a dedicated word-processor unit.

Spreadsheets are important because they do the one thing that computers do exceptionally well and that people take forever to do: lots and lots of simple repetitive calculations. At the heart of any spreadsheet is a column of information, such as a set of prices, that needs to have something done to it, such as adding tax. Before spreadsheets existed, someone would have to look up the prices, do the calculation with a calculator, and then write down the result. Apart from all the time it takes, doing it manually introduces the possibility of mistakes.

The PC spreadsheet, on the other hand, will do all the calculations in a split second and print out the results the way you want, with no extra effort and virtually no chance of errors. And if the calculation has to change – say, the tax rate goes up – then half a dozen keystrokes later, you have all the new figures printed out for you.

Business loved it, and then, as spreadsheets teamed up with good graphing software, anyone who wanted to analyse and display information of any kind soon found that the spreadsheet was an ideal tool. These days spreadsheets are commonly used in all areas: in the home, in the classroom and in big and small businesses alike.

The blank spreadsheet grid may seem a bit awesome, and some of the calculations more than a little complicated, but spreadsheets are easy to master. They can help you out with any project that involves a lot of addition, other calculations or storing information. And once you've got it going, you'll be surprised how quickly you can do complex calculation jobs. ●

The basics

Spreadsheets are the most effective way of dealing with lists of information that need to have some sort of calculation done to them. In the home, this could be something as simple as a shopping list with prices, while a wedding list and an inventory of your household belongings are other examples of household spreadsheets. There are also spreadsheet programs within other packages. Home-finance software is just a spreadsheet that has been tailored to one particular application. You can set up these types of applications yourself using a general spreadsheet package such as Microsoft Excel 2007.

Spreadsheets and the worksheets used by databases have a lot in common. The rows in each represent all the information about a single entry, while the columns group together particular information about all the entries.

Formulas **are a set of calculations, sometimes as simple as adding up a row of entries, that produce the spreadsheet results you want to see.**

Current cell number **tells you which cell you are in.**

Cells **are individual boxes for your data and formulas.**

Rows **go across the screen and contain all the information.**

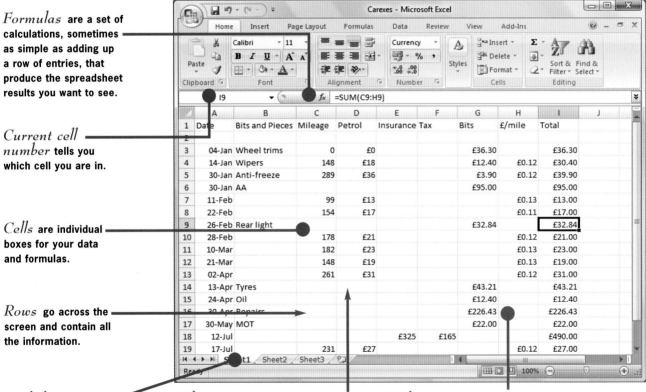

Worksheet **tabs tell you which worksheet you are working on.**

Columns **go down the screen and contain the information about one particular element of all the items.**

Values **are any type of number: this could be a quantity of an item, its cost or its size and these are the elements that are used in all the calculations.**

What does it mean?

- **Worksheet** The large sheet that contains all the data and formulas.
- **Workbooks** A set of worksheets for a complete project.
- **Cells** The boxes that contain pieces of data or calculations.
- **Labels** A text entry in a cell.
- **Value** A number entry in a cell.
- **Formula** A calculation in a cell.
- **Cell address** Identifies a specific cell. Cell addresses work just like map references: cell C24 would be in column C, row 24.

Types of data

There are three separate kinds of information that you can put into a cell: a name or title, called a label; a number or value; and a calculation or formula. In a spreadsheet words are used for the names of the items you are entering and for things such as months and category headings. Your spreadsheet can use words to search, sort and calculate.

Moving around the spreadsheet

Spreadsheets require a lot of simple entering of words and numbers, each into its own cell. Since they are so full of numbers and words, your mouse hand would become really tired if you had to use the mouse to change cells for every entry. Instead, all spreadsheets make use of those arrow keys on your keyboard that hardly ever get used for anything else. Of course, the mouse is essential for moving around to different parts of the spreadsheet.

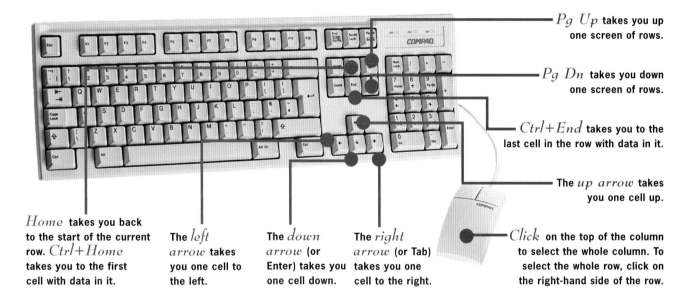

Pg Up **takes you up one screen of rows.**

Pg Dn **takes you down one screen of rows.**

Ctrl+End **takes you to the last cell in the row with data in it.**

The *up arrow* **takes you one cell up.**

Home **takes you back to the start of the current row.** *Ctrl+Home* **takes you to the first cell with data in it.**

The *left arrow* **takes you one cell to the left.**

The *down arrow* **(or Enter) takes you one cell down.**

The *right arrow* **(or Tab) takes you one cell to the right.**

Click **on the top of the column to select the whole column. To select the whole row, click on the right-hand side of the row.**

Adding columns and rows

As you add information to your spreadsheet, you may want to include a new line or column. If you want to add a new line, highlight the row above or below where it is to appear and, with the Home tab selected, go to the cells section of the Ribbon bar (that replaces the menu and Toolbars used in previous versions of Excel). Click on the dropdown arrow beside Insert and select Insert Sheet Rows. The new line will appear and everything will be shifted down or up. Follow the same sequence to insert a column, but select Insert Sheet Columns. If you want to remove columns or rows, follow the same process but choose the Delete option.

Getting the boxes to fit

Spreadsheet boxes usually hold about a dozen characters. While this is easily big enough for most number entries, you may run out of space when it comes to putting in text. When a text entry is too long, some spreadsheets grow taller or the end of the text disappears under the cell next to it. You can alter the width of all the cells in a column by dragging the right-hand side of the column until there is enough space for all the words to fit on one line.

If the number is too big to fit into the cell, you will get something like this. Just *enlarge* **the cell and you'll see the complete number.**

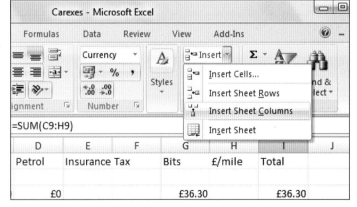

Get started

There are many applications that you can use your spreadsheet for, from doing the accounts for your local club or association to charting your children's heights as they grow. Here we'll try something close to home: a spreadsheet to see how your car costs spread over the year.

The first job is to set up the spreadsheet with the headings you are going to use and then format the columns for the sort of information that is going to be entered into them.

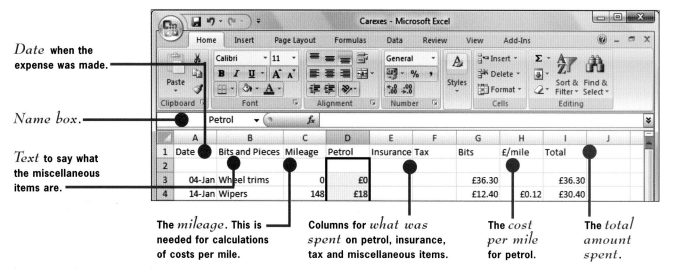

Date **when the expense was made.**

Name box.

Text **to say what the miscellaneous items are.**

The *mileage*. **This is needed for calculations of costs per mile.**

Columns for *what was spent* **on petrol, insurance, tax and miscellaneous items.**

The *cost per mile* **for petrol.**

The *total amount spent*.

Format Cells **tells your spreadsheet that the cell contains a specific type of data that should be displayed as you want. You can choose whether you want decimal places or not, what format to display dates in, and whether to display pounds or pounds and pence.**

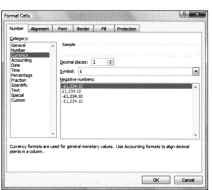

I name this column...

Most spreadsheets let you give each column a name, rather than just a reference letter. Link the numbers in a column by highlighting the cells (for example, cells D2–D19) and type the column name (Petrol, in the above example) in the name box. Naming columns and rows makes life a lot easier when it comes to doing calculations, because you can write formulas in English. Petrol+Insurance+Tax+Bits is much clearer than D5+E5+F5+G5.

Loads of values

If you thought a value was simply a number, then think again. In spreadsheets there are all sorts of values that you can work with: money, dates, percentages or fractions. Each has its particular use, and spreadsheets have special tricks so that they can handle each in a way that makes sense.

Enter the information

Although for some spreadsheet projects you can enter all the data at once, most of the time the spreadsheet is constantly being updated. You can add more information at any time you like, and when you do, all the totals and other calculations are automatically updated.

Calculating

ormulas and calculations are at the heart of any spreadsheet. Once you've put in some data, you can get your spreadsheet to do some calculating. Formulas are sets of instructions that tell the spreadsheet to take the values from specified cells, put them through a calculation, and show the answer.

First you need to find an empty cell to put the calculation in, usually at the end of a row or column. You have to tell the spreadsheet that what you are about to type is a formula, not a word or a number. In some spreadsheets, you do this by typing the @ sign. In Excel you use the = sign.

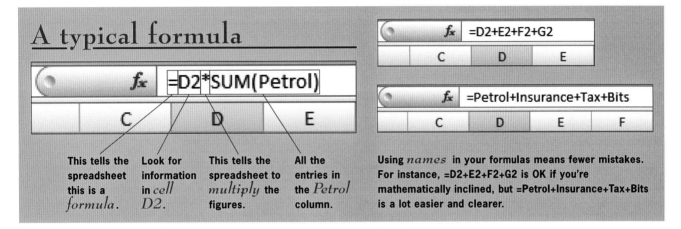

A typical formula

f_x =D2*SUM(Petrol)

| C | D | E |

This tells the spreadsheet this is a *formula*.

Look for information in *cell* **D2.**

This tells the spreadsheet to *multiply* **the figures.**

All the entries in the *Petrol* **column.**

f_x =D2+E2+F2+G2

| C | D | E |

f_x =Petrol+Insurance+Tax+Bits

| C | D | E | F |

Using *names* in your formulas means fewer mistakes. For instance, =D2+E2+F2+G2 is OK if you're mathematically inclined, but =Petrol+Insurance+Tax+Bits is a lot easier and clearer.

Spread the news

Once you've done one formula and it works, use this formula for the rest of the column. All spreadsheets have a Fill option (right), which copies the formula all the way up or down a column or left to right across a row so the totals automatically appear at the end of each column or row. You can see how the spreadsheet can handle a huge number of rows with no more effort than working on a single row.

Working with formulas

When you copy a formula down a column, your spreadsheet uses it to work with each row. This is because the formula is relative. It is telling your PC to look down the row and repeat the calculation using the values from relevant cells. When you copy the formula to the end of another row, it will look at the cells in that row and work on those.

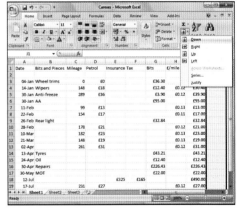

Sometimes, however, you'll want to put in a formula that stays the same whatever you do. You need to turn these into absolute formulas so that the formula always looks *only* at the cells you originally specified.

Different spreadsheets use different signs to make a formula absolute. In

f_x =D2*SUM(Petrol)

| C | D | E |

an Excel or Works spreadsheet, you type the dollar sign in front of any part of the cell address you want to make absolute.

Calculations upon calculations

Now that you've worked out the totals for each item, you can use another formula to add up the results to give an overall total. The spreadsheet will tell you if you've typed a formula that doesn't make sense.

- Invalid Name Error
- Help on this error
- Show Calculation Steps...
- Ignore Error
- Edit in Formula Bar
- Error Checking Options...

More features

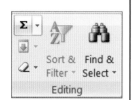

Most spreadsheets give you quick ways to add rows or columns of numbers. You highlight the column and one empty cell at the end and click on the AutoSum button (∑). In Excel it's accessed via the Editing group on the Ribbon bar under the Home tab. Everything in the column is added together, and the result is inserted into the bottom cell (right).

C	D	E
Mileage	Petrol	
148	£18	
289	£36	
99	£13	
154	£17	
178	£21	
182	£23	
148	£19	
261	£31	
Total	£178	

Inside the brackets

Often you will want to use a more complicated mathematical formula, in which you group a couple of mathematical functions together in a particular order. Use brackets to make sure everything is done in the right order. Totals inside the brackets are calculated together before anything else in the formula is worked on.

fx =(Mileage+Petrol+Insurance+Tax+Bits)/7

C	D	E	F	G	H

The spreadsheet will first add the *subtotals* (Mileage+ Petrol+Insurance+Tax+Bits) together and then divide that total by 7.

Hundreds of functions

As well as simple arithmetic, spreadsheets offer hundreds of special functions to help you analyse your information. These can do clever tricks with dates and values, statistical functions, functions that can find words or turn text into numbers and back again, and logical functions that can look at a cell and do different things depending on what is in the cell.

No one will pretend that these special functions are all simple to use. In fact, some are quite complicated, and you'll need a good understanding of statistics or accounting. Since spreadsheets are professional work tools, they need these sophisticated functions to meet the needs of large businesses as well as the requirements of people using them at home.

Logical functions in action

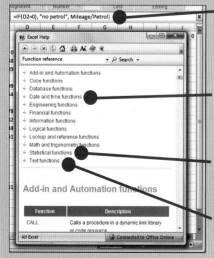

This *logical function* simply says IF there is nothing in the Petrol column (D2=0), then put 'no petrol' in the cell. If petrol was bought, then show the cost per mile (Mileage/Petrol).

Date and Time functions. Dates are converted into numbers, which lets you do all sorts of calculations with items that change over time.

Statistical functions give you an instant way of showing figures like averages.

Text functions find text or change the way that text entries look.

Multiple spreads

Sophisticated 3-D spreadsheets let you work on several worksheets at once. These can pass information from one sheet to another and calculations spread across several sheets as easily as working in different areas of a single large sheet.

Double-check

Double-check a sample result along a couple of rows with a calculator. This will confirm that your formula is working with the right cells and the calculations you've typed in are correct.

Looking good

Now that you've got the spreadsheet working well and showing the right information, you can neaten it up. When you type text into a cell, it is normally aligned left. Numbers are aligned to the right. But you can choose how you want your columns to look. Highlight the whole column and use the Align buttons on the Ribbon bar to align the entries differently. Here, the Center button has been used in the total column but there are no rules: some alignments will simply look better in different situations.

	Date	Bits and Pieces	Mileage	Petrol	Insurance	Tax	Bits	£/mile	Total
1									
2									
3	04-Jan	Wheel trims	0	0			£36.30		**£36.30**
4	14-Jan	Wipers	148	£18			£12.40	£0.12	**£30.40**
5	30-Jan	Anti-freeze	289	£36			£3.90	£0.12	**£39.90**
6	30-Jan	AA					£95.00		**£95.00**
7	11-Feb		99	£13				£0.13	**£13.00**
8	22-Feb		154	£17				£0.11	**£17.00**

Keep it simple

When you are working with long lists of numbers and names, you need to make them as clear as possible. Although you can choose any typeface that comes with Windows, it is best to stick to Times or Arial for clarity. Use bold letters to highlight titles, headings, totals, columns or rows containing the most important information.

Reporting in

Even with the totals and subtotals put in bold, it is still difficult to separate the answers from the mass of numbers and words. And when it comes to printing out the results, you don't want to print pages and pages of spreadsheet data just so you can see the totals at the end of the columns and rows. It makes more sense to put all the results you want to see all in one place as a report, which you can either look at on screen or print out on a single page.

All spreadsheets let you give a block of cells a *name* so you can jump to the area of the spreadsheet where you have put your report information. This means you don't have to scroll through all your spreadsheet data to get there. In Excel 2007 select the range of cells you want to name and click on the Formulas tab on the Ribbon bar and then on the Create Names from Selection button in the Defined Names group.

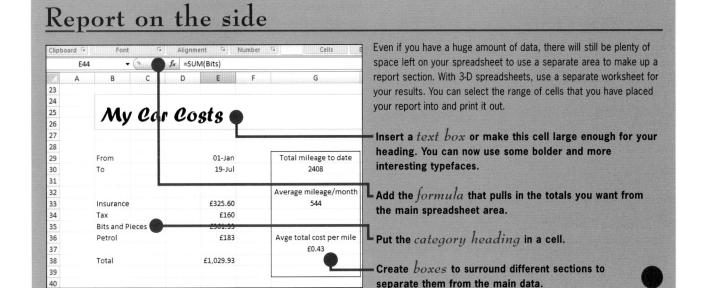

Report on the side

Even if you have a huge amount of data, there will still be plenty of space left on your spreadsheet to use a separate area to make up a report section. With 3-D spreadsheets, use a separate worksheet for your results. You can select the range of cells that you have placed your report into and print it out.

Insert a *text box* or make this cell large enough for your heading. You can now use some bolder and more interesting typefaces.

Add the *formula* that pulls in the totals you want from the main spreadsheet area.

Put the *category heading* in a cell.

Create *boxes* to surround different sections to separate them from the main data.

My Car Costs

E44 = =SUM(Bits)

From	01-Jan		Total mileage to date
To	19-Jul		2408
			Average mileage/month
Insurance	£325.60		544
Tax	£160		
Bits and Pieces	£361.33		Avge total cost per mile
Petrol	£183		£0.43
Total	£1,029.93		

Graphs

There are few spreadsheet reports that can't be made clearer and easier to read by the inclusion of a graph or two. Graphs may not give you detail down to the last fraction, but they do show you what is happening in general and highlight trends. Most spreadsheets have good graphing facilities built in, so it is a simple job to turn your data into a graph. You can place your graph in the spreadsheet or copy it over to a word processor to liven it up.

All sorts of graphs

There are a dozen or so types of graphs that you can choose from. But the most important are bar graphs and pie charts. Bar graphs convert each entry into a vertical or horizontal column and are good at showing trends and how things change from one entry to the next. You can also stack several related pieces of information side by side to see how different categories compare. Pie charts are best at showing how one particular item is split up. You can see how big each section is and which are the most, or least, important elements.

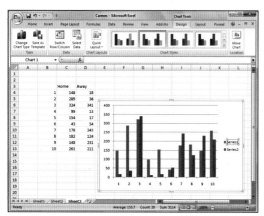

Flat or 3-D

If you want to create a very simple graph, bar and pie charts can be shown completely flat. This is useful if there are a lot of columns and slices in the graph, or if it is vital to produce a clear image, such as when you are creating graphs for display on an overhead projector. But if your graph is going to be seen on screen or printed out in a report, a 3-D graph will look more interesting. You may have the option to change the viewing angle to make the graph more impressive.

Fine-tuning

Don't feel you are stuck with the text and colour scheme that your spreadsheet uses. You can get back into the graph and change the colour scheme and the text style and size to whatever you feel looks best.

If you are using Excel 2007, once you have entered your information on the spreadsheet, go to the Insert tab and select the chart type you want from the Ribbon bar. To see all the charts available click the icon in the bottom right corner of the Charts section. Click on your choice and it will be added to the page. A new tab, Design, appears on the Ribbon bar to let you customise the look and location of the graph.

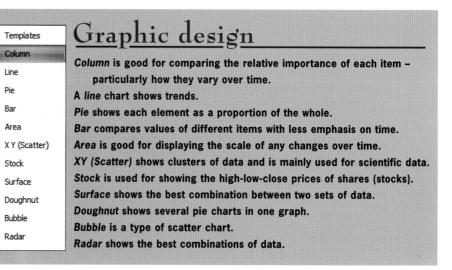

Graphic design

Column is good for comparing the relative importance of each item – particularly how they vary over time.

A *line* chart shows trends.

Pie shows each element as a proportion of the whole.

Bar compares values of different items with less emphasis on time.

Area is good for displaying the scale of any changes over time.

XY (Scatter) shows clusters of data and is mainly used for scientific data.

Stock is used for showing the high-low-close prices of shares (stocks).

Surface shows the best combination between two sets of data.

Doughnut shows several pie charts in one graph.

Bubble is a type of scatter chart.

Radar shows the best combinations of data.

Many options

You'll be glad to know that spreadsheets do not leave you on your own. Many offer all sorts of ready-made files for the most common spreadsheet applications. You can open one up and get going immediately, knowing that all the essential formulas have already been developed for you.

There are additional tools – Microsoft calls its tools Wizards – that will help you make your own spreadsheets and reports. As long as you know roughly what you want to do, the Wizard will take you through the options and start putting in the right columns, rows, formulas and reports.

Working backwards

The natural way of working with a spreadsheet is to put in all the data and then calculate a result. This is fine to see how things are now, but it doesn't help you see how things could be. To do that, you need to work backwards: start with the result and calculate what the data should be to get that result.

What if?

What if you think you can afford to spend a little more on a car. You know how much the purchase price is, but what combination of insurance, miles per gallon and everything else will that allow? You can take the data you have already on mileage and how your existing costs spread over the year, and then enter some totals for petrol, insurance and mileage. The spreadsheet will work back from the totals and fill in the blank data cells. You'll then be able to look at several different sets of options to show what miles per gallon and depreciation and insurance levels you can afford, and how those costs are likely to be spread over the year.

Moving data around

If you want to go beyond the simple database functions of your spreadsheet, you can export the sheet into a database program. Databases work from the same type of worksheet as spreadsheets, so you will be able to start working on your data almost immediately. Software suites such as Works and Office ensure that data can move from one type of program to another without problems.

To and from a word processor

Your spreadsheet results can be easily added into a report written in your word processor. If it is a single report, use Copy to place the information on your word-processor page and it will appear as a table.

If the spreadsheet information forms part of a regular monthly report, use your word processor's Special Paste function to link the spreadsheet information directly to your report document. Each time you update your spreadsheet, the table or graph in your report document is automatically updated, too.

You can, of course, work the other way around, and bring in information from a database or a table in a word-processor document and feed it directly into your spreadsheet.

You can incorporate *spreadsheet results* **into word-processor documents.**

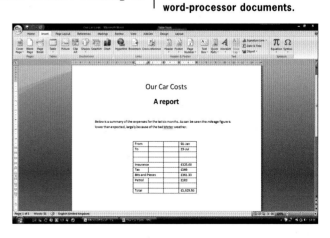

Multiple uses

Although you are not going to be using a spreadsheet as much as your word processor, it is still an important and useful tool whenever you need to do some number crunching. Very few businesses get by without using a spreadsheet of one variety or another, and it will help you manage clubs and associations as well as any other small project that involves lists of things that you have to keep track of and calculate in some way.

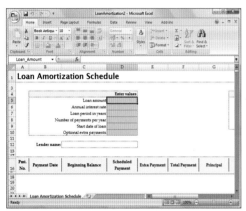

Spreadsheets for finances

Spreadsheets started life as a tool for accountants in large companies, and they have become an essential tool for every company. Now that PCs are available to everyone, and spreadsheet programs have been made much simpler to understand and operate, they can be just as useful for small businesses, the self-employed or anyone helping to run a small club or association.

They will help you keep track of all your financial activities and can be used to create invoices, bills and receipts. Since most businesses or associations need the same sort of spreadsheet layouts and reports, you'll find your software comes with a range of ready-made business sheets, or templates, that you can simply open up and start entering your finances into.

Home finances

In our next chapter, we will be talking about home-finance software that can keep track of your bank accounts, income and expenses. These are basically spreadsheets, although they don't always look like them. In your spreadsheet software, you'll find ready-made spreadsheets that will cover most home-finance tasks, such as making a home inventory.

Spreadsheets at school

Spreadsheets may be new to you, but from primary school onwards, children are getting used to entering data and looking at the results. Spreadsheets form an important part of information-technology teaching, using projects such as looking at the variation in height among the children in a class. The children can put in information about their own height. Then they can start looking at how many variations there are, what averages are and how one measurement is related to another.

To spreadsheet or not to spreadsheet?

For some jobs, such as home finances, you may be more comfortable using a dedicated system rather than the functions in a spreadsheet. If you have a software suite, you might choose to use a spreadsheet instead of a database, as a spreadsheet will also have database and search functions built in to handle the simple requirements of looking for information. For example, a simple list of people and phone numbers can be put into a spreadsheet and sorted alphabetically so it's easy to find a name and number. If you want to do more with the information, you can always export the data into a real database.

7
HOME FINANCE

Easy money

When asked what they would like their PC to do for them, most people reply: 'Anything to get their home finances in order.' A household can have several different bank accounts, credit-card accounts and credit purchases. This is complicated by the usual expenses: the rent or the mortgage, insurance policies, car costs, electricity, telephone bills and the regular income from work and investments. Accounting for the pennies so the pounds can take care of themselves is not always straightforward. And keeping track of exactly what comes in and what goes out requires a juggling act that is beyond most people. So no wonder the computer, with its history of being used for big company accounts, is seen as a boon for helping to keep the household accounts straight.

Accounts packages have been around for a long time. But they weren't popular at first because most of them were designed purely for business accounting. Even if they could handle household accounts, people still needed the skills of an accountant to understand how to use them.

But things have changed. Software systems such as Microsoft Money have moved away from the business approach. They have become more like multimedia programs, with easy-to-use and attractive interfaces that make accounts much less boring and difficult. The idea is to make them so simple to use that you don't avoid putting your weekly accounts into your PC.

Once you are in the habit of putting your finances into your PC, you can get two types of useful information out of your home-accounts package. The first is an accurate view of what is coming in and going out of the household budget. You can check the accuracy of your bank statements and start looking at where the money goes. Once the information is in the PC, it can be sifted and sorted in different ways so you can check what is going on.

And looking into the future and planning your finances is just as important. Can you afford that new car – or even that new computer? What would happen if you paid in one lump sum or used one of the many credit purchase agreements available? Home-finance packages let you look into your crystal ball and see what the best options are and what impact your choices will have. ●

Accounts

Power for finance

Home-finance packages are light users of computer power. A typical program will run on any PC that is powerful enough to run Windows, and will take around 390MB of space depending on the program.

Home-finance programs such as Microsoft Money are aimed at helping you with your personal finances. They make it easy for you to keep track of your money. They can handle anything that involves your income, so you know exactly the state of your financial health at any time.

When you are looking for a home-finance package, you should be sure to get one that meets your needs. Your home finances need a different approach from the one you would use for business. You are not going to need the more sophisticated functions included in business-accounts software.

Even if you have a small business or are the treasurer of a club, you may find some of the home-finance packages are more than adequate.

Accounts for small businesses

If your business or club accounts involve more complex functions, such as stock control, it may be worth considering a business-accounts package. In the past, business-accounts packages were expensive and assumed the person using them was an accountant. The increased interest by small businesses and the self-employed in using PCs has created a new generation of accounts software. This combines the business functions of the bigger packages with the ease of use of the home systems.

VAT's the way to do it

A good home-finance package can handle the essential elements of VAT. If you, your business or your club are VAT registered, you have to tell the VAT office the difference between what you have paid in VAT on buying goods and services and the VAT you have charged your customers.

The theory is simple, but the reality can be a headache. Your PC can take the hassle out of preparing VAT accounts. It will calculate the VAT on any transaction and store this as a separate account. When it comes to working out the accounts, your PC will total all the invoices with and without the VAT, show the amount of VAT that has been paid and charged, and generally do all the hard work for you.

Organising accounts

Once you have installed your software, the first thing you will be asked to do is enter all the accounts that make up your finances. A typical family may have quite an array of accounts. First, there are bank accounts, which may include a current account, an interest-paying savings account, and even a building society account. There may also be investments that are treated as separate accounts, since your home-finance package has special tools to keep track of the ups and downs of an investment portfolio.

Then there are the accounts for credit cards and loans. These may include your credit card bill, your mortgage, a car loan, or the credit payments on a TV.

Virtual accounts

Not every account on your PC has to have a matching bank account, so you can also set up virtual accounts. If you want to save for a holiday, you will

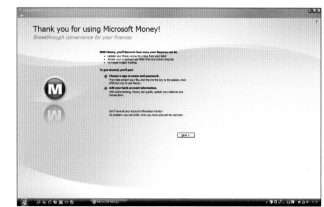

need to keep track of how those monthly amounts you are putting aside are mounting up. A Savings Goal account will keep track of what you are putting aside for that special week in the sun and show you how close you are to reaching your target, even though, in reality, the money is going into the savings account alongside other payments and withdrawals.

Setting up **an account is easy. In Microsoft Money just follow the Wizard to fill in your details.**

Setting up

You can enter all sorts of information about each account, such as contact names and numbers, and whether it pays interest. Your PC will be able to calculate the interest due automatically at any point in time.

When you are setting up your accounts, you can decide whether or not you need to separate out the VAT. For most home users, this should be set to No VAT across the board. But if one particular account relates to a VAT-registered business, you can get the software to calculate the VAT automatically every time a new entry is made.

As with nearly all the functions in a good home-finance software package, you don't have to go through a complex setting-up procedure. When you set up a new account, your PC will ask you all the necessary questions, one at a time. You'll just have to type in the answers.

The current state of affairs

Once you have the framework, it's time to enter your current state of affairs. The important thing is to get your home accounts and the bank accounts synchronised so that your computer's monthly report can be checked against your bank statement.

The starting point for this is to use your most recent statement for each account. The system will ask you to enter the last balance and its date. When you've entered these simple details, your PC has a starting point that matches your printed statements. It will use this as the starting point for all future calculations.

Gather those papers

It is a good idea before you start to get hold of as many of your financial papers as possible and sort them into categories and accounts. If things are missing, don't worry, because you can always add another account or other details later. As well as your financial history, you should also think about any savings goals you might want to work towards in the future. It can be very modest, maybe just £5 a month for a special treat at the end of the year. Set up a Savings Goal and your computer will remind you to put the money in the bank each month and keep track of how your savings towards that specific target are progressing.

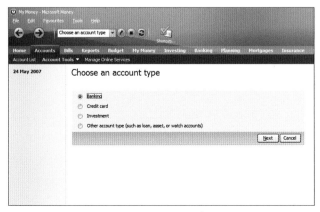

There are lots of different account *options* you can use.

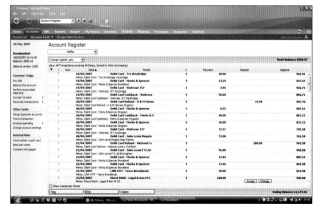

You can look through all the *entries* in any account. There will be a display showing you the current balance, too.

Transactions

our home-finance program coordinates everything you enter into it, using one large spreadsheet. A spreadsheet is like a large piece of paper with lines and columns. Each new entry or transaction is put on a new line, and the amounts involved are put into a column that corresponds to that particular account. There are separate columns for every account and type of transaction and columns for notes about each entry. Printed out in its raw state, this would be a very complex piece of paper.

But you never have to look at the whole sheet. When you need to enter or look at information, the program sorts the relevant entries for that particular job and shows you just what you need to see. With all your accounts centralised in this way, your computer can extract information in all sorts of ways. If you want to look at your current account, the program will take only the entries in the Transaction Sheet that relate to the current account and show you those, with all the totals and subtotals you might need. You may want to look at everything that has been paid in over the past month. Your PC will look at the entries across all the accounts and collate everything that happened over the previous month for you to see. It is this flexibility that makes home-finance packages so useful.

Once the accounts are set up, you can start entering your transactions. Rather than try to describe every different type of entry that your home-finance program can deal with, they are all given the general name Transactions. A transaction could be money going into an account or money going out – or even money moving from one account to another.

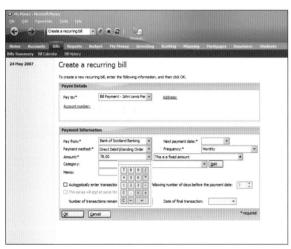

Fill in the *on-screen cheque,* **which has its own calculator, and you can set up recurring bills.**

When you write a cheque or deposit money in an account, you should record it on the PC. As you enter the information, the PC will update the account's balance according to your cheque or paying-in slip.

Entering transactions is no more complex than writing a cheque or a paying-in slip. Your PC asks you more or less for the same information that the bank does: the date, who the money is going to or coming from, and the amount involved. Some programs even display an on-screen cheque for you to fill in and transfer the information directly into the Transaction Sheet. You also have space to type in other notes about the transaction, just as you have on the cheque stub.

You do this when you get a bill to pay or deposit money into an account. Most of the information about the account is already loaded, so this takes only a few seconds. The only other information to add is the transaction's category.

Categorise accounts

Every transaction can be linked to any other transaction throughout the year. And you can group money spent on similar things or income coming from the same source.

On the expenses side, groups that will be regularly used will include home repairs, petrol, holidays, the garden and property taxes. Different sources of income can be grouped together into categories, such as salary, child benefit or interest on savings.

The advantage of categorising all of your transactions is that your PC

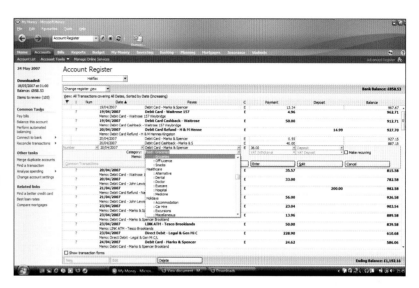

can start grouping them together. Then you can see how much was spent over the year on a particular activity or how much income came into the household from, say, a part-time job. Your program will have a comprehensive list of categories built into it, and you can always add your own.

There are lots of *categories* that you can assign a payment or receipt to. Or you can create your own.

Groups and supergroups

Once you've grouped a set of payments into a single category, you may then find it useful to group a set of categories together into a supergroup. Take the cost of running a car, for example. You would put your fuel costs into the Petrol category, repairs into the Car Service category, and tax and insurance into the Tax/Insurance category. Having done that, you can get your program to tell you how much you have spent in each category, and when.

But you can't find out from this the total amount you have spent on the car. To do that, you have to set up a supergroup, called Car, which groups together the Petrol, Car Service, and Tax/Insurance categories. Now you can see both the overall amount of money spent on the car and individual categories. Regularly used supergroups are those that group all household expenses, income, social security payments, and car expenses together.

You can create larger *supergroups* to tell you the overall costs, or income, from a group of related categories, such as household expenses.

Self-sorting dates

Everything in the Transaction Sheet is listed in date order. It doesn't matter at all if you don't get around to entering a transaction until a few weeks after it happened. Your PC will automatically slot it into its rightful place in the listings.

Cash flow

Y ou'd be surprised how many transactions you know about some time before they happen – the rent or mortgage, standing orders, credit-card payments, car tax and insurance, membership dues and paydays. There are also one-off items that you know about in advance, such as the balance of a holiday payment.

Even if you don't know the exact amounts that are going to be involved, you can enter these future transactions into a financial calendar that keeps track of them. This allows you to see what your accounts are going to look like in a few months' time. For regular transactions such as standing orders, enter the details once. Then it is a simple matter of clicking on the due days each month.

Your PC always knows the date from its internal clock. When you load your home-finance system, the first thing it does is look at the calendar and check for any transactions that are due, or overdue. The system will then tell you what should be dealt with.

Use the *calendar* to put in details of regular payments and income. If the payments fall on the same day every month, you only have to enter the details once and the system will do the rest for you.

Instant transfer

Some transactions will appear in two parts of your system. For instance, with a phone bill, the bill will appear in the telephone account, the amount being added when you pay it.

Back in your cheque account, which is being used to pay the bill, the details of the payment also have to be entered. In theory, this means several sets of entries, but to save you having to move from one part of the system to another, the software will do this for you. When it comes to paying the phone bill, go to the cheque account, which will already have the phone company's details in it, click on the phone company and, if you have already entered the invoice details, most finance programs will take that information and automatically debit your cheque account while updating all the necessary details. This also works when you transfer money from one account to another. Once you have told the system where the money is coming from and going to, it will do the rest.

Balancing

After you have entered your transactions, at the end of each month you need to reconcile where you think you are with where your bank, building society or credit-card company thinks you are. This is called balancing your accounts. Many people already do this each month by checking the bank-statement entries. This is its simplest form. You just check that each item on your bank statement matches the cheque stubs and paying-in slips.

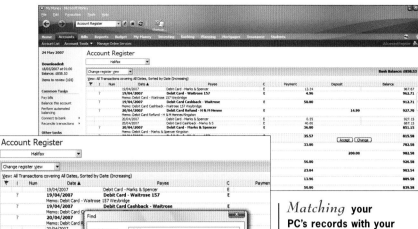

You know the amount, but where is it? Use the *Find* command to sort out those queries.

Balancing your accounts on the PC takes no more time than doing it manually. And it should be quicker because all the information about payments and receipts is at hand. The program shows you the payments and receipts you have entered into your PC. If they are on your bank statement, you check them off by clicking on them. At the bottom of the screen, you can see the current bank balance, the value of items that have not cleared and what the difference is. If everything that you've written has gone through the account, you'll get a satisfying zero in the difference column. Furthermore, with online banking you may be able to download your statement information direct from your bank, into your home accounts package.

Some cheques written near or after the date of the statement won't have cleared. So in the real world, there will nearly always be some amount in the difference column. While this is normal, it shouldn't stop you from looking through the uncleared entries to verify that nothing is amiss. If a cheque hasn't cleared for a couple of months, you can check with the payee that it was received. It is helpful to keep a little more in your account so that it is not overdrawn when a late cheque finally comes through for payment.

Matching your PC's records with your statements is simple. Click the mouse on each entry that is on your statement and you can choose to Accept it or Change it as necessary.

Hide-and-seek

In this imperfect world, paperwork has a tendency to be misplaced. Dates, names and amounts are all needed to be certain that a payment matches an entry in your accounts, but sometimes you may have only one of these pieces of information. This is why the Find and Replace function is one of the most useful in your finance package. Whenever there is a problem with payments into or out of your accounts, Find will usually give you the answers.

The command is simple – it just asks you which category you want to search: the name of the payee, the amount or the date. You enter what details you have and the PC will then find entries that match. This is useful if you have an entry in your bank statement that you can't figure out. Put in the amount and the program will find the matching entry in your transactions.

The match doesn't have to be exact. If it is a credit-card payment for a small amount that includes an unknown extra (such as a postage payment for something you bought mail order), you can ask the system to find all transactions below a certain amount. This will help you narrow down the search and make it easier to find the entry.

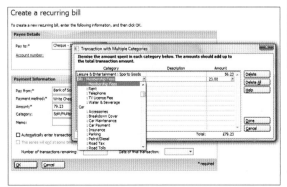

When you create a bill, you can split the total payment between categories. So, for example, a cheque to your fishing club could be split between your regular subscription and some equipment you've bought.

Inventory

As well as keeping track of the cash that is coming into and going out of the house, you can have a complete inventory of its contents. If you can't see the immediate advantage, you may well find that your insurance company will. The best reason for having an accurate inventory of your home and all its contents is to get an accurate value for insurance purposes. Insurance companies say people under-insure their household contents. People always remember the big expensive items – such as the TV, the microwave, the chairs and tables – but not the plants, bed linen, CDs or cutlery. That's where the home inventory comes in. Since you would naturally list things by room, so does the home inventory. It takes you through each room, suggesting the sort of things you should be listing.

What's it worth?

When you enter a value, you have two options: its resale value or its replacement value. Some insurance policies will replace old items with new ones. In this case you will need to enter the current cost of a replacement. Other policies will pay the secondhand value of the items.

In the inventory you can list either value or both. Another option is to enter the purchase price. The inventory will work out the secondhand cost using a percentage of the original price.

As well as an item's value, you can also include a description and other important information, such as serial numbers, date of purchase, original price, and when the warranty expires.

Holiday time

There are all sorts of things you might find the inventory useful for. You could use it for your holidays, for example. There are always things you'll forget to take. Set up a holiday inventory, and when you get back you can update it. When it comes around to holiday time again, you just print out your inventory and everything is listed. The list is also handy to take with you in case you need to claim loss or damage during your trip.

Mix and match

A home inventory can rearrange its information in lots of different ways. You can list everything by room or by category. You can have a listing of everything in the living room or produce a complete breakdown of all your sports gear, no matter where it is in the house. These different ways of listing things can be important when you have separate insurance policies for the car and its contents, a policy for the contents of the house, and one for the building and fixtures. The separate lists can tell you the necessary insurance value for each policy.

1. In Microsoft Money you first need to set up the *Home Inventory* **worksheet. On the Home page, click Customise Content or Layout and select Home Inventory from the Add Content box. Click the Add» button then Done. Under Home Inventory click Go to my Home Inventory.**

2. Use *Home Inventory – Furnishings* **(in listing on left-hand side). The information is stored on one worksheet, but you can select categorised views – of furnishings, or office equipment, for example. This is important if you need to value items separately for different insurance policies.**

3. Use the *Inventory Details* **box to fill in the information. To enter a new item, just click New at the bottom of the worksheet. Keep serial numbers here, and any information needed to make a claim under a warranty agreement.**

8

PRINTING

Press on!

After the screen, keyboard and mouse, the most important device to connect to your computer is a printer. The big difference between a printer and other peripherals is that it affects the way that others see your work. The letters, reports, pictures and graphs that you produce may be the only thing you do on your computer that others will see. And they are all delivered via your printer.

Unlike keyboards or mice, which work in much the same way and differ little in use, there are many kinds of printers. This chapter explores all the options.

There are two main types of printer: inkjet also called bubblejet, and laser. While they all create an image by printing dots on paper, the cost and quality of each type varies enormously. Some produce better-quality prints than others, but may not be within your budget.

When choosing a printer, it is important to know what each type of printer will let you do and what the limitations of each are. Once you've looked at the options, you'll find the number of models that really meet your requirements can be whittled down from the many available to just a manageable handful.

Printing in black and white has been standard since people first started to use PCs, when the idea of colour printing at home would have been just a dream. But now colour printing is no longer a luxury. You can easily, and relatively cheaply, include great-looking, full-colour pictures in your printouts.

Many of you will, of course, already have a printer. Understanding your printer and how it works will enable you to make the most of it, and it will help you to learn how to keep using it without running up big bills to refill the ink or toner each time it runs out.

And don't forget the paper. The right choice of paper can make as much difference to the quality of your printing as your choice of printer. Using cheap paper for work that doesn't leave your house or office saves money. And it can help the environment if you opt for recycled paper. Find out what kind of paper will make an impression on your friends, clients or anyone who reads your printed paperwork. ●

Your printer

There is a bewildering range of printers available that vary hugely in price. You have to choose one that is going to suit your particular needs and finances. First, you need to decide which category is best for you and then look to see which printer in that category is ideal. There are two main types of printer available: inkjet and laser. Each has its own pros and cons.

Inkjets: best of both worlds

Inkjet printers – or bubblejets, as some of them are called – work by spraying ink on to the paper from tiny nozzles in the printer cartridge. For many people, inkjets are the ideal solution since they are relatively cheap to buy and can produce very good results. The fact that inkjets are almost silent when printing makes them worth the investment – your computer's fan is likely to be noisier than an inkjet printer in operation. Typical inkjet printers are fairly compact. And there are several ultra-slim inkjets available that can be used when space is very limited.

Inkjets can handle varying sizes of paper and envelopes. You stack the blank paper in a paper tray, and it is automatically fed into the printer. Although an inkjet printer can be used with a variety of papers, for the best results, paper specially made for inkjet printers should be used.

The printing work is done by the inkjet's printer head, which is part of the ink-refill cartridge. This means that when the ink runs out, you replace both the ink and the printer head using one small cartridge. Because the printer head is replaced on a regular basis, each time you change the ink cartridge, this prevents the head from clogging up. The bad news is that this pushes up the cost of the ink cartridge and makes the inkjet the most expensive to operate of the different types of printer, with the highest cost per page printed.

There is one important thing that an inkjet can do well: it can be used for both black-and-white and full-colour printing. Inkjet manufacturers have found that if they use a specially designed three-colour ink cartridge/printer head, there is little else they have to change to turn an ordinary inkjet into a full-colour printer. So nearly all but the lowest-priced inkjet printers have colour capability. An inkjet uses a lot more ink when it is working in colour, so the operating cost goes up. But when you are printing out black-and-white pages only, you can revert to using just the black ink cartridge, which brings the cost per page back to a normal level.

Most inkjets come with a separate *black cartridge* **so it can be replaced without wasting unused colour inks.**

Lasers: quality at an affordable price

Laser printers create their copies in a way similar to that of a photocopier. A tiny laser beams the image on to a special photosensitive drum, where the image's black areas become charged with static electricity. The statically charged areas then pick up toner, which is ink in powder form. This black-powder image is then rolled on to the paper, and a heating element melts the powder, fusing it on to the page.

Because of their complexity, lasers have traditionally been at the luxury end of the printer range and could cost as much or more than your PC itself. But since more manufacturers have started making them, and more people have started using them, the prices have dropped dramatically. Now there are many laser printers the prices of which are comparable with those of the top-of-the-line inkjets.

Laser printers have many advantages over inkjet printers. The print quality they offer is excellent because the fused-ink system produces very crisp, clear text and images – better than the best inkjets. They are fast, producing several pages per minute, even at higher quality, and are cheaper to run than inkjet printers. Another advantage is that because the ink is fused on to the page, there is no risk of smudging, and laser-printed pages can be handled as soon as they appear.

But laser printers have a downside, too. Normally, they are a bit bigger than inkjet printers, and this can be a problem at home if you don't have a lot of space available. Also, they are less environmentally friendly, producing ozone as a by-product of the printing process. While laser printers are cheaper to run over a period of time, they can be more expensive to buy than other kinds of printers. Plus, although the toner cartridges last a long time, when they do run out, you will be faced with a large bill for a new one. Even though the cost per page is low, this can still come as a bit of a shock.

Colour laser printers are gradually becoming more affordable for home users, although they are still relatively expensive. They are fairly cumbersome in size but offer excellent print quality. A colour laser printer may be well worth considering if you can usefully take advantage of this for business or some other reason. They are good for presentations, pictures and homework projects, for instance, but you might find it more economical to use your old black-and-white laser printer for everyday work.

Photo perfect

While it's easy to send photos to friends and family electronically, sometimes it's good to have a picture you can pin to the fridge door or put in a photo frame on the mantelpiece. Several different types of printer are capable of printing out your photographic masterpiece, including some that are small enough for you to take with you on a trip. In this case, you can print off photos as you go. Otherwise, most normal inkjet printers are able to produce photo-quality prints, while dedicated photo printers use specialist printing techniques.

With inkjet printers, you will usually have to use special photo-paper and printing can be slow. Inkjets that are designed primarily for printing photos will focus on colour quality rather than text quality or speed, and so will be less useful as everyday printers. Some have six-colour cartridges rather than four, which helps to make the colours more subtle.

Many also have a memory card slot and viewer, so you can select pictures from the camera's memory card – and print them out – without going through the PC.

Dedicated photo printers use thermal-dye technology (also called dye-sublimation technology), which enables dye to be transferred from a ribbon on to glossy paper. Each colour is printed in turn and sealed with a clear varnish to give the picture a traditional glossy photo effect. The method used to recreate millions of colours means these printers need a much lower resolution to match the quality of high-resolution inkjets – but the maximum photo size is more limited (typically 4 x 6 inches or 4 x 8 inches).

Space-savers

If space is at a premium, it is well worth considering a multi-function device – that is, a laser printer (or inkjet) that can also be used as a scanner, photocopier and fax machine. While bigger than a standalone printer, a multi-function device nevertheless takes up less space than individual machines would do.

As part of one unit, each function works well with the others. It is certainly a lot easier to set up one machine than having to connect a separate printer, scanner and fax – often from different manufacturers – to your PC. However, as with any other multi-purpose device, you have to remember that if one part breaks down, you lose all the other components while the machine is away being repaired.

Questions to ask

- **Print quality** How good does the printed page look?
- **Speed** How fast will it print each page?
- **Size** Will it fit on my desk/table?
- **Output** Do I need colour or black-and-white?
- **Purchase price** Can I afford it?
- **Running costs** How much is it going to cost to run each year?
- **Noise** Does it have to be quiet?

What to buy

For nearly everyone, the quality of the printed image is the first thing to look at. All printers make up their images as a series of dots. If the dots are quite big, you can see them easily, ruining any illusion of smooth lines and curves. As the dots get smaller and closer together, they merge into one another, creating the look of perfectly straight lines and perfect curved edges. So the quality of a printer is measured primarily in dots per inch – abbreviated to dpi – and the more dots per inch, the better the print quality.

Basic inkjets will probably have a minimum 4800dpi, so a line 25.4mm (1in) long would be made up of 4800 dots. This quality – or resolution – is good for normal letter writing and image printing. The later generations of inkjet printers work at higher resolutions, giving crisper, clearer letters. This also means that the printer can accurately print very small text and the fine details of images and pictures. A basic black-and-white laser printer will usually have a resolution of 600dpi, which is fine for smart text printing – you won't typically be using it for printing a lot of images. More advanced lasers have a resolution of 1200dpi.

Better quality

There is special software that alters the look of the lines and curves just a little, to smooth out the jagged edges that the printer would normally produce. This gives the print quality the appearance of a resolution higher than the printer is actually producing. This is such a good trick that many manufacturers have built the software into their printers so that your printing quality is improved automatically whenever you print anything.

Size

The size of the printer, its width and depth, is called the footprint. If your PC and printer have to sit on one desk, you will probably want the printer to take up as little room as possible, so its footprint has to be small.

Inkjets tend to be medium-sized because you store the paper in the printer. Some inkjets hold the paper up at an angle, so the footprint is reduced, but they are then unable to hold large amounts of blank paper.

Nearly all laser printers are bigger than inkjet printers, so you need to reserve more space. Colour lasers are much bulkier than their black-and-white counterparts.

Speed

If you do a fair amount of printing, you will appreciate a printer that produces pages quickly. A printer's speed is measured in pages per minute – abbreviated to ppm. This is calculated using a test page with enough text and images printed on it to cover about 25 per cent. Assessing printer speeds is not an exact science. The less print there is on each page, the faster the page will print, and if you are printing out many images, you will not reach the printer's quoted speed. It also takes a while for your PC or the printer to do all the calculations necessary to print out the image, so the first page always takes longer than the following ones.

INKJET
LASER

Different types of printers produce different-quality output.

Laser

Laser printers can produce the sharpest printing, even approaching magazine quality in many cases. They contain their own powerful processors and memory, and also have the necessary font or typeface information already loaded in them, so they can do a lot of the processing work very quickly. This means they can produce the fastest prints.

Large box to hold the *complex mechanics* of the laser printer.

The *laser toner* refills will last for tens of thousands of pages. A small laser beams the image on to the drum. The exposed areas are statically charged and pick up the toner powder. Static attracts the toner to the paper which moves on through a set of rollers where heating fuses the powder into a permanent image on the page.

A laser printer uses *A4 sheets*, often holding a large quantity of paper.

Inside information

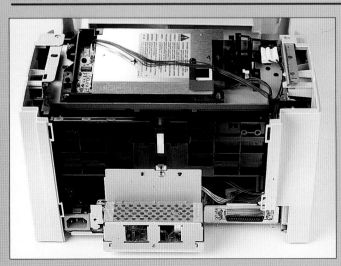

The mechanics inside a laser printer are much more complicated than those of an inkjet printer. Laser printers usually have the details of more than 100 fonts stored in their memory chips. This means that they can work directly with the fonts, thus speeding up the print process.

Large amounts of memory help speed up the laser-printing process further. Home laser printers have anywhere from 16MB to 1GB+ of RAM installed. And a high-power processor handles the complex task of creating high-quality text images, rather than letting the PC do all the work.

As well as the usual connections, some laser printers have sockets for connecting directly to a network system.

Inkjet

Inkjets represent a good compromise for many home-office and small-business users. They deliver remarkably good-quality printouts and do not cost too much to buy. Although they are not particularly fast, or the cheapest to run, their attractive colour printing is especially useful when it comes to putting together presentations, business reports or homework projects.

Most inkjets have a black cartridge and a three, or more, colour cartridge. The black, which gets heavier use, can then be replaced separately, without having to waste any unused ink in the colour cartridge.

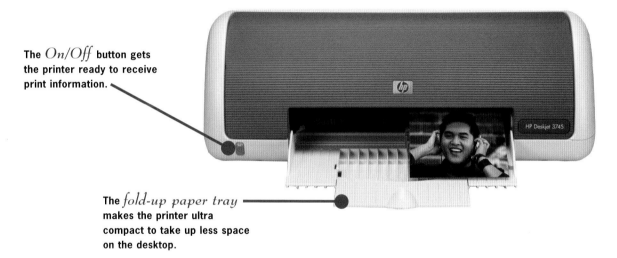

The *On/Off* button gets the printer ready to receive print information.

The *fold-up paper tray* makes the printer ultra compact to take up less space on the desktop.

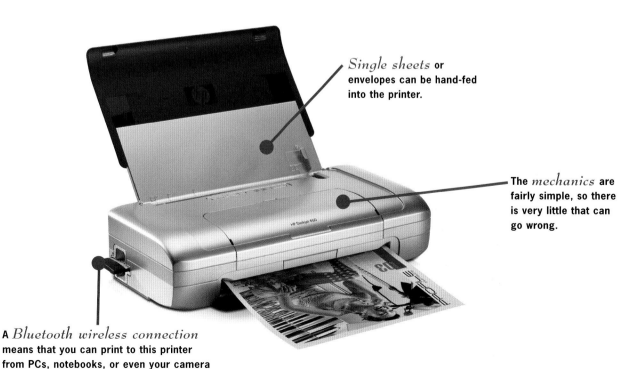

Single sheets or envelopes can be hand-fed into the printer.

The *mechanics* are fairly simple, so there is very little that can go wrong.

A *Bluetooth wireless connection* means that you can print to this printer from PCs, notebooks, or even your camera phone, if they have a similar connection.

Drivers

When you connect your printer to your PC, the connections are standardised and the leads all fit. But it won't print anything from Windows unless you tell Windows what sort of printer you have.

This is because every type of printer uses different software instructions to make it print. Windows has to translate the image you have created into instructions that your printer can follow.

This is the job of the printer driver, a software program that translates the image data for the printer to use. Installing a driver is simple. When you install Windows, you are asked what printer you have. You can choose from over 1,000 printers for which Windows has drivers.

If your printer isn't on the list, check its instruction manual; it may tell you that it works in the same way as another printer. Alternatively, the printer will have come with a disk that contains the right driver for it.

Who does the processing?

Many printers now come with their own processors and memory. Many laser printers and some inkjet printers also have details of all the common Windows typefaces built into them. So, instead of your computer having to do all the work in creating the page, it does some preliminary calculations and sends off a simple set of instructions. The printer's processor will do the rest. This is just like having two computers working on your print job rather than one and will considerably increase the printing speed as well as allow your PC to move on to the next function.

Printer control

Printing is a background operation, which means that your computer does all the calculations involved in creating the images and sending

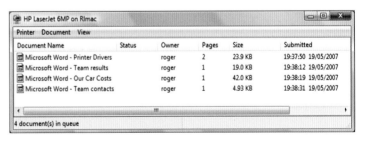

them to the printer while you get on with other things. You don't even have to wait for one print run to finish before you tell your computer about the next. If there are several documents to print, Windows creates a line of print jobs, and as each job is finished, the next is sent off to the printer automatically.

Windows controls it all through the Printer menu. As soon as you click on Print, a printer icon will appear in the bottom right-hand corner of the screen. If you want to see how a particular printing job is progressing, or want to pause or cancel the jobs in the print line, just click on this icon.

Connecting

A printer is one of the easiest things to connect to your network. Most modern printers connect via the USB port, using a standard USB cable. Connect one end of the USB cable to the printer and the other to the PC, switch on and Windows Vista will automatically detect your new printer. So it is ready to use straight away.

However, for some of the more advanced features – such as troubleshooting and cartridge cleaning – many manufacturers provide their own printer management software. You install it like any other program, and it will, typically, add an icon to the Taskbar so that you can access it easily.

As well as the connector lead to the PC, the printer needs to be connected separately to a power supply. The easiest and safest way is to use a multi-outlet power strip or surge protector, which can be used to switch on or off the power to the computer and all its peripherals.

If you would like several PCs to share the same printer – perhaps you have a desktop PC and laptop, or have set up a family network – a wireless connection would be best. This enables you to send documents directly to the printer from wherever you are in the house, without having to go through another PC. Some printers come already wireless (Wi-Fi)-enabled, but if not, you can add a wireless adapter to allow your printer to be accessed wirelessly from around the home.

Printers are able to operate independently of the PC in other ways, too. Many photo-printers let you print images direct from the camera's memory card, and some all-in-one printers (multi-function devices that can print, scan, fax and copy) will operate as a fax or copier without the PC it is attached to being turned on.

Typically, new printers connect via a *USB cable* **or a** *wireless connection*.

All together now

If you have several computers connected together in a network and prefer not to use Wi-Fi, they can still all share the same printer. When you click on Print on your screen, the instructions are sent around the network to the printer. Your job joins the line behind those already requested by other people on the same network. Higher-quality laser printers have special connectors so that they can be hooked directly into the network system.

You don't have to use a network to share a printer. If you have two or three computers and want to use one high-quality laser printer, you can use a switch-box. The computers plug into a small box that has a switch that allows you to select which computer is going to work with the printer. This is a crude but effective way of sharing a printer.

It can be useful to have two printers, or more, for different types of work and the switch-box idea can also be used to feed the output of one computer to a selection of different printers. For instance, you may want to use a laser printer for its high quality and an inkjet for everyday output.

Portables

E ven if you are on the move, you can still take a printer with you. There are several very efficient portable printers that can slip easily into your briefcase. Portable printers work just like ordinary printers and connect in the same way to the laptop computer's USB port or sometimes wirelessly through an infrared or Bluetooth connection. While the printer has to be wide enough to handle an A4 piece of paper, they are usually very slim and compact to take up the minimum amount of space. The Canon Pixma iP90v, for example, is just 310mm wide x 174mm deep and 51.8mm high (12^1/$_2$ x 6^1/$_2$ x 2in).

Some portable printers are more portable than others. Some have internal batteries, while others use an external battery power pack that plugs into the printer and takes up a little more space. All offer the option of connecting to an outlet, often using an external adapter. If you are staying in a hotel and just want to be able to print out documents, it is the size of the printer, rather than battery power, that is most important. Some business users, however, may want to visit customers, work on projects on their laptop, and print out the results on the spot. Turning someone else's office or home upside down looking for an outlet doesn't give the right impression, so in these circumstances battery power is an essential feature. The computer and printer can be quickly connected together and the hard copy printout produced there and then.

The *rechargeable batteries* of the portable Hewlett Packard Deskjet 460 give you enough power to print up to 450 pages per charge.

Quality

Because the printer is small it doesn't mean it is going to perform significantly worse than a full-size desktop printer. The resolution of many portables is similar to a desktop version at up to 4800dpi. There are no compromises on speed, either. You can usually get around eight pages per minute out of an inkjet portable. While some portables use black ink only, there are others that will work in full colour, and even print at photo quality.

The only real limitation on the portable printer is its lack of input and output paper trays. Adding a reasonably large paper tray would make the printer too big, so most allow you either to feed in individual sheets or to use a small paper feeder. The fact that ink capacities are often smaller than with desktop printers, and that the batteries may only last for a few dozen pages, makes the portable suitable for occasional print jobs on the move rather than for running off large reports.

Printing with no printer

Away from home and desperately need a hard copy of something you have done on your laptop? Provided your computer has a fax/modem, you can get it printed even if you don't have a printer with you. Simply fax the document to anyone with a fax machine and you have an instant hard copy of what you have done.

DIY refills

Each time the ink runs out, you can save money by buying alternatives to brand-new inkjet cartridges or laser toner cartridges. You can, for example, refill a cartridge with laser toner, or buy a recycled cartridge. But whether you buy from the manufacturer or one of the many on-line stores offering cheaper replacements, you need to make sure you get the right kit for the make and model of your printer.

Inkjet cartridges

When you replace an empty inkjet cartridge, you are paying at least as much for the new cartridge itself as for the ink it contains. So re-using an empty cartridge by filling it with ink can save money. Many companies produce inkjet refill packs that contain a bottle of ink, a syringe or filler bottle, and a seal to put over the filler hole on the cartridge. Although refilling an inkjet cartridge is a simple job, it can be messy and many kits come with light plastic gloves to protect you from staining your hands with the ink. Be wary of buying a universal inkjet refill kit, rather than one for your specific printer. It won't be a perfect match for the particular demands of your model. So, potentially, it could damage the cartridge head and may not provide the best performance.

New *inkjet cartridges* (1), and *laser toner cartridges* (2) should all be simple enough for you to install at home, but make sure that doing so does not affect your warranty.

Refuelling your inkjet

Remove the filler-hole seal and refill the cartridge to around half to three-quarters full. Then seal the filler hole again with the sealing pin or adhesive foil. The cartridge must be left to settle for an hour so the ink can find its way fully into the cartridge nozzle. While this is happening, some ink will drip out of the nozzles. You can save around a third to half the cost of a cartridge by refilling it, and you can refill cartridges several times. The print quality will deteriorate just a little, and sooner or later the cartridge nozzle will clog up and need replacing, so have a spare cartridge handy as well as the refill kit.

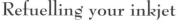

Laser toners

For a laser printer, you usually have to buy a combined toner cartridge/printer drum unit, which is considerably more expensive than buying just toner. These are sealed units that cannot be refilled at home.

However, there are several companies that will refill and refurbish used drum/toner units, saving around a third of the cost, although the performance may not be quite up to the standard of a new one.

A few laser printers have long-life drums and are designed to be refilled with toner. This will save a reasonable amount of money, especially if the printer is being used a lot. But toner powder has a tendency to get everywhere, so handle with care.

Paper

The paper you use can make a big difference to the overall look of your documents. If you are interested enough to choose your printer carefully, you should also spend some time finding the right paper. When you send any document out to other people, whether it's for business, for school or for the bank manager, you will want your document to look and feel good.

The first decision to make regarding your paper is how good you want it to feel. Photocopy paper is the cheapest you can buy. Although it does the job, it will not provide the quality feel of better paper. But the choice isn't just about the quality you would like to have. The clarity of your print depends on the paper working well with the print process you are using.

If the paper is too absorbent for inkjet printers, the ink being sprayed on to the paper will spread, making the edges of the letters slightly fuzzy. So paper makers have come up with papers designed to absorb the ink uniformly and give your printing a cleaner look. This is even more important when printing colour pictures. If you really want these to stand out, you should use specially coated inkjet paper. Coated paper produces really clear colour images but costs much more than ordinary inkjet paper. If you have a photoprinter – or an inkjet capable of printing out high-quality images – you will need photo-quality paper to do the images justice.

Laser printing, in which the ink powder is fused into the paper, also works better if you use paper that has been developed especially for it.

Because laser printers are usually associated with the highest quality, you will find that there is also a wide range of luxury papers available for this type of printer. Wove, linen and laid paper finishes are all available to really enhance the look of your documents and make the right impression.

Buying paper

It used to be quite difficult to find paper for computer printers, but now office-supply stores offer a wide range of paper, usually packed in reams of 500 sheets. You may find that stationery, office or computer supply companies that sell by mail order offer a wider range of specialised papers, as well as slightly lower prices, provided you buy in large enough quantities.

Put on some weight

The thickness of paper is measured in grams per square metre (gsm). The heavier the paper's weight rating, the thicker and firmer the paper.

gsm	70	80	90	100	150	200	250
Basic photocopy	☺	☺	☺	☺			
Good-quality			☺	☺ ☺ ☺ ☺ ☺ ☺ ☺			
Card					☺	☺ ☺ ☺	

Storage

Your printer cannot hold a whole ream of paper, so the rest has to be stored. Paper should be kept flat, out of the light, and in a box so the edges don't get damaged. Make sure the storage area is dry, as paper will quickly absorb dampness in the atmosphere, and this produces a blotting effect.

Fonts & images

All text is printed as fonts, and fonts are stored in your computer not as pictures of letters but as a set of equations that say where the lines and curves should be and how thick each part of the letter is. There are several standards for fonts, the most common being TrueType and PostScript. With most lower-cost printers, the font information is stored only in your PC. When you want to print out a document, your PC will pull out the relevant fonts' equations and create the page ready for printing.

Some printers have extra memory and processing power built into them. These printers can store fonts or take over some of the processing work needed to create the page. Whenever you use these fonts, the printer takes over the calculating function, thus speeding up the printing process. Many such printers also let you load your own regularly used fonts into their internal memory so they can be used by the printer, too.

Grey from black-and-white

While hard-edged black-and-white is ideal for letters, you need to have lots of different shades of grey or colour for pictures. Although your printer can produce only black dots on white paper, it can still give the illusion of printing shades of grey by using halftoning. This converts the photo into a pattern of dots that gives the illusion of degrees of grey.

In magazine printing, halftoning is done by making the dot size bigger or smaller. A large dot with no white space around it will create a dark grey area, whereas a small dot with some white space looks light grey. Printers cannot change the size of the dots, so they split the image into little squares of 2x2 dots or 4x4 dots and make those darker or lighter by printing more of the dots, or pixels, in the square. The more dots in each square, the darker the little square appears. If you use a 4x4-dots square, then you have up to 16 possible shades of grey. To get a nearly realistic level of 256 shades of grey, you need a 16x16 square. But if you split the picture into large squares rather than single dots, the resolution – the ability to print fine detail – is reduced. A printer that produces 600dpi on text will perform to 150dpi on pictures with 16 shades of grey. On 256 shades, it will be about 37dpi.

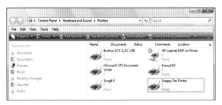

Print a fax

If you have a fax/modem, you can send faxes by using dedicated fax software or you can treat the fax/modem as though it were a printer. When you install your fax, you can load the fax system as a Printer driver. When you want to send a fax, click on Print and select the fax/modem as the printer. This will send the page to your fax software. This is a quick and easy way of sending faxes.

Printing to disk

If you want your pages printed professionally, you need to put your file on a disk to take to a bureau. If you are using well-known desktop-publishing or word-processing software, it is possible the bureau will have the same software and you can take just the desktop-publishing or word-processor file. If not, you can use one of the PostScript printer drivers to create the page's image, but instead of sending it to a printer, you can store it on disk. The bureau's printer will take that image and print it out directly on to its system.

Colour

If you want to print in colour, you will probably be working with an inkjet printer. But how do you get a full-colour image from a printer that has only three ink colours? When you were at school mixing paints, the primary colours were easy: red, blue and yellow. You could make green, orange and purple from those, and then all the other colours by mixing the primary colours with one of the secondary colours.

Colour separations

It gets a little more complicated when it comes to printing. The white light from a light bulb or the sun hits the printing ink on the page, which absorbs all the light except for the colour the ink represents. So you are taking light away to get the colour. This is called a subtractive process. The subtractive primary colours are magenta (red), yellow and cyan (blue).

The printer's software takes the image of the page to be printed and creates three separate images using an electronic colour filter. One is for the cyan content of the page and its pictures; one is for the magenta; and one is for the yellow. These are called colour separations and all colour printing, whether it is done at home on your inkjet printer or by a large magazine or newspaper printer, uses separations to create a colour image.

The inkjet printer's software sends the three images to the three separate sets of inkjet nozzles that are built into the colour inkjet cartridge. The cyan image is sprayed on to the page by the cyan nozzle and at the same time the yellow and magenta images are being placed on the page. So you end up with the full-colour image you started with, made up from just three sets of different coloured dots.

A touch of black

In magazine printing the image is split into four different filtered images, the fourth being the black, or the key, image. Although adding CMY (cyan, magenta and yellow) together will produce black, it will not be as pure and crisp as using CMYK (cyan, magenta, yellow, key) printing, which uses black ink for the key outlines and shadows. For the best-looking pictures you should consider a CMYK inkjet rather than the CMY types.

Using CMYK printing, which adds the black *key lines* to cyan, magenta and yellow, gives the picture stronger definition.

9

SENDING FAXES

Face fax

Time was when a fax machine was an amazing new gadget that up-to-date companies showed off in their front offices and reception areas. Now the fax is an accepted part of office machinery and, even with the advent of the Internet and e-mails, it remains a useful method of sending documents. Official letters or quick notes scribbled on a piece of paper can get to their destination within seconds of leaving your hand.

In the home, fax machines haven't proved quite so popular. Their size has deterred people, and the cost of a fax machine had to be evaluated, especially if it was not going to be used very often. Enter the fax/modem. If you have a PC, then you probably have a modem. With the power of your PC behind it, your modem can double as a fax machine that sends anything you are working on straight from your PC to a fax thousands of miles away.

With the modem doing all the transmitting and fax software included in both Windows and in the software you get with the modem, you essentially get a fax machine for free. The fax/modem is ideal for anyone working from home, part-time or full-time, but it is also a way to send faxes to friends and relatives. As home PCs are becoming more universal, so is the home-based PC fax. If you forget to show someone a copy of a letter you have sent, you can fax it. Do you urgently need a copy of the school's activity list for next week? Call another parent and ask them to fax it over. Are you writing a letter of complaint? Fax it for more immediate attention. ●

Fax/modems

To send and receive faxes from your computer, all you need is a fax/modem and some fax software. This often comes free with your modem or there are several reasonably priced programs available on-line, such as SnappyFax, used here. Windows Vista Ultimate comes with its own fax program built-in. Turn to Chapter 11 On-line for all you need to know about modems.

Usually, your PC will come with the modem built-in. If you need to add one, you can buy your fax/modem as an internal card that plugs into one of your computer's expansion sockets or as a stand-alone unit that connects to one of the USB ports. External modems tend to be more expensive than their internal equivalents, but they are slightly easier to install and set up. On the other hand, once an internal fax/modem is installed, it doesn't clutter up your desk and you can almost forget that it is there.

PCMCIA Cards

You can also fax when you are on the move by plugging a fax/modem PCMCIA card into your laptop; or prepare your faxes on your notebook PC and then send them all at once when you get to a phone.

Plugging in a fax/modem

At the back of the fax/modem is a pair of telephone sockets and it will be supplied with a lead to connect direct to your telephone wall socket. Your normal phone plugs into the other socket at the back of the fax/modem. This arrangement lets you use the phone and the fax on the same line.

Fax/phone switchers

If you are using a single phone line, you may want to buy a fax/phone switch-box which has separate connections for your phone and fax/modem. This answers the phone with a short message telling your caller to hold on. It then pauses and if it hears a fax-machine signal it will switch the call to your PC's fax/modem with a ringing signal that 'wakes up' the fax software. If it doesn't hear a fax tone, it switches to your phone line and starts ringing your phone.

One line or two?

If you receive only a few faxes every now and then, it makes sense to use one telephone line for both fax and telephone calls. If you receive a lot of faxes, you will probably find it worthwhile to invest in a second phone line just for the fax.

Computer fax vs fax machine

Fax machines and fax/modems both have their advantages and disadvantages. If your faxes are generated mainly on your PC, then the fax/modem is cheaper and more convenient. It also has more flexibility and takes up less space. On the other hand, a fax machine has a built-in scanner to handle any document wherever it comes from, and it doesn't require that you leave your computer switched on all the time to receive every fax.

Fax/phone/scanners

There is another way to get a fax up and running with your PC, which combines the best features of the stand-alone fax and the computer fax. These multi-function centres are fax machines that also link up with your PC. You can feed paper into them for quick faxes and paperwork you haven't created on your PC. But the link with your PC means that you can still send faxes directly from your computer and do all the other things you can do with fax software, such as sending faxes to groups of people and storing received faxes on your hard disk. These machines can also function as a scanner for your PC, as a printer and as a photocopier.

Quality

If you receive faxes regularly, you'll have noticed a huge variation in their image quality: thick lines down the middle, jagged edges to all the lettering or whole pages fed through askew. What causes these problems is the quality of the fax's scanning section: how well it has been adjusted, how smoothly it feeds the page through and how clean it is.

When you send a fax from your computer, the file information is converted directly into the fax format, so bypassing the scanning operation. You can always recognise a fax that has come from a computer. It looks like it has come straight out of a printer.

Voice-mail modems

You can go one step further with your fax/modem and buy a voice-mail fax/modem, which uses your PC's microphone and will record and play, or receive and store, messages on your hard disk. These add all the facilities of a good answering machine to your PC and are as easy to install as a normal fax/modem card.

Speedy faxes

The slowest fax machines used to send fax data out at 2,400 bits (the computer's basic number system) per second. Now the fastest fax systems send out data at 14,400bps, which is over five times faster. The faster the transmission rate the quicker the fax is sent and the cheaper it is to do.

Fax basics

When two fax machines are connected via a telephone line, the first thing they do is exchange some basic information about the fax being sent and how quickly the two machines can send and receive the fax information. This process is called handshaking and is the reason for all those funny fax tones when you first make a fax connection.

When the handshaking is finished, the fax machine starts feeding the sheet through, scanning lots of thin lines across the page. The scan turns the areas of black and white that make up the text and pictures into a series of computer numbers that are sent down the phone line as warbling tones. The receiving fax machine turns this information into instructions to print the identical black-and-white areas on to its blank fax paper.

Your page is scanned in thin *lines* **by the fax machine.**

PCs do it differently

Your PC fax works slightly differently. The pages that you have on screen are first converted into a new image and stored in your PC's memory or on the hard disk as a fax file. The fax/modem then dials the number and calls up the fax image, a line at a time, and sends it to the fax machine at the other end to print it out on its fax paper.

When you receive a fax, the PC fax/modem stores the incoming fax on your computer's hard disk as a fax file. From this it recreates a fax image that you can see on screen, print out, or turn into a picture that you can use in any of your applications.

Files or faxes?

Since your PC's fax hardware is based around a modem, your computer can choose to send your fax as a file instead. Say you have used Microsoft Word to create a letter and your fax/modem to send it to someone else who, as it happens, also has a PC with a fax/modem and uses Word. Instead of turning everything to and from fax images, your message can be sent simply as a Word document file that the user at the other end can call up like any other Word file.

Fax-software systems do this by using a system called binary transfer. When your fax/modem starts the handshaking process it checks if the other fax is a PC-based fax/modem geared up for binary transfer. If the answer is yes, your PC will send the document as a Word file instead of a fax image. The two PCs can work all this out themselves. You are not aware of anything different except that you have received a perfect word-processor file that you can edit and print out, rather than a fax image that you can only look at.

Setting up

Fax software will handle all your basic faxing needs. No matter which software system you decide to use, you first have to set it up with some basic information about you and your phone number. Once you've loaded your fax software, you will be asked a few questions about your system.

Enter your details

Your name and phone number:	This will appear at the top of each fax you send.
Modem details:	What type of fax hardware you have and how it is set up.
Page size:	The same as your usual page size (A4).
Cover page:	Do you usually want to send a cover page?
Resolution:	Do you usually want to send standard quality faxes or high-resolution images that will take twice as long?

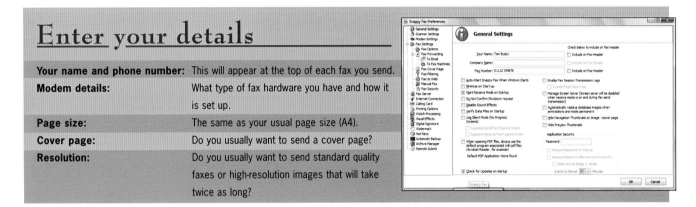

The printer fax

When you install your fax/modem, you should check that it has also been included in your list of printers. For everyday faxing, the easiest way to send a fax directly from your word processor, or any other Windows application, is to press the Ctrl+P keys together to open the Print box and select the fax printer from the dropdown box beside Name: and send the fax from there.

Secure faxes

Whatever fax software you use, there is usually a way of sending your messages securely so that they can be opened only by the recipient. Often the message can be accessed only by entering a password.

See it first

Some PC fax systems let you decide what happens when a fax arrives. You may choose to have it automatically printed out or to display an on-screen message or icon that tells you that a new fax has been received and stored on your PC. Others may show the fax on screen after, or even during, fax transmission so you don't have to wait to see what it is all about.

Snappy Fax, like all fax software, has a *fax viewer* so you can look at a fax on screen without having to print it out first.

Various *tools* for improving the fax – such as straightening it or removing some of the speckles – are shown as icons along the bottom.

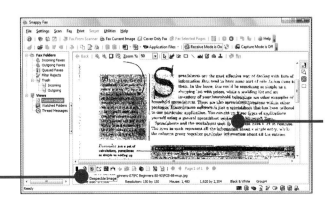

Read your fax *on screen*.

In and out

When it comes to receiving faxes, whenever your PC is switched on, and no matter what you are doing, the fax/modem is always in the background, monitoring the phone line and waiting for it to ring. What it does when the phone rings depends on what you have entered in the Fax Receive options.

If you are in an office, set up the fax to answer after a certain number of rings. The fax/modem answers the phone after the set number of rings, sends out the fax handshaking signal, and waits for a response from the other end. This is the option to use if your PC is connected to a separate fax line.

If you are at home, choose Manual Answer. When the phone rings, pick it up. If it is a fax, you can click on the fax button and your fax/modem will take the call and receive the fax. This is the option you should use if most of your phone calls are from people who want to talk rather than send faxes.

Sending faxes

When you are working on a letter, spreadsheet, image, or any other kind of document you want to send to someone, you don't want to be wasting time saving files, opening up fax software and finding files to convert to fax format before you even start selecting who to send it to. With the fax system set up as a printer, you send a fax just as though you were printing it on your inkjet or laser printer. But instead of the sheet being printed at your desk, it turns up on a fax machine that can be thousands of miles away.

STEP 1 First *select* **what you want to fax. It can be an entire document – like your family newsletter – or a selected area of text.**

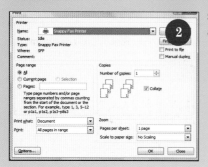

STEP 2 Choose your fax as your *printer*.

STEP 3 Your *fax system* **will now ask you to whom you want to send the fax.**

STEP 4 Click on *Finish* **or** *Send* **and your PC takes care of the rest as a background operation while you move on to something else.**

Broadcasting faxes

Most faxes are messages to be sent to a single person. Occasionally you might want to send the same information to a whole group of people. With an ordinary fax it can be time-consuming feeding the same sheet of paper through the machine over and over again, manually dialling the different numbers.

With your fax/modem you can tick off as many names in your address list as you like. Your PC will go through the list one by one and send the same fax to each of them, with individualised cover sheets. It takes only a little more time to organise sending a fax to 100 people than it does to send a fax to one.

Send now/send later

You'll usually send faxes the minute you've prepared them. But you can also save them and get your PC to send them later. This lets your PC concentrate just on the job of sending faxes. You may find that faxing in the background takes up enough of your PC's processing power to slow down whatever else you are doing, and sending faxes after you've finished working on your PC avoids this.

The other advantage is more interesting – it's cheaper to phone in the evening and at weekends when the cost for national and international calls is significantly reduced. By faxing after hours, you can save quite a lot of money, and you can just leave everything to your PC.

Set it up and sign it

Since you produce most of your faxes using your word processor, it makes a lot of sense to create a standard fax layout to use every time you want to send a fax. Then all you have to do is write what you want to say and send it.

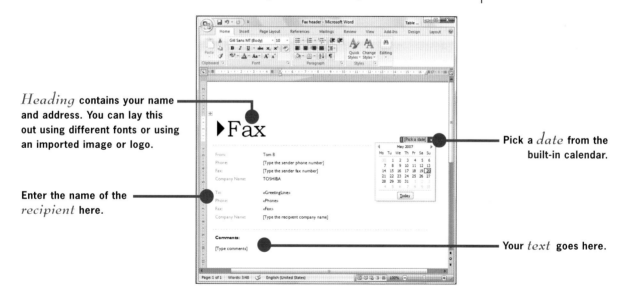

Heading **contains your name and address. You can lay this out using different fonts or using an imported image or logo.**

Enter the name of the *recipient* **here.**

Pick a *date* **from the built-in calendar.**

Your *text* **goes here.**

Signing off

When you receive a fax, one of the clues that it has been sent from a fax/modem is that it doesn't have a signature at the bottom – this is because you can't type a signature. Yet adding a signature is easy. First, write several signatures on a piece of paper and scan it into your PC. Then use a paint program to select the best one to import into your fax sheet and adjust the image so that it is the right size.

Don't worry if you don't have a scanner. Send the signature to yourself from someone else's fax, preferably set to high resolution. You can now turn that fax into a picture and continue as before.

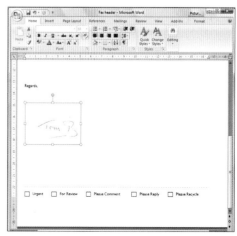

Who's there?

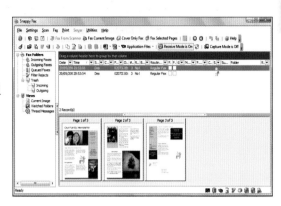

I f you want to know who you have sent a fax to, it's easy enough to find out. The fax software keeps a record of every time it sends or receives a fax. You can look up in the fax log exactly what was sent and when. If you are sending faxes when you are away from your PC, the send log will tell you which faxes were successfully sent and which didn't get through.

Get a little help

Although faxes are received and stored as images, what is on the page is usually text, which would be more useful as a word-processor file. There is a magical piece of software called Optical Character Recognition (OCR) that can do the conversion for you, instead of you typing it in.

OCR software, which is included in some fax-software packages, scans the fax and sees if it can read the letters. Provided the fax is clean and the text is not too small, then good OCR software can produce remarkable results. You'll always need to double-check the copy against the original fax image, but usually it is very easy to spot the occasional errors.

Your *logo*, scanned into your computer and held as a picture file.

The *recipient's* details, put in directly from the fax address book.

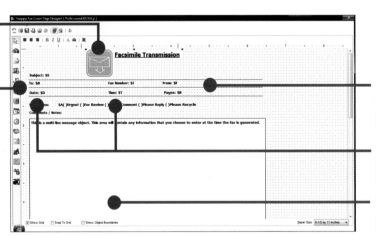

Your *details*, taken from the information you put into the system when you first set it up.

The *date* and *time* of transmission are entered for you automatically.

You can type in a short *note* on the cover sheet before you send the fax.

Cover sheets

When you use a fax machine to send a fax, you can add a cover sheet with your own name and number and the recipient's name and number on it. Instead of typing this up each time, your PC fax can do it all for you.

When you enter someone's number in the fax address book, you'll also include their name and the name of their company. When you send a fax, the software takes all of this information, as well as your details and any logos you might want to add, and creates a cover page which is then sent in front of the fax. Every cover page is completely personalised without you even having to think about it. Snappy Fax includes its own Cover Page Designer so you can customise the default templates to your taste, or create your own from scratch.

Clean up!

Spring-cleaning is a good excuse to go through the house with
a fresh eye to tidy up, reorganise and throw out all the things
that have accumulated over the year. We don't always do it
in spring: it is sometimes prompted by an impending visit by
a relative or just because you are in the mood.

Well, things are no different with your PC. It has a great capacity to store
all sorts of clutter on its hard disk, and it can do with a good clear out from
time to time. It may be because it's spring, because you're about to load a
big new program, because you're about to make the transition to the latest
version of Windows, or just because you feel like it.

Housekeeping on your PC has a lot of benefits. After you've finished, you'll
have more space on your hard disk. You'll also have a PC that works faster,
looks better and is tailored a little closer to the way you would like to work.

Even if there isn't too much in the way of things to
delete, your computer's files can always benefit from
some reorganisation so that you know exactly where
everything is.

And, like any house, where things get worn out over
time and need some attention, your PC can often do with
a bit of repair work. There are all sorts of ways that you
can make sure your PC is properly maintained, with
very little effort and without taking up too much of
your time.

There are many elements of your software that
were set up when you first started running your
computer and have never been touched since. So
you continue to work the same way, not
because it suits you and your family best
but because you never got around to
looking at the alternatives. While you are
spring-cleaning, you can also add,
remove and change parts of your
programs and your PC's general setup to
get it to work the way you want to work.
And even if you haven't yet bought your
PC, looking at the kind of things you may
be doing after a few months will prepare
you for taking care of it properly. ●

Cleaning

Why not take this opportunity to give your whole system a good clean up, starting with the outside? Unplug everything from the mains and then clean the computer and the monitor. Use special cleaning cloths, which are sold by computer suppliers, or a cloth lightly dampened with a cleaner designed for plastic and metal surfaces. Antistatic wipes will help stop the build-up of dust, especially on your monitor. Watch out for the air vents on top of the monitor and at the rear of the computer and make sure they are clear of dust and fluff.

If you have an older mouse, remove the mouse ball, check the rollers inside and clean them with a cotton bud. If you have a laser or optical mouse, a wipe over is sufficient. Don't try to remove any of the parts. This may also be a good time to replace your mouse mat, or at least clean it. Most material mats can be cleaned by immersing them in warm soapy water, rinsing and letting them dry. But mats are so cheap now that it may make more sense to replace them. And if you haven't already got wrist supports for the mouse and your keyboard, now is a good time to add them to your shopping list.

Give scanners and printers a gentle wipe. Make sure that the scanner's lens or window is clean, as any marks will translate into spots or lines on your scanned copies. If you have a laser printer, run cleaning paper through it to pick up any stray toner dust, but do not try to clean inside any type of printer unless you really know what you are doing.

CD and DVD drives need occasional cleaning. Use a special cleaning kit. These look like CD or DVD discs but have a cleaning area, which clears dirt off the heads inside the drive. CD cleaners designed for hi-fi CD players will work just as well as those specially designed for CD-ROM drives.

If you want to get deeper into the crevices of your PC, consider buying a commercial PC cleaning kit. One of these usually contains an anti-bacterial cleaner – safe to use on plastic, coated metal and glass – to remove finger oil, grease and dirt, as well as specialist brushes and strong, lint-free cloths. A mini-vacuum attachment is also handy to get into those awkward places of the keyboard or PC where dirt gathers. Most come with adapters that will fit nearly all makes of vacuum cleaner. For the keyboard, a spray can – or air duster as it is sometimes called – and special nylon strip brushes are also included.

Shake it all about

Your keyboard's keys can get quite dirty, so they will need cleaning. Turn the keyboard upside down and gently shake it to remove any debris that may have dropped between the keys. You can also gently use a soft small paintbrush to help clear the spaces between the keys or a small can of compressed air to blow out the dust.

Spring-clean shopping list

- PC cleaning kit including vacuum cleaner
- CD/DVD drives cleaning kit
- Mouse mat
- New CD/DVD discs, plus a disc-storage box or two
- Keyboard and mouse wrist supports
- Antistatic screen wipes
- Spare ink cartridges

Organise

Spring-cleaning includes reorganising what you want to keep and throwing away the rest. Keeping your filing straight is an important job and you should look at your PC's filing to make sure everything is in a logical place. It's not just neatness for its own sake: with so many files on your PC's hard disk, some are going to be almost impossible to find again without good organisation.

Whether you are filing on a PC or in a real filing cabinet, you use a tree directory system. The directory starts with a main root store, which has branches off it. Those branches have branches off them, and so on.

The filing cabinet is the root directory, where everything you are looking for is kept. The drawer marked Letters is the first branch off the root directory; the section in the drawer marked Customers Letters is the next branch off that; and the A–G compartment is yet another branch. This filing system has been used for centuries as a very natural way of working, and your PC's hard disk should be organised in a similar way.

Windows Vista takes the filing cabinet idea and calls the separate filing areas Folders. Use Explorer (shown here) to look at the way your files are organised. The folder tree in Windows Vista is called the Folders list. You can access it from the Navigation pane in any folder, by clicking Folders at the bottom of the pane. Looking for a file among the thousands on your hard disk is easy if you have organised your filing properly.

In Windows Vista, a *folder* containing more branches is marked with a ▷ rather than the + found in earlier versions of Windows.

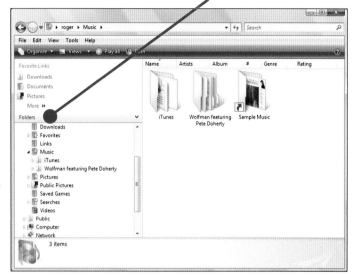

Change a name

It's a good idea to give your folders a name that clearly indicates what they contain. To rename a folder, click on its name and then type over it with the new name. Remember, when you use the application or program that generated those files, it will be looking for the folder under the old name. So the next time you run the program, you will have to tell it the new name.

More but smaller folders

Don't be frightened of creating more folders, or directories, to separate your various files into smaller compartments. It is easier to find a file among just five or six others in a small and very specific folder, rather than sifting through 40 or 50 files in a big general folder.

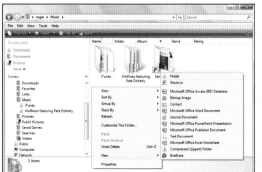

Right-click on the area where you want the new folder to be, then select New/Folder. The New Folder's title box is now highlighted so type in the name you want to use.

Folders and files

You can move folders and delete them in just the same way that you handle individual files. When you drag and drop a folder to a new position, all of its files and subfolders will also be moved automatically.

Disk care

Your hard disk is your computer's library. It is the storehouse for all your files and programs. Like a library, it has to be properly maintained if it is going to do its job properly. The best tools for taking care of your library are the utilities supplied with Windows.

To find some of the main hard-disk maintenance tools, double-click on the Computer icon on your desktop. Use the right mouse button to click on the disk drive that you want to work on. Then click on Properties. You'll see the

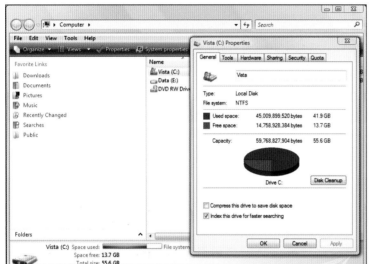

Properties box, which will show you how much disk space you have used and how much is left. Note the amount used so you can see how much space you create by tidying up the disk.

The tools

Press the Disk Cleanup button to access the program that will scan your drive and tell you which files and folders can safely be deleted. Click on the Tools tab and you will see the Defragmentation section.

On the mend

Over the years your hard disk can get damaged. Tiny areas of disk often become unstable. Fortunately, when your PC is writing new data on to your hard disk, it checks what it is doing. If there is a problem, it will mark the area as being unusable. Some of the problems your PC finds may not be faults on the disk, but a problem caused by something else – such as someone bumping into the desk while the PC is trying to write a file. So there may be nothing wrong with the area now marked as faulty. After a while you could end up

Check Disk to the rescue

Check Disk is the repair kit within Windows Vista that tests your hard disk and fixes any problems it finds.

To launch Check Disk, go to Computer, select the drive you want to check, right-click and select Properties. On the Tools tab under Error-checking, click on Check Now. This shows two options (shown right):

This first option will check the system files only.

Option two is the most thorough check. It looks for any part of the disk with problems and attempts to recover any readable information. It also checks for file system errors.

As Windows can't check the disk while you are working on it, it asks if you want to run Check Disk the next time your PC starts.

with a hard disk that has perfectly good areas cordoned off as being unusable. Windows Vista comes with its own repair kit, called Check Disk. This will go through your hard disk and test every bit of it, looking for errors.

Defragmentation

When your hard disk stores a file, it doesn't always put it all in one place. The hard disk has its spaces set out in clusters. Windows looks for the first available space, which could be a gap between two other files, and starts pouring the new file into it. If the gap isn't big enough to hold the complete file, Windows goes off and finds the next available gap and puts the rest of the file in there. In this way, a large file may end up spread all over the disk.

Even though the file is split up, your PC can still retrieve it because it creates a special index that tells it where all the fragments of the file are located. This fragmentation of your data tends to get worse as fragmented files are deleted, leaving more small gaps for the next file you save. Since your PC has to keep searching backwards and forwards to find all the parts of the file, a fragmented hard disk slows up the retrieval of files.

Windows comes with a Disk Defragmenter that will go through your disk, find all the files, and then clear space to rerecord each of them so that each one is a continuous run of clusters. The rewriting is almost always perfect, so you don't need to worry that anything will be lost or altered during the defragmentation process.

Even if files on your hard disk are not very fragmented it is still worth *defragmenting*. For maximum effectiveness, you can set your Disk Defragmenter to run weekly – or however often you choose.

Get it done for you

Microsoft has produced a separate set of facilities in Windows Vista that can be set up to run tune-up programs automatically. Task Scheduler can run the programs at regular times each week or month, so that your disk is well maintained. You can set common tasks, such as Disk Defragmenter, to run regularly at different times of the day or night so the maintenance work won't interrupt your work.

Health check

Every now and then a computer virus hits the headlines when a company contracts a nasty one that does a lot of damage to the information on its computers. There are about 70,000 computer viruses floating around, varying from old, easy-to-detect and relatively harmless ones, to some difficult-to-spot examples that can destroy all your data. Although the chances of your PC catching a virus are relatively low, it is still something you need to guard against.

What's a virus?

A virus is a small program designed to hide itself on your PC. It cannot do physical damage, but it can give instructions to your computer to do anything from displaying an unwanted message to wiping your hard disk. A virus can be built into an otherwise innocuous program, or it can hide itself away in an e-mail attachment. It is called a virus because, like a real virus in the body, it has the ability to replicate and pass itself on. It does this by copying itself on to your PC's hard disk and then using your e-mail program to send itself on to your contacts and infect other computers.

Who are the culprits?

People who create viruses fall into two main categories. There are those who just want to prove how clever they are at programming. These people usually produce a benign virus that displays a message on your screen that is often linked to a special occasion. Then there are those who want to prove how clever they are and have an axe to grind against the world in general. They produce the most damaging viruses.

How to protect against a virus

The best way to solve a virus problem is not to catch one in the first place. Viruses can be caught from the Internet and e-mail, the latter being the most common. It is worthwhile to invest in virus-protection software that will spot a virus and chase it out of your system.

It's also possible to catch viruses from a CD or DVD made on another PC, so try to avoid using discs copied from other PCs. When you first put a copied disc in your PC, you must run the virus checker before doing anything else. If the disc has a virus, let the virus protector remove it.

Make it a routine

Try to get into the habit, and get your children into the habit, of checking any discs coming into your house for viruses. Explain that it is their software, as much as anything else, that will be destroyed by a virus. You can set anti-virus software to check your PC each time it is switched on. This will mean that there is a longer delay between pressing the On button and having Windows finally loaded, but it guarantees that your PC is checked for intruders before they can do any damage.

Running virus detectors

There are several virus protection software packages around, including those from Norton and McAfee. There are also some good ones available as shareware on disk or from the Internet. The only problem with downloading anti-virus programs is that some unsavoury characters have created anti-virus programs that actually contain a virus, but these are usually spotted before they spread too far.

Prevention is better than cure

1 Use a *virus checker* to check your e-mails, any CDs and DVDs that have been made on another PC, or even a USB drive you might connect to your PC. In a few minutes you will know whether it is clear or not.

2 You can set your virus detector to check any *new file* that comes into your PC from a disk or via your e-mail or Internet browser. Alternatively, it can check your *whole system* for infection every morning or every week, depending on how likely you think it is that you will catch a virus.

3 New viruses appear constantly and unless you have the latest version of your virus checker, you will be vulnerable. *LiveUpdate* is a service from Symantec (www.symantec.com) that can protect you from new viruses.

How a virus detector works

Virus detectors work in several ways. Like a detective, some will go through all the program files that could carry a virus and check on the number of computer data bits that each uses up. For a program file, this amount should hardly ever alter. But if the program catches a virus, this amount will change.

Some look for the fingerprint evidence. Most viruses give a tell-tale sign of their presence, and some anti-virus programs use lists of fingerprints to identify them. Other systems look for suspicious characters, and investigate anything on your hard disk that is out of the ordinary.

Can my PC catch a virus from commercial software?

The companies that copy commercial software are very careful. Any disk that comes to them to be copied is thoroughly checked, so it is very unlikely that commercial discs, whether CDs or DVDs, will carry a virus. You do have to be careful if you share a rewritable disc or USB drive that has been used on another PC.

Compress

You can make better use of your disk space by using file compression. File compression uses a mathematical technique that looks at all the data that you are trying to file away and takes out any unused, duplicate, or spare data. In the end you get a file that is much smaller, but that can be expanded back to its original form. The data compression used on your PC is called lossless compression, which means that when the file is read back it is exactly the same as the original. There is no way of telling whether the file has gone through a compression process or not.

When you store files on CDs or DVDs, compressing them means you can fit more on each disk. When you back up your files, the backup software can also compress files so they take up less space. Compression can also be used to reduce the size of a file when you are sending it by modem. Since the file is smaller, it takes less time to transmit, leaving you to get on with something more useful.

There are many different types of file-compression systems, but the most common is PKZIP. You will recognise a PKZIP file because it will have the file extension .zip.

Zip by shareware

There are various software systems designed to zip and unzip files. Nearly all are available in shareware from Web sites on the Internet, or on shareware CD-ROMs and shareware disks in computer stores. Don't forget to register your copy if you use it.

Squeeze a folder

In fact, you can also compress files using Windows Vista itself. Go to Computer and double-click the drive and then click through the folders until you're at the location of the folder you want to compress. Right-click and select Send To, from the pop-up menu, then Compressed (zipped) Folder. Rename the folder something suitable. You can compress files by simply dragging and dropping them into the compressed folder you have just created (you can tell which folders are compressed by the zipper on the front of them). To extract all the files or folders from within a compressed folder, right-click it and select Extract All.

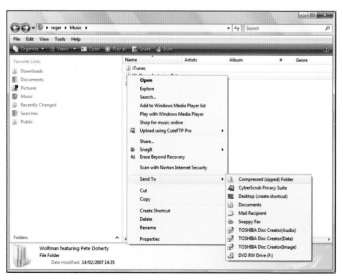

ON-LINE

All lined up

There has been an explosion of interest in using computers on-line. 'The World Wide Web', 'surfing the net' and 'the information superhighway' are all phrases associated with the worldwide community that has been created by people using their computers and a phone line to talk to each other.

Linking your computer to the outside world via your telephone line is one of the most useful and exciting aspects of home computing. You are sure to be impressed by the amount of information available on the Internet and the limitless possibilities it has to offer.

If there are others interested in your favourite subject, you'll be able to find them on-line with a crowd of people all pooling their knowledge. It doesn't matter where they are in the world. You can leave messages and talk to others using your computer keyboard for no more than the cost of your Internet connection. Australia on the cheap? It's possible on-line.

On-line means being able to use the telephone line in different ways. With a modem you can communicate with others via e-mail and you can turn your computer into a fax machine at no extra cost. There are also on-line games which enable kids to play against others down the road or on another continent. You can go shopping on-line, order the latest CDs or DVDs via your computer, and have them delivered by post.

Going on-line turns the home office into a real extension of the workplace but mobile phone systems make it possible to access the Internet from anywhere – the middle of a field, a motorway rest stop, or even the beach.

In this chapter, we will take you through all the possibilities that going on-line opens up for you. But the Internet also has a dark side – the spread of pornography and extremist political material. This is of real concern, especially to parents. We will show you how to be wary of coming across unsuitable material on-line accidentally and how access to it can be restricted. ●

How to buy

T here are internal and external modems. External modems are about the size of a small paperback book and usually connect to the computer's USB port. They have small status lights at the front that tell you about the modem link. An internal modem fits into one of the expansion slots inside your computer and becomes part of your PC. For a dial-up modem, an internal model is more convenient. With a broadband connection – which gives you an always-on link to the Internet – you will be given an external modem.

The type of modem you need to buy depends on whether you will be using a narrowband or broadband connection. In practice, the likelihood is that you will want to use both at some time or other.

Your phone still works

Most modems have a second socket to plug your telephone into. When your computer is off or the modem is not in answering mode, then your phone will work normally, as though the modem isn't there. If your modem doesn't have an extra socket to connect your telephone into, then you need to get a two-way telephone adapter. This will give you a pair of sockets into which you can plug your modem and your phone.

Dial-up modem

A narrowband connection is the conventional dial-up Internet access. You use the modem to connect to your Internet Service Provider (ISP) over your normal telephone line. Typically, you will be charged either by the minute for however long you are connected, or by a monthly subscription, which allows you unlimited access. For this type of connection you need a dial-up modem. The better the modem, the faster it will transmit the data, which is important if you are on a pay-per-minute tariff. The less time you need to be connected, the less you have to pay in phone charges and on-line fees. You should be looking for a modem with a speed of 56,000bps (bits per second) – also referred to as 56K – the fastest available for a conventional dial-up modem.

Nearly all these modems will be able to send and receive faxes, unlike broadband modems. This is the main reason you would want a conventional dial-up modem if you have a broadband connection. Don't forget, though, a dial-up modem does also give you a back-up connection to the Internet if your broadband connection fails.

Internal or external? The pros and cons

Whether you choose an internal or external modem is a matter of preference. There are pluses and minuses to both types.

Internal	External
GOOD POINTS Takes up no additional space on your desk. Doesn't need to be connected separately to the mains. Leaves one more USB port free.	**GOOD POINTS** Can be installed or repaired without taking the lid off the computer. Status lights show what is going on with your modem and fax connections.
BAD POINTS Have to take the computer apart to install or repair. Doesn't have status lights to monitor modem activity.	**BAD POINTS** More desk space needed.

a modem

Broadband
The type of broadband modem you choose will depend on the type of Internet connection you have. In the main, there are two options – ADSL or Cable.

ADSL
You can turn your ordinary phone line into a high-speed data connection with ADSL (Asymmetric Digital Subscriber Line). As a minimum, most home users will have a 512 thousand bits per second (Kbps) connection – about ten times faster than a normal modem – although anything up to 8MB or faster is available for home users. How fast it will be depends in part on how far you are from the exchange.

Your ISP may provide the option of a broadband modem or a wireless router, such as BT's Home Hub. With the Home Hub, the router is connected to your broadband link. Any wireless-enabled PC or laptop can connect wirelessly to the Internet through it.

If you choose to have the modem, it needs to be connected directly to one PC (although other computers or laptops can connect to the Internet through it). Installation is simple and you can easily do it yourself.

Cable
This uses the same line that brings TV and telephone signals into your home. Potentially, cable can offer faster connection speeds – up to 20Mbps – which would mean you could download a music track in a couple of seconds. But speed is affected by the contention ratio – that is the number of users who 'share' the same bandwidth. Installation is usually done by an engineer.

The *network map* in Windows Vista shows how the computer is connected wirelessly to the hub (2WIRE227) that houses the broadband modem.

Buying Narrowband versus Broadband

Narrowband
You just need a phone line and modem

Your phone line is blocked while you surf the Internet – unless you pay for a second line.

The longer you're on-line the more you're charged. For regular surfing, look for flat-rate packages, which mean you can surf when you like for a fixed monthly cost.

Broadband
You need to be within a certain range of the exchange to have an ADSL broadband connection. Broadband modems can be around three times as expensive as a regular modem.

You can make phone calls over the same line as an ADSL connection.

Broadband connections are generally more expensive but it is a 'fixed' monthly amount, so no surprises.

Modems

As soon as the computer stopped being something that had to have a room all to itself and became small and cheap enough to be used on a desk in an office, people started looking at ways to get one computer to talk to another. If computers are in the same building, they can be linked together with cables creating a network of computers that pass information back and forth using a very fast and reliable system. With wireless adapters, they can send data wirelessly.

It's for you

Early PC users soon looked to the phone system as a way of spreading computer links to any house with a phone. But phone lines are designed for people to talk to each other, not computers. When you try to send data signals down the phone it doesn't work. So the modem was developed as a way of making computers seem like people by turning data into electronic speech.

What's in a name?

The modem takes the data and turns it into sound by modulating tones to represent bits of computer data – the 0s and 1s that make up all computer information. The sounds are sent down the phone line and the modem at the other end takes those sounds and demodulates them, turning them back into digital data. The name modem comes from these two functions: MODulator/DEModulator.

This is a great idea in theory, but in practice there are several drawbacks. First, the phone system can't carry much data. Early modems could transmit only 300bps. At that rate it would take over three hours to transmit a full-screen colour image. Then there is the problem of static and interference on the line. The data that makes up a file or a message has to be perfect and a crackle on the line can cause the receiving modem to make a mistake.

Parcel delivery

The modem sends your data in small parcels that include additional bits of information that allow the receiving PC to check whether each parcel of data has been perfectly received. If there has been a problem, it reports back to the modem transmitting the information, telling it to send the data again.

ADSL, or broadband, modems work in a similar way to conventional modems. But they turn your ordinary phone line into a high-speed connection by sending the data at a different frequency from the voice traffic. This way you can make a phone call and surf the Internet at the same time!

V signs

For conventional modems, each new speed is set out in an internationally agreed standard, which is given a V number. The latest one for 56k modems is v.92.

Fitting

If you don't want to take your computer apart to add a modem, an external modem would be the right choice. They are simple to connect, but you must make certain that you have a spare socket to plug it into.

An external modem, whether narrowband or broadband, is usually connected to the USB port. Then it is simply a matter of connecting your modem to the mains, using the power lead, and to the telephone socket. If you have a separate line for your modem, connect the line socket on the modem to your telephone wall socket using the cable supplied. However, if you want to use a telephone on the same line as the modem, buy a double connector and plug both the modem and the telephone into it. It is also possible to route the telephone through the modem by plugging it into the phone socket on the modem with the adapter lead supplied.

Internal modems

Internal modem cards are almost as simple to fit. First turn the PC off and then unscrew the lid. Firmly slide the modem card into a spare expansion slot and replace the computer's lid. The internal modem doesn't need to be connected to a power outlet; it just has to be connected to the phone socket.

Broadband modems

To install an ADSL modem, you need to plug a microfilter – usually supplied by your ISP – into each of the phone sockets used with that line. This separates the data chanel from the phone line.

Typically, with the newer broadband connections, your service provider might provide you with a router rather than just a modem. The router will usually include the modem as well as a hub that connects to any other PCs you have on your network. The connection to this hub can be wireless or wired. If wired, it is connected by Ethernet cables. This way any PC, laptop, or even a games console on your home network can connect directly to the Internet without having to go through a dedicated computer.

Connect an external modem to your PC via the *USB port*.

The *wireless antenna* enables you to connect to the Internet from anywhere in the home.

These *Ethernet sockets* allow you to connect other PCs, or a laptop, that are on your network to the Internet.

The *data connector* links the modem or router to your telephone line.

Software

You can use your modem with several types of communications software. A dial-up modem will usually come with fax software and may also have trial software for going on-line. With an ADSL or broadband modem, Internet access is through the Internet Service Provider (ISP) who is supplying the connection. For example, with an ADSL modem it could be BT or TalkTalk. With a cable modem it will be through the cable provider, such as Virgin Media.

Setting up the software

After you've installed your modem, you'll have to tell your communications software some basic information about it, such as which port it is connected to and its fastest transmission speed. You may also have to check settings for the fax part of the communications software. Many software packages will do this for you. Windows has settings for a range of the most commonly available modems. You only have to call up the right one and Windows will do the rest.

Once you've set up your communications software to work with your modem, you have to set it up to work with the modems at the other end of the telephone, that is with your ISP. Often the software supplied with the modem will run a Wizard that takes you through this process step by step.

Sort out the settings

The first thing to be checked is how fast your modem and the modem at the other end can transmit data. Most modems will agree on a suitable transmission speed automatically.

When you first make a connection between two computers, neither side knows what is about to be sent, at what speed it will be sent, or even which part of the long stream of signals coming through the telephone line represents the important file information. To make certain it all works properly, systems known as protocols put the stream of modem data into a fixed format.

Stop bits and pieces

The data to be sent is packaged into parcels of either seven or eight bits per parcel. Then, at the end of each parcel is an indicator, called a Stop Bit, to say this is the end of the parcel. Parity is one way that modems can check that the data has been received correctly, but not all systems use it. There is also a system for the modems to tell each other that they are ready to transmit or receive. This is called Xon/Xoff.

Setup details

Different on-line services use different combinations of Stop Bit, Data Length, Parity and Xon/Xoff settings. When you set up your connection to an on-line service, your communications software makes sure that it will work with the service.

Uploading and downloading

Taking a file from a web site, bulletin board or a service provider is called downloading. You can send a file to the service provider by uploading it. The process is virtually the same when either downloading or uploading.

Kermit makes perfect

A crackle or static may cause the modem to make a mistake. If you are typing a message live to someone, that person can ask you to retype the words. When you are transferring files from one computer to another you need a similar system to ensure that the file is received perfectly.

This is where protocols Kermit, X-modem, Y-modem and Z-modem come in. These automatically check that the data has been received correctly. Each works slightly differently from the others, and which format is used is worked out automatically when it is time to transfer a file.

Service providers do it for you

If you use one of the larger service providers, they will usually provide a CD or DVD with the software to get you on-line. Alternatively, you can get Windows itself to help. The Connect to the Internet Wizard will guide you through the necessary steps. The first choice is the type of connection you want – wireless, broadband or dial-up. Simply fill in the details asked for and click Connect to get on-line.

On-line warning

The Internet is a male-dominated society, with estimates of just 30–40 per cent of users being female. You should be aware that it carries adult and pornographic material, topics that have generated a number of headlines in the media.

To put it into perspective, users usually have to search out this type of material, but it is possible to come across it accidentally. Some adult sites use seemingly innocuous names or variations of well-known sites. Mistype or misspell the URL for the site you want and you can end up with a nasty surprise. Although many service providers will try to block some of the more extreme sites, it is a good idea to use parental-control software to prevent your children from accidentally accessing adult Internet sites.

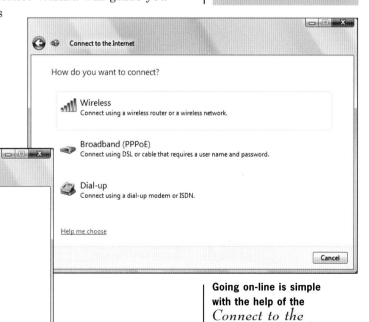

Going on-line is simple with the help of the *Connect to the Internet Wizard.*

Logging on

Real access to the power of the worldwide network of computer systems comes when you sign up with an Internet Service Provider (ISP). Put all these on-line networks together and you have the Internet. It started in 1969 as a way of connecting three computers run by the United States military. Over the years it has grown to hundreds of millions of users, each with a computer address and each with access to all the public material on computers connected around the world.

What's a service provider?

There are two main types of service provider. The first, such as AOL, are on-line portals. They offer you access to information and forums – groups of users with an interest in common – that are controlled by their own computers. Access to their services is sometimes free, sometimes for a fee. They may also offer a gateway to the Internet and your own unique e-mail address which you can use to send and receive messages and files to and from anywhere in the world.

The service providers promote themselves with adverts in computer magazines or give away their software on the covers of magazines, so you will easily be able to find out how to contact them and get an idea about what services they offer and how much they charge. If you know people who are already on-line, ask them about the service they use.

The cost

The second – and largest – group of ISPs mainly provide you with access to the Internet, either by a broadband or dial-up connection. The increasing competition among service providers means that they are offering cheaper services. Most on-line services have now removed their set-up cost or membership fee as a way of attracting new users, but some providers will still charge you a monthly subscription whether you use the service or not. For dial-up subscribers, the fee will include at least a few hours of on-line time for free per month. With other service providers, there will just be charges for the time spent on-line.

You will also have to pay for your phone call to the service provider's own phone links (called nodes). If you are in a city, there will nearly always be a node just a local phone call away. It doesn't matter where you are sending a file, you only pay for the call to the service provider's node.

Regular Internet users will find it more cost effective to have broadband access to the Internet via cable or ADSL (Asymmetric Digital Subscriber Line). Broadband connections are always open and allow you to connect to the Internet at up to 200 times faster than the fastest modem. Most services charge a monthly fee for unlimited use, which varies according to the speed of the connection.

Which service?

The number of major players in on-line services is continuing to grow and the options and services they offer are continually being improved. Some names to consider are:

On-line services
- AOL
- Yahoo
- MSN
- Tiscali

Internet Service Providers (ISPs)
- Orange
- BT
- Demon
- Pipex
- Virgin
- Fasthost

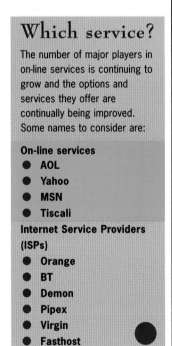

What you get

The aim of the service provider is to provide you, the customer, with as much in the way of interesting, stimulating and informative on-line services as possible. Some users find these services so comprehensive that they hardly ever go elsewhere on the Internet.

Forums, messages and conferences

One of the most consistently active parts of any service provider's facilities is its forums. These are used by people with a common interest, such as photographers or musicians or people interested in family history. There are forums for hundreds of different topics. In a forum, you can have open or private e-mail conversations, access a large catalogue of files on the topic or even contribute by uploading some of your information. An electronic conference is just like a real conference, with lots of people on-line together, each contributing opinions and ideas. A conference can involve a lot of people or can be as simple as a chat between you and just one other on-line forum member.

Investigate **what others know about the subject or add to the worldwide knowledge base with your own information.**

Click on the *link* **to go to the board for that topic. You can talk with others, ask a question or just read what others are saying.**

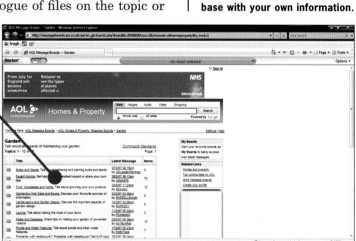

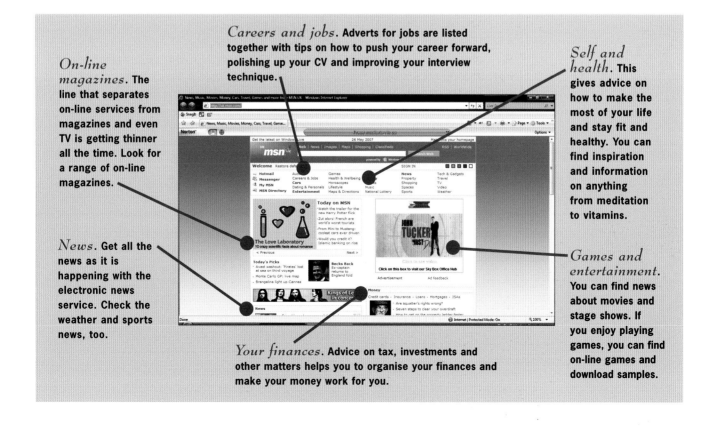

On-line magazines. **The line that separates on-line services from magazines and even TV is getting thinner all the time. Look for a range of on-line magazines.**

News. **Get all the news as it is happening with the electronic news service. Check the weather and sports news, too.**

Careers and jobs. **Adverts for jobs are listed together with tips on how to push your career forward, polishing up your CV and improving your interview technique.**

Self and health. **This gives advice on how to make the most of your life and stay fit and healthy. You can find inspiration and information on anything from meditation to vitamins.**

Games and entertainment. **You can find news about movies and stage shows. If you enjoy playing games, you can find on-line games and download samples.**

Your finances. **Advice on tax, investments and other matters helps you to organise your finances and make your money work for you.**

The Internet

I f all you could do with the Internet was exchange messages, it would be of only limited interest. But all these network routes from your computer to any other on the Internet are also available for you to use like a computer-oriented phone system. You can go to remote computer sites and look at the information and files that they have stored especially for public access and either just view them or download the files for your own use. The Internet has its own file-transfer protocol (FTP), the protocol which ensures that the data gets to you intact.

Service providers **make surfing the Internet simple and fun.**

This is the point at which the Internet starts getting complicated. As the system grew, several different ways of accessing other computer sites were established. There are newsgroups that are very similar to FTP sites that have large stores of files, discussion groups and the Internet Relay Chat (IRC) system – the on-line equivalent of CB radio. So, instead of having just one type of on-line system, you have to negotiate several different types if you want to get at all the computer sites that are available on the Internet.

All webbed together

The good news is that an idea called the World Wide Web, also known as the Web, developed by the European Laboratory of Particle Physics (CERN) in Switzerland, makes access to many of these systems infinitely easier.

Not only does the Web remove much of the complex typing needed to get to a remote computer system, it does two other important things to make the Internet really work for you. The first is that it offers a Windows-like graphical interface that can deliver images, sound and even movie clips directly from a remote computer site to your desktop PC. This makes using the Internet very attractive and accessible to anyone who can operate a simple computer system. The second feature is that it can automatically make links to files located at many different sites by just clicking on a section (a 'hot' button) of the web page you have on screen.

Wandering the Web

Service providers give you all the software you need to browse through the millions of pages of information and entertainment that are available on the Internet. The software for browsing around the Web is called, naturally, a web browser, and there are now two main browsers: Microsoft Explorer and Mozilla Firefox. When you see a site you like, you can store its address in your Favorites (Bookmarks) folder for quick access at any time. Many Internet sites add sound or animation features, which need additional software to play them. These additional software modules can be downloaded from a web site and then plugged into the browser you are using.

Home sweet ome page

An increasing number of individuals and companies like the idea of their own home page, which can display information and pictures about themselves and has links to direct you to other sites of interest. With a little effort in learning HTML, the computer language that makes a web page work, you can create your own web page, which your service provider will display usually as part of your subscription charge. There are also free services that offer personal web pages, for example MySpace.

The amazing web site

A web site is a treasure chest of information and entertainment. When you go to a site you'll see a starting menu page with words and images that are linked to hotspots. When you click on one of these hotspots, you are whisked off to another web page that takes you deeper into the topic. This may be on the same web site or it may be a link that automatically sends you to another web site on another computer, maybe in another continent.

Everyone is getting on the web-site bandwagon. Whatever your interest, there'll be a web site that has something to say about it. Want to know more about the latest films? Most major movies have their own web pages. Want to shop? There are web sites that will sell you anything from a bottle of wine to an airline ticket. Just want to be entertained? There are a vast number of just plain fun web sites that have great graphics and now add animation, sound and even video. To get them to run smoothly, it's best to have a broadband connection.

Servers and clients

On the Internet, a server is the computer that serves you web sites, files and messages, and your PC is the client. The problem with having so many thousands of web sites and servers is knowing how to find what you're looking for.

You certainly can't go looking at every site in turn to see if there are any files with likely sounding names. It would take years on-line. Fortunately, there are a mass of search sites ready to come to your rescue…

Search engines

Search systems have lists of Internet sites and many of the files they contain. They use a list of keywords taken from the sites to get an idea of what they are about. If you know the name of the file you want, you can just type it directly into the search box. If you have a general topic of interest, you can type in a keyword and the search system will give you a list of sites that may be of interest.

Once you've found a few useful web sites, you'll see that they have lists of other, like-minded sites. The web site's hotspots will link you directly to the new sites at the click of the mouse button.

Clicking on a *hotspot* will whisk you off to another web page.

Search engine or directory?

The Web contains a fantastic wealth of information. Whether you're looking for information on Bob Dylan or a recipe for pumpkin pie, it'll be on the Web, but how do you find it?

There are two basic kinds of search sites – search engines and directories, although the distinction between them is blurring. A web directory is usually best if you want to find links around certain topics (for instance, a listing of on-line clothes stores). Search engines are best when you want all the information possible on particular ideas or people (such as the writings of Winston Churchill).

Searching the Internet

● **www.google.com** and **www.altavista.com** Search engines like these are automated systems that use 'spiders' or 'webcrawlers' – software that automatically searches for sites on the Web and copies information about them into huge databases that can then be searched. Google is currently the most popular search engine on the Web.

● **www.yahoo.com** and **www.about.com** Directories such as these are listings of web sites that have been selected and sorted into related groups by human editors.

● **www.scoot.co.uk** One of several sites where you can search for information about businesses in your area.

● **www.ask.co.uk** A search site that has a natural language engine so you can type in questions as you would ask them (rather than keywords) and get a list of web sites with possible answers.

● **www.dogpile.com** A metasearch site, i.e. your query is automatically sent to several search sites at the same time.

● **www.shopsonthenet.com** There are many sites where you can search on specific topics. For example, this site is a searchable directory of shops that are available on-line.

E-mail

The Internet creates a way for computer systems to link their messaging and file-exchanging functions. Along with your Internet connection, most ISPs will give you your own personal e-mail address. With Internet e-mail you can send text messages, and even attach documents and photographs, to anyone in the world who also has an e-mail address. The message can be as long as you like and it will arrive at its destination within minutes of being sent.

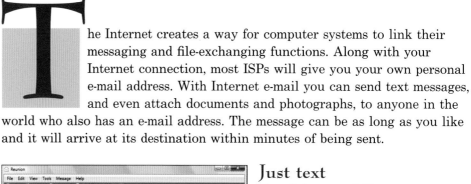

Just text

E-mail is essentially a text system. It combines the friendliness of a phone call with the efficiency of a fax. If the recipient has the same word-processing system as you, click on attach, then click on the file you want to send and it will be sent with your e-mail.

If you are sending a document as an attachment to someone who has a different word-processing system from you, it is important to convert it into what's called ASCII text first. All word processors can handle ASCII text, but you may lose formatting features, such as type style and size.

Addressing your electronic envelope

When you join a service, you are asked for your own electronic name and address. Most service providers let you use variations of your name. The address lets the Internet know how to get the e-mail to the right person and follows an established format:

There is always the @ *separator* to separate the name from the address.

The type of service provider. Co. means it is a *commercial service*.

smithjones@demon.co.uk

The person's *e-mail* name.

The name of the *service provider*.

The *country*.

Finding people on the Internet

The easiest way of finding someone's e-mail address is to ask them. If they have sent you a message, their address will be included in it, and all you have to do is copy it across to your e-mail address book. Windows Mail makes it easy. Simply click the e-mail address beside To: then right-click and select Add to Contacts.

Failing that, there are several directory systems that can be used, but none of them have a comprehensive listing of the millions of e-mail addresses.

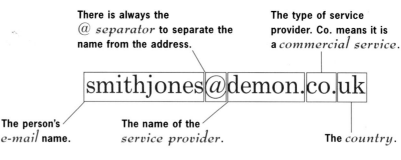

Return to sender

E-mail can take a rather tortuous route to get to its destination, going through several different computer centres before it gets there. The exact route is added to the start of the message, so if there is a problem, you may be able to track down where the hold-up was. If the mail doesn't get through, the computers report back to each other and you will get a message that the e-mail failed to arrive.

Etiquette

The vast majority of e-mail messages are polite, courteous, informative and fun. And, like any other club, the on-line community has its own rules of etiquette to keep it that way. When you join any on-line group, there is always an FAQ file about the group and any etiquette that applies to it. FAQ stands for Frequently Asked Questions. This will give you guidelines to what is expected of you. If you are unsure, ask the Sysop, moderator, or anyone else who happens to be in the chat room. You will also find other users helpful.

Little and often

Keep your messages short. You can make a point in a few sentences. This will be quicker to read and is more likely to get a response. You have plenty of opportunities to cover different topics in separate mailings rather than try to cover a lot of ground in one. Because other users won't necessarily have seen the start of your on-line conversation, it is sometimes nice to include a snippet from the mail you are replying to.

Junk mail

You can use the on-line systems to broadcast a file or message to many people. But don't do it unless you have a good reason. It clogs up the system with unwanted messages and files, and no one likes unnecessary mail. It will usually be regarded as spam, or junk mail. There is so much unsolicited mail that regulations have been brought in to try to stop it.

Generally, the advice is if you don't recognise the sender of the message, don't open it. Be particularly careful if it has an attachment because this may well contain a virus.

Don't SHOUT!

Even if something is upsetting, DON'T SHOUT BACK WHEN YOU ARE TYPING BY USING CAPITAL LETTERS. It's not much fun to read too many capitals.

Flaming last resort

Some messages provoke a heated reaction. If you see something that really gets on your nerves, you can respond in heated verbal terms. Letting off steam in this way is called flaming. If you want to use immoderate language, flame in a private e-mail. But don't forget that to libel someone in e-mail is just as much an offence as it is in any other written form.

☺ Smileys

When you talk to someone face to face or on the phone, there are all sorts of clues you get about the real meaning behind their words, whether what is being said is meant nicely, affectionately, humorously or angrily.

On-line, only the words come on the screen, so it is quite possible for your light, humorous remark to be taken as a deadly insult. One way of solving this is to add <s> or <g> at the end of the sentence, meaning smiling or grinning. There are also the smileys, which use keyboard characters to create the picture of your face as you are writing.

Here are a few of the more useful smileys. Turn the page on its side to see how they work.

:-)	Happy	:-(	Sad
:-D	Laughing	:-||	Angry
:->	Devilish grin	:-o	Shocked
:'-(	Crying	;-)	Winking

Here are a few less useful, but fun, smileys to describe people. See if you can figure out what they mean (the answers are below).

:-i	=:-)	:-[
8:-)	8-)	:-)>

:-i Smoker	8:-) Little girl	:-)> Beard
:-[Vampire	=:-) Punk	8-) Wearing glasses

☺

Faxing

If you've looked through the ads for modems, you will have seen that they include a fax function. The fax machine is an important method of communication in business. It is simple to use and can send pages of documents anywhere in the world in seconds.

A business has little difficulty in justifying the cost of a fax, but at home it is different. For the convenience of sending or receiving an occasional fax, you wouldn't consider buying a fax machine, let alone finding the space for it and adding a second telephone line. But with a fax/modem, all these problems disappear. You get the fax function with the modem. It doesn't take up any space and it will have voice/fax switching built into its software so you don't need an extra phone line.

Where do I put the paper?

Rather than scanning a real piece of paper, your fax/modem software takes the image created by your Windows program and turns it into a file of fax data ready to send. This is all done inside your PC. Apart from the convenience of not having to print the page first and then feed it into a fax machine, the fax/modem produces a better-quality fax, simply because the page hasn't gone through the printing and scanning process.

Using Print or Send

Many software packages will let you fax your document directly using the Print command. This saves you having to load up your fax software. Instead you use the fax like a printer. Press Ctrl+P to open the Print box and select your fax/modem as the printer and continue with your usual printing routine.

Fax incoming

Receiving a fax is even easier. The fax/modem is connected to the phone line. When the phone rings, the software will automatically detect a call and answer it. If it is a fax, your PC will receive and store it; if it is a regular phone call, it will pass it on to your telephone.

You can set up your fax/modem software in lots of ways. If you only rarely get faxes, you can tell the fax/modem to ignore all incoming calls. If you pick up the phone and find it is a fax, you just select Manual Receive from your keyboard and the fax system will take over. This is a lot nicer for your friends and relatives, who can find the squawk of your fax trying to talk to them very irritating.

To store & to print

Your fax/modem will store all the received faxes on your hard disk. You can have your PC print them as soon as the fax has been received or leave them stored in the computer until you are ready to print them out later.

Background faxing

Faxing, like printing, can be done as a background operation. Having told your PC to send a fax, you can go back to doing your normal work on the computer while, behind the scenes, your PC is busily creating the fax pages and sending them off.

On the move

With a laptop computer, you can hook up to an on-line service from just about anywhere. You can either plug the laptop PC into any phone socket or link up with a mobile phone.

Mobile modems

Whichever way you want to work, you will need to add a modem to your laptop PC. The external portable modem is like a regular external modem, only smaller. It connects to the laptop PC using the standard connector and has a socket for a phone lead to connect to the telephone socket. Portable modems use the same basic electronics as the larger desktop PC versions, so they can work at high speeds and offer fax and modem transmission.

The credit-card modem

Modem miniaturisation is taken to an extreme with the new generation of internal modems. Instead of using a standard internal expansion slot, laptop PCs are adopting the PCMCIA adapter standard. A PCMCIA modem is a small credit-card-sized device that plugs into a slot on the side of the computer; the slot can take a whole range of different plug-in peripheral units. The slot-in-and-use convenience of the PCMCIA standard makes it ideal for portable communications.

The great on-line from the great outdoors

External and PCMCIA modems have to be connected to an ordinary phone line. Digital mobile phones, however, work well with computers, and the digital system bypasses the traditional modem. Several digital mobile phones are equipped with special adapters to connect the output of the laptop computer directly to the mobile phone, giving fast and reliable on-line connections. On some systems, data can be transferred by infra-red or through a Bluetooth connection.

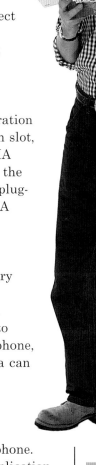

WAP phones

With WAP phones, you don't need a PC at all. You can surf the Net direct from your mobile phone. WAP stands for wireless application protocol, which is a global standard for enabling mobile devices to access the Internet. It's a fast, convenient way to get the latest news, stock prices, and weather reports, or even to buy the latest CD or book online. But while a WAP phone gives you Web access on the move, there are drawbacks. WAP phones have small screens, so the information they can display is limited, and writing e-mails or other messages using a mobile phone keyboard is slow and tricky.

The trend towards using *cellular phones* **with laptop computers and credit-card-sized modems means you can be on-line while you are on the move.**

Home and away

Many of the larger service providers, such as AOL, have access points throughout the world. You should be able to log on using a local or national call, rather than having to call back to your native country. You should always check where the nearest access sites are before you leave home. When you call and log on with your password, the system will react exactly as it does at home.

Shopping

Many banks and stores think that on-line shopping and on-line banking will be important to every household in the future. If you have a PC and a modem, you can contact a variety of stores to browse through what's available, order what you want, and have it delivered to your door.

You won't need a PC

On-line shopping is too big to offer just to households with PCs. With the arrival of hundreds of digital TV, satellite, and cable TV stations, little black boxes connected to your TV that contain a modem and computer processor will hook up to the telephone socket. With a simple remote control, you can highlight any product being shown on screen and press the Order button, and the system will automatically make the call and electronically place the order for you.

On-line stores

The virtual shopping centre has all the shops you are likely to see in any city centre – if not more. On-line you can get just about anything you want, from palm-tree seeds to the latest style in trainers. There are department stores, such as Amazon(www.amazon.co.uk) and John Lewis (www.johnlewis.com), auction houses, such as Ebay (www.ebay.co.uk), on-line food stores, with home delivery from all the major supermarkets, sports shops, book shops, electrical goods shops, garden centres and so on.

The costs of setting up and running a virtual store are a lot less than a physical shop, so on-line prices can be substantially lower than in the high street. You do need to allow for delivery charges though, unless your goods are downloadable – like music or videos. With the rise of broadband access, on-line entertainment has become big business. On-line music stores, including iTunes (www.itunes.co.uk) and MSN Music (entertainment.uk. msn.com/music), have revolutionised music buying. These stores let you sample part of a music track for free. Then, if you like it, you can buy it and download it instantly to play on your PC or music player. And it's not just music. You can also buy audio books, videos, TV shows and even full-length films 'on demand'.

Secured nets

Most on-line stores use secure servers so you can confidently place your order using a credit card. It means you can do the whole transaction electronically from your screen by typing in your address and credit-card number and whizzing that over the Internet to the web-site shop. The electronic shopping and banking systems encrypt the information into a secret code before it leaves your PC. Your details can be unscrambled by the electronic store or bank only. To everyone else the information is meaningless. The key that unlocks the encryption can have up to 18 billion billion combinations, so it's about as secure as you can get.

12 CREATING IMAGES

Quick draw

Thanks to the computer many of us are discovering artistic talents that we never knew we had. With the popularity of digital cameras it has never been easier to snap a picture and upload it to your PC. Once on your PC, you an use graphic software to manipulate the image – to remove red-eye, for example, or make the picture brighter – or use it as your inspiration for a painting or drawing.

To begin with, the photo is a handy base for your drawing. You can use painting and drawing software to trace over it electronically, to add effects and so on. Then, once you see how easy the software is to use, there will be no holding back your creative talents.

For kids – and many older first-time PC users – using painting and drawing software is a way of exploring the workings of Windows and practising control of the mouse. Nothing increases your mouse control more than trying to draw a perfect straight line or circle completely freehand. We are surrounded by computer-generated images in magazines and newspapers and on TV. Simple cartoon-like pictures and complicated, magical images are all achieved with painting and drawing programs that can run on your PC.

But painting and drawing isn't just for fooling around. Although you can produce lighthearted pictures, you can also produce illustrations, images and graphs that support the most serious documents. Drawing systems are an important part of industry. A huge number of manufactured or built products – from the smallest toy to the largest building – start life as a drawing on a PC.

Computer graphics are used to liven up reports with graphs and simple pictures. With the latest generation of drawing, presentation or picture-editing software, anyone can make professional-looking images, regardless of their abilities. Painting, drawing or photo-editing provide very different ways of making pictures. We'll show you what the differences are, and which to use. This is the time to experiment. You can do as much as you like without wasting any paper, ruining your photo, running out of paint or needing to sharpen a pencil. Your only limitation is your imagination. ●

Painting and

Painting and drawing have developed as two entirely different ways of producing pictures on your PC. Painting is the artistic approach for producing pictures that look like real paintings and for working on photographs and other scanned images. Painted pictures give you a full range of brush and paint effects so you can sketch or paint in any way you like. You can take real images, scanned or downloaded into your PC, and change and alter them in ways that cannot be detected. And you can produce spectacular effects using the various mixing, merging and filtering tricks.

Drawing, on the other hand, is for making more technical images, graphs and plans. Everything you see is made up of a series of straight lines, curves, squares, circles, rectangles and ovals. While a drawing program can make excellent cartoon-type pictures, it won't let you re-create the 'Mona Lisa' on your computer screen. What it will do is let you make attractive illustrations, graphs and drawings to be used in documents, either for home or office use, no matter what your drawing skills are.

Paint **programs produce bitmapped images that can look just like real photos or paintings.**

Bitmaps and vectors

If a picture looks like a photo or a painting, then it's a painted (bitmapped) image. Each coloured dot, or pixel, is given a number that tells the computer what colour it is and where it is on the screen. The sharpness, or resolution, of the image depends entirely on the number of dots, or pixels, used to make up the picture – the more pixels per square centimetre, the better the image will look.

Even a picture that fills the screen at the lowest Windows resolution will be made up of 600 rows of 800 dots in each row (nearly 500,000 pixels in all). Since every pixel is listed in the image's file, these files can get pretty big. Several megabytes or more is not unusual.

Pictures created by drawing programs are called vector files and store the picture information in a totally different way. They tend to look like cartoons or graphs. If you've placed a square on the screen then what is stored is information about your square's size, position and colour. The description of a big square or circle takes up no more file space than a few bitmapped pixels, and so vector files take up very little disk space.

Because everything you draw is stored in the file as a separate item – a square in this position, a curve there, a straight line here – even after you've

Vector **programs give less artistic-looking results and are better suited to producing simple things like graphs.**

drawing

finished drawing you can still pick out any of the elements and change their colour, position and size or remove them altogether without affecting anything else in the picture.

Zoom

If you zoom in on a bitmapped picture, the quality of the image declines as you begin to see the dots – just like looking at a newspaper through a magnifying glass. But when you make a vector drawing bigger or smaller, you are telling your PC to recalculate the position and size of the squares, lines and circles in the picture. So when you zoom in on a vector drawing, the picture is recalculated and displayed or printed at the best quality your PC can produce.

Display your work

If you want to work on your photos and images and get them exactly right, you will need the best colour resolution you can get out of your PC. Go to the Windows Display and make certain the colour settings are set to Highest (32bit), as this will approach photographic quality.

As you increase the number of colours shown on screen, you will notice your PC reacts more slowly. If you are doing a lot of drawing and painting work, you should think about using an accelerator video-display card. Increasing the amount of RAM in your PC or the memory in the video-display card will also help to speed things up.

Put it on paper

All printers will produce reasonable black-and-white copies of your images. Printers are getting better all the time, but they won't be able to produce prints that are as good as a well-printed magazine or a photograph. Having said that, the best inkjet printers working on the latest high-gloss 'photo' papers will produce near-photo quality. But if you want an image printed out perfectly, go to a good DTP bureau which should be able to produce a high-quality print or photographic slide from your PC's picture file.

A vector drawing should look *smooth*, no matter how much you magnify it.

Input devices: Your PC's brushes and pencils

● A mouse or trackball can be used for both bitmapped and vector drawing.

● A graphic tablet (right) is a book-sized tablet with a pressure-sensitive surface that can detect the point of a stylus being drawn across it. The tablet is the nearest a graphic artist can get to real painting on a computer.

● Scanners are used to turn a photo or picture into a picture file that your PC can work with. For near-photographic quality, you need one that can capture the picture's subtlety of shading and colour, preferably a 24-bit scanner.

● If you have a video capture card, you can capture stills from your TV, VCR, or camcorder. These are then stored as bitmapped pictures just as though they had been scanned.

Paint tools

A typical paint program is Paint that comes with Windows. In Paint, you open a new picture and you'll get a blank sheet of electronic paper. Click on the pencil icon and start drawing on the screen by holding down the left mouse button and moving the mouse. Doodle as much as you like until you get the hang of it.

Once you've got the idea, click on the brush. This time you get a choice of brush sizes and shapes, and each has its uses. Click on an angled brush and see the calligraphic effect it gives to curves.

Have you ever wanted to be a graffiti artist in the comfort of your home – and no cleaning up afterward? Then click on the Airbrush. This will give you a choice of three spray positions. The smallest is like holding an airbrush close to the paper, which produces a small but very dark spray. Using the larger options gives lighter sprays over a wider area.

As with a spray can, the longer you hold the airbrush in one position, the more paint you spray on. Try moving the spray across the screen going very slowly first and then speeding up.

Outlined or filled in?

When you draw a rectangle or an oval, you can show it as an outline and have it filled in with colour, or you can have it as a coloured shape without an outline, depending on which box you select. The line colour is always the foreground colour. You choose a fill colour by changing the background colour.

Write on!

Adding text is easy. Click on the text button and then map out the space you want the text to fill – usually a long thin area. Now you can type the words. Click on the right mouse button and call up the Text toolbar to change fonts and sizes. When you are happy with your text, clicking on any other tool

Lines, curves, squares and circles

Circles, ovals, squares and rectangles – in fact anything that needs perfect curves or straight lines – are easy to do in Paint, as it has special buttons dedicated to doing just these things.

To draw *straight lines,* use the Line button and select how thick you want the line to be. Put the cross-hair where you want the line to start. With your finger on the mouse button, move the mouse, and a line will appear. With your finger still on the button, you can move the line and make it longer or shorter. For a perfect corner, release the button momentarily and press it again to start the next line at the end of the first. To get lines that are perfectly horizontal, vertical, or at a 45° angle, hold down the Shift key while you are drawing.

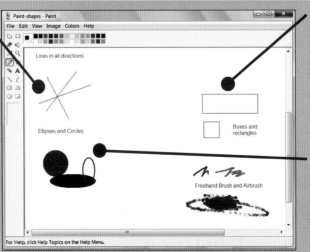

For *rectangles* and *squares,* click on the screen where you want one of the rectangle's corners to be. Click on the Rectangle button and, as you drag the crosshair across the screen, you create a rectangle. Holding down the Shift key will produce squares rather than rectangles.

Ovals work in the same way. Click on the Oval button and drag the crosshair across the screen for wide/fat ovals, or up and down for tall, thin ovals. Holding the Shift button down turns ovals into circles.

Easy ART PROJECT

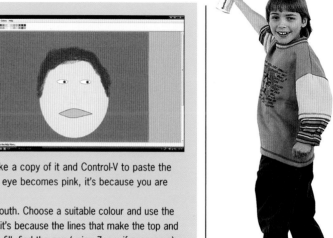

Use the oval button to create a filled circle. Try a skin colour by going to Edit Colour and typing in the values 20 for hue, 200 for saturation, and 210 for luminosity.

Use the Oval for one eye (don't forget to change foreground and background colours) and add a black circle for the pupil.

Put a select box around the eye, then press Control-C to make a copy of it and Control-V to paste the copy onto the screen. Move the eye to the right position. If the eye becomes pink, it's because you are still in transparent mode.

Use the Curve tool to make the bottom and top lines of the mouth. Choose a suitable colour and use the paint can to colour the mouth. If the whole face changes colour, it's because the lines that make the top and bottom of the mouth aren't quite touching. Use Undo to clear the fill, find the gap (using Zoom if necessary), and connect the ends with a small line. Now it's freehand time. Do your best for the nose with the Pencil or Brush and add the hair with the Airbrush. Now try the other tools to fill in the background.

button will place the words permanently into your picture. But remember, once you have exited the writing mode, the words become part of the image, just like the writing on a drawing. If you want to change anything afterwards, you have to rub out the words and replace them.

Cleaning up

If you've slightly overshot a corner or made other little mistakes, you can clean up your picture with the Eraser. This will rub out anything just like the eraser at the end of a pencil. For large areas, click on the big eraser. For fine work, use one of the smaller options. For really careful work, zoom into the picture using Magnifier (shown as a magnifying glass icon in the Toolbar). The thumbnail (right) shows where you are in the picture. You can also use the pencil to correct single pixels.

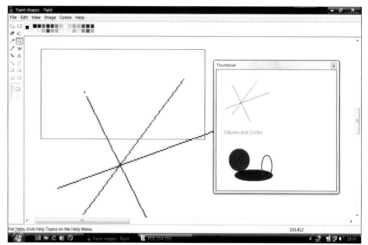

Oops!

Simple mistakes can be eliminated as they happen. Say you are drawing a line and it goes too far. If you are still holding the left mouse button down, pressing the right button will remove the line you have just drawn. Now start again.

If you have finished the line and let go of the mouse button, but then decide that the line isn't right, go to Undo in the Edit menu (or press Control Z). Undo undoes the last drawing action. You can use it to remove the last three additions to your picture.

Manipulating

Copy it

You can copy from other pictures by copying the part you want to the Windows clipboard and pasting it into your own picture. Remember that many programs come with large collections of ready-made images, cartoons and backgrounds that you can add to your own pictures.

Once you've done some painting you still have a whole set of tools to alter what you've done. You can change the whole picture or select a part of it for changing by using the select buttons. You can cut and paste parts of pictures as you choose. Simply surround the part you want to use and Copy or Cut it out and then choose Paste. You will see a new copy in the top left-hand corner of your picture, and you can drag and drop this anywhere you like. By pressing Control-V repeatedly you can use Paste like a rubber stamp.

You can flip an image over or spin it around by using Flip/Rotate, which you'll find in the Image menu. Flipping has the same effect as reflecting the image in a mirror and rotating spins it around.

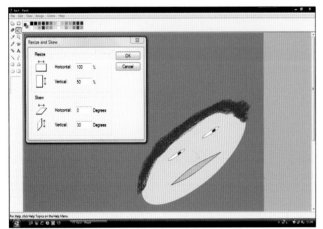

Squeeze me

Any part of the picture can be stretched or squeezed. Draw around it using the Select tools. You will see a dotted line rectangle with small square handles on the corners and the centre of each side. Place the crosshair over the handle and use the mouse to squeeze or stretch the image. If you use the corner handles, you can shrink or enlarge the image without distorting its shape. You can do the same thing using the Resize/Skew option in the Image menu, this time typing in, as numbers, the new size. From this dialogue box (shown left) you can also skew the image, squeezing it sideways or upwards.

Colours

Paint and draw programs give you control over both the foreground and the background colours, and you can change them as you go along. The foreground colour is your paint can colour – the colour that appears when you use the Brush, Pencil or Spray can. The background colour is what lies underneath – the colour of the paper you are working on. The background colour also sets the colour used to fill squares and circles. When you use the Eraser to rub something out, the background colour is revealed underneath.

Foreground **colour to paint with.**

Background **colour for the paper and fills.**

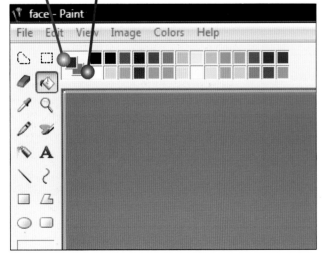

In most programs – we use Paint for this example – you choose your foreground colour by clicking on the Paint Can, then selecting the colour with the left mouse button. To select a new background colour, click on the Paint Can and choose the colour with the right mouse button.

In Paint you'll have a range of 28 paint pots to choose from, but you can also mix your own colours with Edit Colors in the Colors menu. This gives you another 20 cans of colour to work with.

Go to Define Custom Colours and select your own custom colour by moving around the colour matrix block until you find the one you want. You can use it immediately or save it in a custom-colour paint can that you can use again.

images

Fixing your digital images

Since the digital camera is so popular nowadays, it makes sense to use Windows to help you get the most from your images. After all, most of your digital pictures will be stored on the PC. On page 160 we show you how Windows Photo Gallery can help you load and organise your photos.

As an added bonus, this program also comes with a small but useful group of tools for retouching and editing your digital images. The four main areas it will fix are exposure, colour, cropping and the removal of red eye. You can alter these manually or let Photo Gallery Auto Adjust it for you. First, you need to open the photo you want to alter in Windows Photo Gallery, then click the Fix icon in the top toolbar to open the Fix pane on the right-hand side.

One of the main ways to improve a photo is to increase the contrast. To do so click on the Adjust Exposure and move the Contrast slider that appears a few notches to the right. This will work best with outdoor shots.

Red eye (the sinister-looking red glow in the pupils that comes when people look directly into the flash) can spoil many a good photo. To remove it, click the Fix Red Eye option in the right-hand pane. Click and drag a rectangle around each of the eyes – one at a time. To make it easier to place the rectangle on the affected area, zoom in by using the magnifier icon on the left of the control bar.

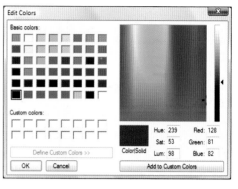

You can create your own colours in Paint using *Define Custom Colors* **under Edit Colors in the Colors menu.**

You can rescue a dull picture by adjusting the *contrast.*

Drawing

Although drawing programs share a lot of functions with Paint, there are some very important differences. Pictures created with drawing programs are full of shapes – each one entirely separate – that are put together by you to create the picture. Rather than painting on a piece of paper, drawing is more like making a felt picture, in which pictures are made by laying different small shapes on to a background card. Microsoft Office 2007 comes with its own set of drawing tools that can help you create a variety of shapes, with 3D effects and more.

One advantage of the Office Drawing Tools program is that, even when you think you've finished the picture, you can still go back to it and move single pieces around, change the order in which they are laid on top of each other, and add more pieces.

To add a drawing to a document in Word, you first need to create a drawing canvas. To do so, go to the Illustrators group, click Shapes and then New Drawing Canvas. The Format tab for the Drawing Tools is added to the Ribbon. Add a circle, by going to the Insert Shapes group, selecting Oval from Basic Shapes and holding the Shift button down as you draw on the canvas. Make a couple more. If you then go to the pointer tool and place the arrow over one of the circles, you can select it, move it around the screen, and change anything about it you want. Stretch it, shrink it, squash it, change its colour – whatever you do affects only the object you've selected.

Drawing programs construct pictures using any number of different shapes.

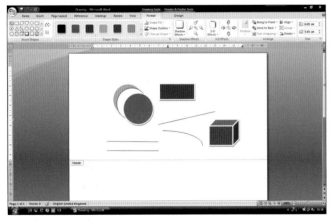

From A to B

As well as moving the mouse to create your picture, with Drawing Tools you can simply set the start and end points of the line. Click on the line icon in Insert Shapes, then click anywhere on the screen – that is your line's starting point A. As you move the mouse around, the line is automatically drawn to the cursor. Click again and you've set your line's end point B.

You can alter those points at any time. Use the arrow button and click on the line. You can move it, change the start and end points, change its colour and thickness, even turn it into a dotted line.

Circles, wedges and squares

The same applies to any other object. When you create an object, you are telling the computer what shape and colour it is. Your PC uses these instructions to recreate your picture every time you call it up.

Layer upon layer

Just like a felt picture, what you see finally depends on which objects or shapes sit on top of each other. Each time you draw an object it will automatically be placed on top of anything that is already drawn on the paper. But you can change the order in which objects are layered by using the Bring to Front or Send to Back instructions in the Arrange group.

Create a star and make a *copy* and colour it. Click on the copy and put it behind the original.

Grids

If you are producing graphs or other technical illustrations, you will find it important that you place blocks or other objects in straight lines. Doing this by hand is very difficult, so the Office Drawing Tools give you a grid to work with. The grid is really just like graph paper, except with paper you always see the squares. The squares appear only on your monitor. So you can easily make sure your columns and lines start and stop in the right place.

But maybe you are still not sure your control of the mouse is good enough, even with the grid lines to help. Then switch on Snap Objects to other Objects in the Grid Settings. As you draw, your PC will automatically help position everything accurately.

A choice of fillings

With Drawing Tools, you have a wide range of fillings that you can put into your shapes. There are solid colours, outlines, lines and graduated tints, which move slowly from one colour to another. Gradations can make an ordinary image look very professional. Gradations give a 3-D feel to your objects, turning circles into balls and squares into almost tangible cubes.

Join the group

Often you will need to handle a selection of objects as though they were a single item. You can do this by collecting them into a group. Hold the Shift key down, and click on all the objects you want to group. Now select Group in the Arrange menu. Try moving the group around and you'll see that now everything moves together. Anything you can do with a single object – moving, resizing, copying, layering, changing colour and so on – you can also do with a group.

You may have created a group to move a whole part of the picture from one point to another. Now if you want to change something within the group, select Ungroup to separate it back into individual parts.

Write-on

Unlike Paint, which turns text into part of the picture itself, the Drawing Tools treat text just as a word processor does. You can type in your words and change their size, font and colour. You can align the words left, centre or right. Best of all, you can always come back and change the text at any time you like.

Line styles

When you are drawing lines in, you can change both the thickness of the line and its style. You are not restricted to a continuous line: with Drawing Tools you can just as easily produce a dotted or dot-dash line by selecting these in the Shape Outline menu.

Freeform

In the Drawing Tools you'll find a Scribble tool that works like the pencil in Paint. As you draw, it creates your shapes out of numerous short lines.

Photography

The digital camera has turned everyone into a photographer. It's easier than ever to achieve reasonable quality images, and your computer is a natural place to store them. You can even improve them using basic image manipulation software, or share them with others via the Web, e-mail or print-outs.

There are several ways of transferring your photos to the PC. If your computer has a card reader, the easiest way is to plug your camera's flash memory card into it. If you don't have a built-in card reader, there are several inexpensive ones available that plug into a spare USB port. Alternatively, you may be able to connect your digital camera directly to your PC using a USB cable. Once connected, most cameras will appear as a disk icon in your Computer folder, and you can then copy and move files in the usual way. Alternatively, some software programs will start copying over the photos automatically once they are connected to the PC.

Set up a picture gallery

Windows Vista makes it simple to keep track of your pictures once you've uploaded them by including Windows Photo Gallery. You can also organise, edit, print and share them – all from one place.

To open the program go to the Start menu, All Programs and click on Windows Photo Gallery. Clicking on the camera icon next to Recently Imported shows the images you have just uploaded. Alternatively, you can look at all the pictures – sorted by the date they were taken, the folder where they are stored, any ratings you have given or any tags you have applied (for example, if they are pictures from a family occasion you may have tagged them as 'Birthday Party').

At the top of the gallery are the tools for editing and sharing photographs. Click on the image you want to change and select Fix. The image editor opens on the right-hand side of the screen. With this, you can adjust the colours, the brightness and contrast, resize the image and even remove red eye. Then click the e-mail button to attach it to a message, using your default mail program, or send it to your printer. If e-mailing it, the Attach Files box opens so you can select the size of image – from small to large – that you want. The pixel size is also shown, along with the size of the file once it's converted to an attachment, so you can make sure that it's not too big. Click Attach and the file will be formatted and attached to an e-mail, ready to send. For printing, a photo printer is ideal but most inkjets can print at photo quality on special paper. Click on the arrow beside Print on the top toolbar and select Order Prints for your photos to be sent to a digital printing company.

After you have uploaded your photographs into Windows Photo Gallery, they will be displayed automatically as a series of *thumbnail images.*

13 MULTIMEDIA

No limits!

Multimedia is the reason that many families buy a PC for their home. Your multimedia PC can merge information, images, movies, music and speech into a single program that can inform, educate and entertain – all at the same time.

Multimedia programs can be educational and take young children through the basics of reading or maths. For older children, there is a wide range of software on topics from dinosaurs to music. And for everyone there are the multimedia reference works that go far beyond the usual text of an encyclopaedia. Mixing sound clips, colour pictures and movies, multimedia turns learning into a more entertaining experience. Learning can be so much fun that users have coined a new name for these types of software: edutainment.

For the business user, multimedia can radically overhaul the way information is presented. A sound clip of just a few words can be used to explain the complexities of a graph. Adding multimedia to a presentation – mixing animated graphs, sound and even video – makes a great difference in the impact the presentation has on an audience.

And then there is pure entertainment. With a multimedia PC games can offer real sound and fast-moving video. You can even turn your PC into a TV. Multimedia not only brings you into the world of playing multimedia programs from CDs or DVDs, you can also make your own. With multimedia you can do virtually anything with your PC, from adding short sound bites to a word-processed document to making your own multimedia TV show.

Interactivity is a key element of many multimedia programs. It means being able to move around the available information in any order you want, with the PC helping you to navigate, rather than dictating where you have to go next. It is a bit like a reference book, in which you look up references and move around the book to delve deeper into a topic. But an interactive multimedia program will do all the searching for you and come up with a whole range of text information, images, video and sound clips to explain the topic more clearly. You can harness this power to a high-quality colour monitor and a sound card that can record and play to full CD or DVD quality. There is virtually no limit to what a multimedia computer can offer. ●

Multimedia

Take a good PC, add a CD or DVD player to run the latest multimedia software, and a sound card and speakers to play sound and music, and you have the essence of a multimedia PC. Most new home computers have all the important multimedia functions already built into them, so all you have to do is plug in the PC and you are ready to go. This is particularly so with PCs running Windows Vista. With the Home Premium edition of Vista comes Windows Media Center, which is pretty much all you need to run a full home entertainment system. It also offers a spectacular range of multimedia effects with a program called Aero that helps you manage the windows on your PC.

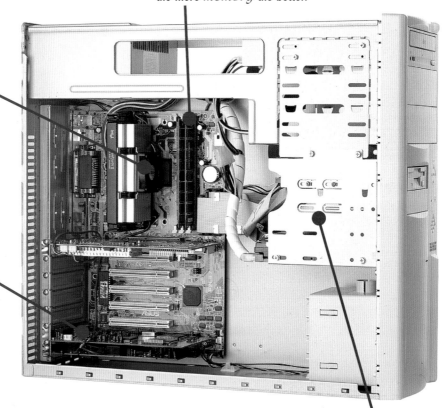

Microsoft recommends a minimum of 1GB of RAM just to run Windows Vista smoothly, so the more *memory* the better.

At the heart of a PC is the *CPU*. A 800MHz CPU is sufficient for Vista's requirements but higher speed chips would be preferable.

Windows Vista has an Aero feature that requires a powerful *3D graphics card*. The card needs to support DirectX 9 or above and have at least 128MB of dedicated memory (you can get away with less if you have a fast processor).

The biggest development in look and feel with Windows Vista (compared to earlier versions of Windows) is thanks to *Aero*, which comes with all the Home Premium editions. It's not included with Home Basic, however. The Aero glass effect gives folder borders a transparent look, Flip 3D lets you shuffle through a stack of open windows by pressing the Windows key and Tab, while Live Preview presents a thumbnail view – with animation, if appropriate – of an application or document.

Multimedia PCs need a larger than average *hard disk* to store sounds, images and movies. In addition, you need at least 15GB of free space to run Vista.

Inside your multimedia PC you will find all the essential elements that make it perform: the CD or DVD drive, to access the programs; the sound card; and the powerful central processing unit and video card. You will also find a large hard disk so that you can comfortably store multimedia programs, audio and image files.

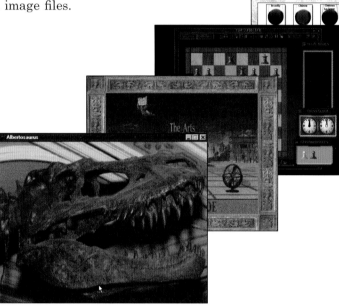

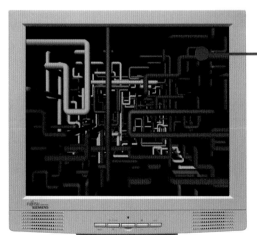

A good display card and *monitor* make the most of multimedia's full-colour images and speed up video playback.

Software

The reason for buying a multimedia PC is to run multimedia software. These amazing programs mix information with pictures, sound, animation and video clips in a way that makes the most complex topics accessible and interesting. There are thousands of multimedia titles available, ranging from educational and reference works to games. Although home multimedia has only been around for a few years, many of these titles are well put together.

Education

Kids can use the PC to draw, write, make music or learn about their world. Multimedia encyclopaedias and dictionaries are designed to capture their attention and enthusiasm. These edutainment programs make education fun.

The more sophisticated edutainment software goes straight to the heart of subjects being taught in the National Curriculum. Such programs are particularly useful for special projects, background information and hobbies.

Adults, too

Multimedia is not all kids' stuff. Some of the most successful titles are bought by adults. Grown-ups' CD-ROMs range from computer golf to adventure games. Art, movies and music are particularly well represented. Other edutainment titles include architecture, history and astronomy.

And if you ever wanted a complete set of encyclopaedias but never had the wall space or the cash to buy them, a multimedia CD or DVD will give you the equivalent of a 30-volume set with the bonuses of sound and video.

Controller

Multimedia is as much about games as anything else, and multimedia computers often include a socket for a joystick controller. It is much better suited to game playing than the mouse or the keyboard.

Kit stop

MPC, short for *Multimedia PC*, **was a standard for the recommended configuration for a PC with CD drive. The logo is not seen much now, in part because nearly all new PCs for the home market are multimedia PCs.**

As well as a DVD or CD drive and a sound card, your PC needs to have the right combination of processor power and memory before it will properly play multimedia programs. This is because the computer's workload increases dramatically when you want to hear and see high-quality sounds and pictures. For example, a photographic-quality colour image that uses nearly 17 million colours will demand three times more memory to store and display than a simple 256-colour image.

PC performance

The faster Pentium PCs will work with all of today's multimedia programs. These very fast processors are able to handle the large amounts of picture and sound information being played from a good multimedia program. The amount of internal memory that your computer has will also dramatically affect how smoothly it will play multimedia. Your computer must have at least 1GB of internal RAM to handle Windows Vista and run multimedia programs smoothly. However, 2GB is recommended if you are serious about using your computer for sound and moving images.

The constant demand from games players for better onscreen images has led to graphics cards becoming ever more advanced. Most will enable you to do some basic video-editing on your PC. Such cards provide all the hardware necessary for video capture. In addition, they may have a television tuner, so you can watch all your favourite soaps on the PC. Cards like these store video in the MPEG standard, the same system used by DVD movies. But video does take up a lot of hard disk space so make sure you've got plenty of gigabytes spare.

Sound waves

Sound cards on multimedia PCs have gone way beyond simply playing the beeps you hear when you turn on your computer. They are now almost a complete orchestra in a box. Previously most sound cards used a system called FM Synthesis to create their sounds, which used a special synthesiser chip to imitate real sounds.

Now most sound cards use wavetable synthesis. This involves real sounds being recorded (sampled) and stored digitally on the card – notes from a real piano for example. The wavetable controller or engine then plays back the recorded sounds to simulate pieces of piano music.

Most sound cards also come with a MIDI (Musical Instrument Digital Interface) system, which enables musical instruments, such as keyboards, to be plugged in and controlled by the PC for recording and editing sounds.

Look to the future

As time passes, computers will continue to become more powerful and multimedia software will make more demands on your PC. Inevitably a PC that is right for today's multimedia programs may not be able to handle programs being produced in a few years' time. Yet all is not lost, because you can upgrade your computer to meet future needs. If you need more memory, you can simply plug some more in. If you need a high power, movie-type display card, you can replace your existing card with a new one. For more sound features, just replace the sound card. Invest wisely now and you will have a PC that can grow as the technology changes.

Better pictures

The bigger and better your monitor, the higher the resolution you can use without it either flickering or looking too small and fuzzy. The two important aspects of the multimedia monitor are its resolution and refresh rate. On a 19in screen you can get a high resolution of 1280 x 1024. But if you tried to pack more pixels into the same size screen, the detail would be too small to show up easily. The refresh rate is also important for traditional CRT (Cathode Ray Tube) monitors. To make sure there's no onscreen flicker – you should look for a figure of 85Hz or above. With the increasingly popular flat panel (LCD) monitors it's not so important as the individual cells don't dim. An LCD monitor is fine with a refresh rate of 60Hz.

Identifying sound files

Sound files can be identified by their file extensions – that is the characters on the ends of their names – and most can be played by Windows Media Player (which comes with Windows) or RealPlayer. Portable music players, such as Apple's iPod (below), can be connected to your PC to download your music files. The most common types of music file are:

.mp3, MP3
MP3 is a way of shrinking sound files that makes digital music easier to handle and speeds up the time it takes to download songs from the Internet.

.mid, MIDI files
The file format for storing MIDI songs.

.wav, Waveform Audio Format
The standard format for storing sounds in Windows.

Windows comes with its own **Media Player** that will use the soundcard on your PC to play back your music.

Bits of colour

Sometimes the colour performance of a PC is described as 8-, 16-, 24- or 32-bit. This tells you how many binary bits are used by the PC to describe the colours in each dot, or pixel, on your screen.

8-bit colour = Up to 256 colours = Minimum for multimedia
16-bit colour = Up to 65,536 colours = Video quality
24-bit colour = Up to 16.7 million colours = Photographic quality
32-bit colour = Up to 4,000 million colours = High-end graphics

Music

MIDI

The MIDI (Musical Instrument Digital Interface) data system creates a simple set of instructions that tells the synthesiser about the note you want to play. MIDI instructions contain information about the note's pitch, length, dynamics and the type of sound that you have chosen. Because these are stored as simple instructions, rather than complete recorded sound samples, they take up very little disk space. MIDI synthesised music will need 30KB of hard disk space per minute of music, compared to 600KB per minute for even the lowest-quality recorded sound.

Your sound card's built-in synthesiser not only produces the sounds for most of your computer games, it can also be used to make your own music. If you don't have a musical instrument you can use your computer keyboard and a mouse to create your own tunes using the sequencer software that is often bundled with the sound card.

Instead of recording the actual sounds of a music track, the sound card's internal synthesiser plays the tune from a simple set of instructions using the MIDI system, which was developed for electronic-music keyboards.

These MIDI instructions tell the synthesiser which notes to play and for how long. They are stored as a MIDI file with the extension .mid. Games and multimedia software use MIDI and the sound card's synthesiser to create music and sound effects.

Sing-along-a-PC

You can buy CDs with a range of MIDI music files of popular songs. You just load the file from the disc and the PC will play the music for you.

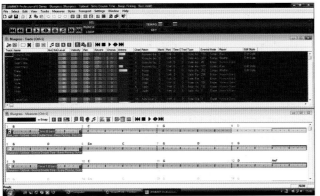

The *sequencer* is like a word processor for sound.

Because these are files of instructions you are in total control. You can speed them up or slow them down or change the pitch. You can also change the instrument sounds, turning a keyboard solo into a guitar solo or altering the balance between the different synthesised instruments.

These MIDI disks are available in music shops so you can use them as an accompaniment to your own musical efforts – on another instrument or just singing along in karaoke mode.

FM and Wave

Previously, the most common type of synthesiser chip on a sound card was an FM synthesiser, which recreated sounds by merging different tones. Now, more advanced sound cards have WaveTable synthesisers that use a store of short recorded clips of musical instruments. You are listening to real sound, so the sound cards with WaveTable synthesisers sound much more realistic.

Making music

You create and store your own synthesised music using the sequencer, which is a word processor for music. Instead of typing in words and setting font size and styles, with the sequencer you enter notes and choose what type of instruments they should sound like. Many sound cards have an extra socket that can be used either for a games joystick control or as a MIDI connection to an electronic keyboard.

With a keyboard connected to the sound card you can play music directly into the sequencer, and the PC will store every note exactly as you play it. If you make a mistake, you can then use the sequencer to manually edit out or change any wrong notes.

Images

A multimedia PC can handle a wide range of images, both still and moving. Photographic-type images are usually bitmaps, where the picture file contains information about the colour of every pixel (or bit) in the image. Drawn pictures are often created using vector drawing packages. These make a picture from circles, lines and squares that are stored as mathematical equations which tell the PC to display, say, a square of a certain size, shape and colour in a particular position. The bitmap images are good for photos and scanned images, but they take up a lot of disk space. The vector drawings are good for simpler images and take up less room on the hard disk.

Getting a new image

There are lots of ways to include images in presentations. A selection of artwork usually comes with your software in the Clip Art program, and more can be downloaded from the Internet; or you can create your own drawn images using a painting or drawing program (see pages 151–59). Most computer stores stock CD-ROMs full of photographic and drawn images. Alternatively, using a scanner, you can scan in your own images.

Another way to get images is to use a video-capture system. Some multimedia PCs have video features, and some include an internal TV tuner so you can use the monitor as a TV. With video capture, as you see the images from the TV or your VCR, you can capture a single frame and use that as a picture.

Talkies

Still images are only half the story. Many multimedia CD-ROMs also contain animations and video clips. All multimedia PCs can play these using software programs that read and create the images. But the quality is often dependent on the speed of the computer's central processor and the amount of memory it has installed. Real TV produces 25 images every second, but some PCs may not be able to read, decode and display 25 full-screen pictures or frames that fast. So you will get a smaller image that plays at a slower frame rate. Many cards have movie electronics to take over these image calculations so you get smoother playback. This is called hardware decoding. Specialised image-capture systems let you record video clips onto your hard disk so you can add home movies to your own multimedia shows.

Off to the movies

Many multimedia DVDs/CDs include TV-quality video, using a system called MPEG. Although there are software-only programs to decode MPEG images, they will suffer from jerkiness unless you have a very powerful PC. To get full-colour, full-screen video images with stereo digital sound there are display cards that include MPEG decoding, or you can add a separate MPEG decoder card. There is also a range of video CDs (VCDs) of movies and TV programmes that use the MPEG system. These look just like audio CDs but contain movies instead of music.

Multimedia

A new PC is as likely to come with a DVD drive – even a DVD rewriter – as it is a CD-ROM drive. The steady growth in popularity of DVDs is also mirrored in Windows. When Windows XP was launched, special third-party software was needed to play DVD films. Now, in Vista, DVD playback is built in so you can play DVD movies on your PC without any additional software.

In fact, DVD drives are not expensive so you may want to upgrade your CD-ROM drive to a DVD player. A DVD drive has the advantage that it will also read CD discs. Alternatively, you can buy combo drives that run a DVD player plus a CD rewriter, so you can burn files to CD.

DVD rewriters are also becoming increasingly common. In the past, DVD-burners were available in two competing formats – DVD-R/RW and DVD+R/RW. This caused some difficulties because a disc recorded in one format wouldn't play in a drive using the other format. However, all new DVD burners use combo drives that can read discs from both formats.

Disc tray **will hold either the standard 5in discs or the small 3in discs sometimes used for portable applications or, previously, CD singles.**

Front panel button **to open or close the CD tray.**

Headphone socket **for listening to audio DVDs/CDs.**

Faster and bigger

Other factors to consider are speed and size. CD speeds are increasing all the time and a read speed of more than 48 (shown as 48x) is fine. Most DVD burners can write to disc at 16x, which means you can burn a complete standard-sized disc in about six minutes.

Double-layered DVDs – great for backing up files – increase the disc's storage capacity from 4.7GB to 8.5GB. However, burning is slower – usually a maximum of 10x – and for a home movie the disc won't work in most standalone DVD players.

Recordable discs

Recordable discs usually have a distinctive gold or green data layer. They are useful for storing a backup of important files or a home movie you want to keep – once the information is burnt into the disc, it is locked in permanently and is impossible to erase.

Recordable discs are used in many professional applications. Software developers use them to test software before they go on to press thousands of discs, and radio stations use them as a simple way of storing and playing their jingles. Blank discs are not expensive and, once recorded, will play on virtually all other PCs and most standalone DVD or CD players.

Discs that can be erased and reused around 1000 times are available, but these rewritable DVD and CD discs are not always playable on older drives or household players.

drives

Speed may not be an important factor if, for example, you want a DVD player only for the purpose of watching films on your PC. Where it does make a difference, however, is in reading data files, such as those that come with computer games. The next generation of DVD burners has again been developed in competing formats. Blu-ray is very expensive but you can burn up to 50GB on a single disc. The other new format is HD DVD, for which players – but as yet no burners – are available.

In the driver's seat

In order to work with a multimedia drive or a sound card, your computer needs to know how to control it and extract data from it. This is the job of the device driver, a small software program that tells the computer all about the new hardware and how it functions. Device drivers are usually transferred automatically to your PC's hard disk during the new hardware's installation and set-up procedure. After that, they are automatically loaded every time you switch on your PC.

The computer also needs separate software drivers to know what to do with specific types of multimedia, such as CD Audio, MIDI or video files. Usually, these are placed automatically into your PC's device manager section when new multimedia software or hardware is loaded. These drivers will be loaded when Windows is run without you having to do anything more.

Keeping it clean

The small laser beam inside your drive is focused on the playing surface of the disc using a tiny optical lens, which can get dirty over a period of time. You can easily clean it by using one of the many cleaning disks that are available in computer or music stores. A cleaning kit designed for household audio players will do just as well on your multimedia drive.

Make your own DVD

Create your own multimedia experience with Vista's DVD Maker. It lets you combine videos and photos – and add a soundtrack or special effects – at a click of a button. You can then burn your multimedia entertainment to a DVD or CD to watch on a TV or the PC. To launch Windows DVD Maker, go to the Start menu and select it from the All Programs menu.

Multimedia

The CD was launched in the early 1980s, at the same time that the first PCs were coming into the shops. The main plan of its inventors, Philips and Sony, was to replace the LP with a longer-playing, better-sounding, scratch-proof, digital audio disc. But they also realised that it could be used to hold computer programs, since the CD is simply a carrier for digital information – a vast number store. On music CDs, these numbers carry digitised sound. But they could just as easily be carrying digitised images, digitised movies or the data that makes up a computer software program.

CD-ROM

The proper name for a music CD is CD-DA, which stands for Compact Disc-Digital Audio. Computer CDs are called CD-ROMs, which stands for Compact Disc-Read Only Memory. The Read Only part means that the information on it is pressed permanently into the disc itself when it is manufactured. It is not possible to record on to it from your PC.

A CD-ROM is capable of holding at least 650MB of data, and is fairly inexpensive to make. This is what made the CD a runaway success for delivering storage-hungry software such as multimedia programs. Now the arrival of double-sided DVDs able to hold 17GB of information means even the most space-hungry program can fit on a DVD.

Inside a disc

The CD-ROM is made of polycarbonate pressed with small pits in a spiral track and backed by a reflective aluminium layer. These pits represent the binary ones and zeros that the computer uses as data. If you stretched this track out it would be nearly 3.7 miles (6km) long. Unlike the spiral track on an LP which starts on the outer edge and works inwards, the CD's groove starts in the middle and works its way out to the edge. This aluminium layer is extremely thin and would fall apart if you tried to handle it, so it is coated on to tough, clear plastic.

Green CDs

Polycarbonate is a plastic that does not naturally break down very easily. There is a lot of waste polycarbonate during the manufacturing of a CD/DVD. Most disc plants try to recycle as much of their waste polycarbonate as possible, to save them from having to buy more raw material. Some countries are making strict laws about what happens to such recyclable products as CD/DVDs when they are no longer wanted by the consumer. In Germany there are moves to make CD/DVD manufacturers responsible for the correct disposal of unwanted discs.

Discs

When you put the CD into the CD-ROM drive, the small solid-state laser focuses a beam of laser light through the plastic on to the aluminium layer which then reflects the light back on to a light sensor. When the laser beam hits a pit in the surface, less light is reflected back. The sensor can read this as a 0 or a 1 and passes the data on to the computer.

Correcting errors

One of the reasons that discs are not easily affected by surface marks is that the data recorded on to them also contains error-correction information. Instead of putting the data on to a disc as one long continuous stream of numbers, it is split up into tiny bursts, or blocks, of information. Each small block includes a way of letting your computer check that all the data has been read correctly. If there is a small scratch that hides some of the disc's data, the computer can recalculate what is missing.

All change

The technology behind the CD has continued to evolve. First, there was the recordable CD (CD-R) and later a rewritable CD (CD-RW) where information could be written to the same disc a thousand times.

While the CD is still going strong, the DVD – Digital Versatile Disc – has come into its own with Video, as it is able to hold much more data. It too has evolved with recordable and rewritable discs. As DVD discs can deliver better-than-TV-quality video on your PC screen, they have become the format of choice for home screenings of the big Hollywood films and for the new wave of high quality video games. Sound has moved too from basic radio quality up to CD-stereo quality with cinema surround-sound. Multimedia is no longer confined to disc. More and more web sites are adding sound and moving images, so you can get the multimedia experience on the Internet.

High-density CD

Once, 650MB capacity of CD sounded like a lot of storage, but it is soon eaten up by multimedia software, especially if it contains a lot of audio and video clips. High-density recordable and rewritable DVD discs have between five and 15 times the capacity of CDs.

Whereas the high-density floppy took you out of kilo (thousand) bytes of data storage into mega (million) bytes of storage, rewritable DVD moves up into the world of giga (billion) bytes of storage.

What's ahead

The next generation DVDs are already emerging. Unfortunately, in an echo of the old VHS versus Betamax video recorder war, there are two competing formats – Blu-ray Disc (BD) and HD DVD. Blu-ray Discs currently have more capacity than their rivals – 25GB for a single layer disc and 50GB for a dual layer, compared with 15GB and 30GB respectively for the HD DVD. However, HD DVD has faster read times, which produces smoother playback.

Handling Discs

Despite the early claims of indestructibility, discs can still be damaged by dirt and grime. If the surface becomes badly marked, the laser will not be able to read the information buried inside the disc. So always handle the disc by its edges or by its centre hole and try not to touch the playing surface. Put the disc back in its case when you have finished and don't leave it in the drive. If the disc gets dirty, clean it with a soft cloth dampened with warm, slightly soapy water.

Edutainment

Here is an example of an edutainment multimedia CD-ROM, taken from the Encyclopedia Britannica's CD-ROM Space – Discover Astronomy & Space Exploration. Many other CD/DVDs work in a similar way. These edutainment programs use a mix of traditional index systems and point-and-click to find information. The beauty of such programs is that you can go from one topic to another, with the computer doing all the searching for you. The images are all in full colour and can be printed, so they can be included in projects. Unlike a book, Space provides sound effects, sound clips, 3D models and videos, and also includes links to on-line sites where you can continue your research.

A Toolbar on the left enables you to access *external tools* to help you, so you can, for example, add a memo, highlight some text and copy it, or start up your web browser.

The easiest way to explore space is with your *mouse*. As you move over the central image, different constellations and planets appear. Simply click on these to find out more. In the screen that opens you'll see – and hear – further details of what lies behind these heavenly shapes.

Unlike regular computer programs, Space takes over the *whole screen* with a magnificent view of the galaxy as seen from Earth. Traditional Toolbars help you navigate around the CD. Click on 3-D Worlds, for example, and you can see a list of the virtual 3-D simulations of the solar system and its planets that are available.

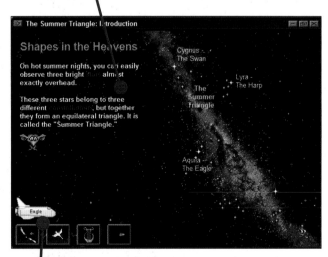

At the bottom of the picture are several boxes and as you move over them a *Challenger spacecraft* appears with details of what information they contain.

You will see that certain words are *highlighted*. Click on them to get a clearer explanation of what the terms mean.

To make it more interactive, clicking on one of the spacemen *icons* will launch a fun effect. For example, how does Saturn compare in size to Earth? Click on the space figure icon and you will see that it would take nine planet Earths to fit side by side along Saturn's diameter.

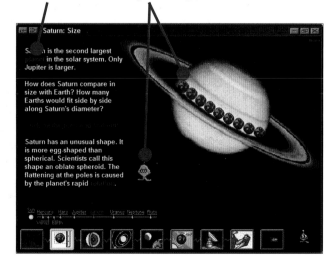

EDUCATION

A class act

Computers used to be impressive luxury items for schools. Now they are just another essential feature of school life used by every child. Far from making children passive users of high technology, replacing a good understanding of basic skills such as reading, writing and arithmetic, computers are helping kids to improve their skills in every area and enabling teachers to produce more individualised teaching materials.

Using the computer is seen by children as a reward in itself, especially as educational software is designed to feel more like computer games than lessons. Nevertheless, tucked into all the colour graphics, animations and sound effects is a huge amount of information to reinforce the teaching being done in class. And, as children move up in the school, the computer becomes just as important for finding information. Multimedia CDs on topics from dinosaurs to robots use sound, pictures, animation and video clips to make even the most complicated topics understandable and accessible.

The pattern is being repeated in the home now that the cost of computers has dropped to a level that has brought them within reach of families, and the advances in technology have made them very easy to use. Using a PC as an educational tool is the most powerful reason for investing in a computer for the home. Children can use it to build up their expertise in many areas, from the basics of reading and counting in the earliest years to helping prepare for exams.

It's not just the younger generation who can broaden their horizons with a home PC. Whether you want to grapple with a foreign language for your holiday, go through a multimedia course on wine, or learn more about classical music and art, there is a wide range of titles to choose from. Knowledge is not just obtainable from CDs or DVDs. There is a vast research library online that is available to you with virtually a click of the mouse. You can explore all of Shakespeare's texts, get a web page translated on the fly or take a dip into some of the millions of entries available in the online encyclopaedias. So sit back and start learning about learning with the aid of your PC. ●

The educated

Home education and edutainment software are among the most demanding software in terms of what hardware you need to run them. Educational titles nearly all run under Windows and use it to integrate sounds, pictures and movie images, all in one package. This makes it essential that you have a good-quality multimedia PC.

The *CD* or *DVD drive* will be working hard on many educational titles to deliver all the audio, data, text, animations and movie clips contained on the discs.

There is an amazing amount of information available from the Internet and the various on-line service providers. A fast *modem* will give you access to computer files all around the world.

The *screen and video driver card* for the monitor should preferably be SXGA with a resolution up to 1280 x 1024 pixels showing millions of colours.

The sound quality on the discs was once poor compared to the picture quality. But things have much improved, so opting for good *speakers* will make a noticeable difference, especially for those titles that deal with music-related topics.

Many educational programs need a *printer*. Learning word processing or drawing on a PC loses its appeal if you can't print out the results. Images and text can be printed out from all the reference works. A laser printer offers the best quality, but the results from an inkjet are almost as good.

Inkjet printers are generally cheaper and have the advantage of colour printing.

Use a *Disc rack* so that the discs are always handy and don't have to be searched for each time you want to run the program.

Most *sound cards* will work very well with educational titles, as nearly all are at least CD quality.

Speed is needed to make sure images come on screen quickly and to avoid any hold-ups inside your PC when sound and movies are being played. An *800MHz processor* is the minimum needed to run Windows Vista but the faster the better.

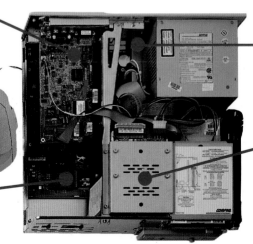

Lack of *memory* can also slow down your edutainment titles a lot. When running Windows Vista with edutainment software at least 1GB of RAM is recommended.

Although the software comes directly from the disc, most titles can also be installed and run from the hard drive so it's wise to have as large a *hard disk* as possible. Consider 80GB as the minimum.

PC

Start at the beginning

It is a good idea to get your child used to switching the computer on and off, loading the programs, putting in the CD or DVD discs and getting the printer going. These are basic skills that are fun, satisfying and add to a sense of responsibility and control over the PC. It also means they can get everything up and running without having to be supervised all the time.

K is for keyboard

Learning how to use a keyboard is best done while writing things in the word processor. Most of the ways a keyboard works are easily picked up, but one technique that does have to be learnt is using two keys together, such as pressing Ctrl and P at the same time to get the Print dialogue box and, more importantly, getting a capital letter by holding the Caps key down with one finger while pressing a letter.

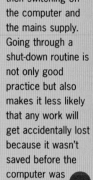

Children, and many adults new to a keyboard, press the Caps Lock key to lock the keyboard into capital letter operation, press the letter and then press the Caps Lock key again to cancel Caps Lock. This is slower and it is easy to forget to switch off the Caps Lock. So try to build up the two-finger approach.

Change a letter, not a word

When children find they have made a typing mistake they tend to use the Delete button to erase everything back to the mistake and then retype it. Get your child used to using the keyboard arrow keys to move to the mistake and delete the wrong letter. It's easier to do this with the arrow keys than with the mouse, as it can be hard to highlight a single letter with a mouse.

Considering how much time most kids will spend using the computer later on in life, typing skills are very low on the list of computer education priorities. While one-finger typing can reach reasonable speeds, touch-typing will always be faster and easier and can be mastered with learn-to-type software.

Mouse time

Learning to use the mouse may take a little time. It is quite natural for a child to hold the mouse a little way above the mouse mat and move it, not realising that the sensor underneath has to be in contact with the mat. Drawing programs are good practice for moving and clicking the mouse, and using it to access different functions in the menu bars. Refine skills with a word processor, using the mouse to highlight specific letters, words and lines, and to move things around.

Saving

As well as learning to switch on the computer, you should also go through the switch-off routine of saving the work, closing down the program, closing down Windows, and then switching off the computer and the mains supply. Going through a shut-down routine is not only good practice but also makes it less likely that any work will get accidentally lost because it wasn't saved before the computer was shut down.

Educational

Because educational software is aimed at the family rather than computer enthusiasts, it can be found in a wide range of shops. However, computer stores and computer games stores usually offer a wider range of titles. In the high street, check out newsagents and stationery retailers, radio/TV suppliers and bookshops. More specialised software is often available by mail order, so look through some of the computer magazines. Your school's computer or multimedia specialist will also be able to advise you on where to get specific titles if you are having trouble getting educational software.

Although the disc and packaging you get costs little to produce, the price you pay has to cover the development of the software, and this can run into large amounts for each title. Because they are now seen as a common consumer product, like games, educational CDs and DVDs are gradually coming down in price. Some do cost more, but that may be because of the type of information they contain.

Follow your PC's instructions when *loading software* **from a CD-ROM.**

Loading your software

Most educational software is supplied on CDs or DVDs. You put the disc in the CD/DVD drive and it will usually run automatically. Depending on the program, it may run from the CD or DVD rather than from your PC. The software will load a relatively small set of programs to control the disc. When it has finished loading, the control program will be on your hard disk and you will have an icon to click on when you want to start the software. When you want to run the software you must first put the CD/DVD disc into the drive and then click on the appropriate icon. The control software will then investigate the drive and start loading the pictures, sound and text from the disc. If you have forgotten to put the disc in the drive, or put the wrong one in, then you will get a message telling you what to do.

Other programs will install themselves on your PC and run from there. When you first insert the disc in the drive the software takes over and loads itself on to your hard disk. Once loaded, all you have to do is click on the title's icon to run it.

Teachers' packs

Software companies are starting to produce packs for teachers so that they can use standard software in the classroom. Microsoft has what it calls Resource Packs for Education. These consist of a selection of classroom activities that accompany a particular program, such as the Encarta encyclopaedia. Each pack includes teacher's notes, pupil worksheets, a wall chart and templates on disk for teachers to develop their own activities. It also includes a video to show how technology can be used in the classroom. If you are interested in finding out about teachers' packs, contact your local education authority.

software

Noises

You might be wondering why children's writing or drawing packages still need a multimedia computer with sound. For a start, they use lots of noises to accompany on-screen activity such as selecting menu items. While you may find these noises irritating after a while, kids love them. Many of these programs include multimedia elements, so that noises, effects and music can be added to the on-screen text. Drawing programs often have the ability to create animations with accompanying sound and music.

Software on the cheap

When PCs were first developed, there were no software programs available on individual topics, such as learning a new language or how to manage your money. Fortunately, some people with computer-programming experience solved this problem simply by writing their own programs. Many of these amateur programs are good value and may exactly match your needs.

The reason they are cheap is that they are shareware programs, which you can try first and then send money to the authors if you like them. Freeware is software that people have produced for the fun of it rather than for profit, or just simply low-cost programs. Such programs vary in quality enormously. Although some are very simple, others like the chemistry lab simulator shown here can give commercial software a run for their money. Look in computer magazines for shareware companies, and for shareware CD-ROM discs in computer stores, or investigate the Internet forums on your particular area of interest.

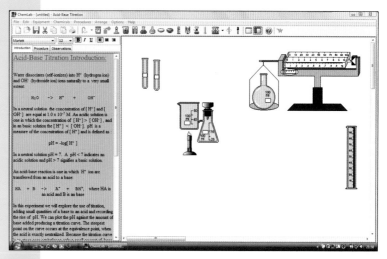

Key stages

You may see some software referring to Key Stages and Attainment Targets. This is all terminology relating to the English National Curriculum. Your child's total school syllabus is split up into four separate phases, Key Stages 1 to 4. The Key Stage sets out what is being taught in any particular school year. The details of what is to be taught in each of the core subjects are set out in the National Curriculum. The school tracks what each child has covered and this is ticked off as an Attainment Level. So these show what has been taught at school and learnt by the child.

Different teachers cover areas of the syllabus in a different order and children naturally learn at different rates, so there will be considerable overlap of the Attainment targets reached by each child. At the end of primary school, your child could be studying anything from Attainment Level 2 work up to Attainment Level 5 work.

KEY STAGE	AGE RANGE	SCHOOL YEARS	ATTAINMENT LEVELS
1	5–7	1–3	1–3
2	7–11	4–6	2–5
3	11–14	7–9	3–7
4	14–16	10–11	-

Young kids

Very young children can use the computer to help develop the basic language, maths and science skills that are essential to their development in the early years at school. There is a lot of software that will grab children's attention and reinforce these skills while they think they are just playing on the PC.

For young children, up to the age of about eight, the most important thing is for you to work with them on the computer. Despite the sophistication of your PC, the instant computer teacher is still a long way off, and the PC should be used alongside books, magazines, television, radio, CDs and DVDs as one of many ways to help your child grasp the basics.

Counting

Learning to count is one of the naturally fun things for kids to do. Adding things together — a favourite is adding and taking away sweets — has started many on the route to proficiency in maths. There are several counting and early-maths software packages that use colourful cartoon characters to reinforce the basics of counting, adding and taking away.

Writing and drawing

Words and pictures are all around us, not just in books, but in cards, animations, leaflets, notes, magazines, comics and on badges. These can all be brought into play to help teach writing and drawing and stimulate the imagination. Many programs can produce quick and attractive results, such as a colourful birthday card for Grandma. But they also have enough depth and flexibility for working on more elaborate projects. Software packages such as Discover Painting for Kids and Creative Writer 2 build up ability in both areas.

Creative Writer 2

Creative Writer 2 helps children who already have some grasp of writing to expand their horizons. You don't need to read a manual to understand how to use it. Max, your funny-looking on-screen friend, will explain what the buttons do and offer general advice. There are lots of colours and special effects, which can all be easily accessed.

Creative Writer 2 starts off with an *ideas generator* to begin a story.

There are lots of ready-to-run sections for making *badges*, *posters* and *cards*.

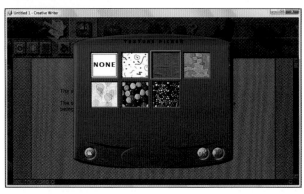

Write the words, add pictures or textured backgrounds and go over the spelling. Use the *spelling check* to see if you've missed any misspelt words.

Spelling

Spelling is an area that computer software enhances by posing questions (disguised as various forms of games), keeping track of the scores and repeating areas that are problematic. Programs have key vocabulary lists and work through the words, moving from simple ones to more complex and difficult spellings.

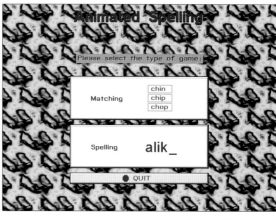

Animated Spelling **makes spelling a game.**

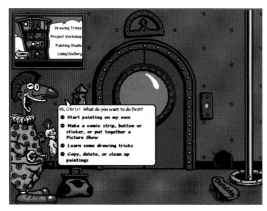

A good *drawing program* **covers a lot of things beyond just making simple pictures on screen.**

Art

Art and drawing programs are good for experimenting with shapes and colours. There are hundreds of patterns and painting tools in software programs. There are 3-D tools for creating drawings that use perspective. Experimenting increases the appreciation of what different types of drawing and painting materials do.

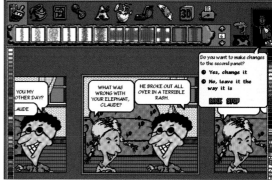

Make *comic strips* **without having to completely redraw each frame from scratch. Each image can be built up from different backgrounds and characters.**

Reading

The multimedia computer is ideal for helping with reading. It can deliver the words on screen at the same time that the words are spoken through the PC's sound system. It's just like a read-along CD, but with total control and a lot more visual impact. These programs often add in other functions such as painting, so that there is more than one reason for wanting to use them.

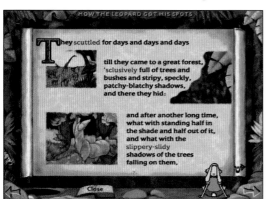

Click **on any part of the picture to see and hear its name. Words are highlighted as the story is told.**

Science

Topics like space and how your body works may seem a bit advanced for primary school children, but with a good story, lots of graphics and sounds, and a game or two, the topics come to life in a very accessible way. The number of software packages on specific topics aimed at younger children is still fairly limited, but the numbers are growing, as families no longer wait until their children are 9 or 10 before investing in a PC.

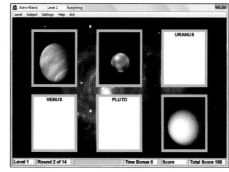

Explore the *solar system* **with Astro-Mania. It has a game, IQ test and study resource to teach kids about the planets.**

For your

The edutainment software that you are most likely to come across first is the reference CD-ROM. Encyclopaedias, dictionaries, and a whole range of specialised topics, from films to dinosaurs, have some very informative and entertaining software that covers the topic in reasonable depth and in a way that is easily understood by adults and older children.

A complete reference library

A single disc can contain all the basic reference books you'll need for everyday use: a dictionary, thesaurus, atlas, almanac, timeline and dictionary of quotations. Alternatively, you can access the same resources online, through their websites. Here we look at Encarta (encarta.msn.com).

Thesaurus **to find alternative words.**

Dictionary **to look up the meanings.**

Encyclopaedia **of the hows, wheres and whys.**

Search **gives you a quick way to find the information you want.**

Related Items **provides links to other relevant information.**

Atlas **to find out more about places.**

Find any *country* **or** *major city*.

Select the type of *map* **you want – whether it covers time zones, political boundaries or ecologies.**

Not only can you find the definition and origins of the word, you can also hear how it is pronounced by pressing the *speaker icon*. **You can even translate it, by clicking the Translations tab or find similar words by selecting the Thesaurus tab.**

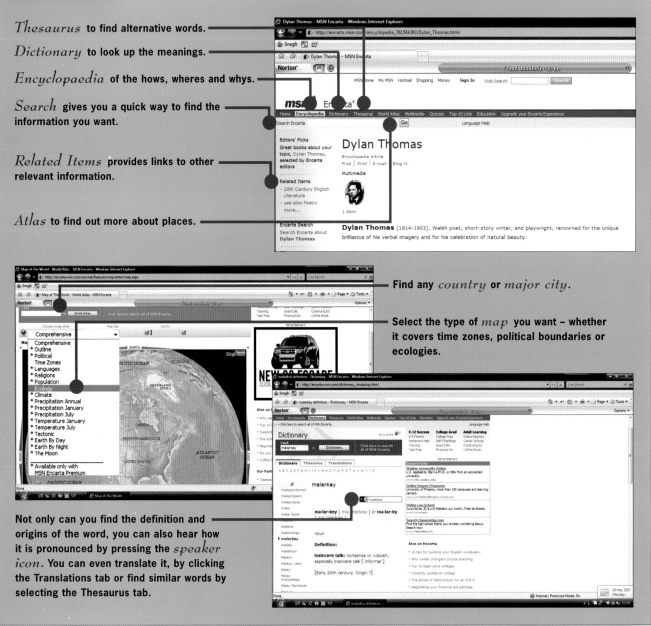

reference

Work your way around

Most reference CD-ROMs work in a similar way. Once you've learned to use one, you'll find the rest are easy. Atlas of the Ancient World from Maris Technologies (maris.com) is a typical example and shown here.

This is your *main screen*. **Find your way around the disc by:**

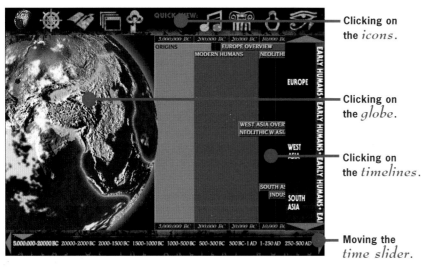

Clicking on the *icons*.

Clicking on the *globe*.

Clicking on the *timelines*.

Moving the *time slider*.

There are 274 *maps* to peruse. With a click, you can find out how particular features are distributed or bring up boxes of information.

See the *artefacts* of the time and place and them in their culture.

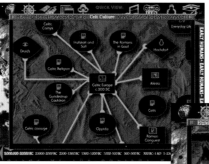

Every civilization has its own *road map*, containing links to all the relevant facts.

Explore 10 *virtual reality recreations* such as the tomb of Queen Nefertiti.

Navigate through time and move around the globe with *interactive maps*.

See scenes from *everyday life*, presented in the appropriate artistic style. Click on the activities to make the images move.

Encyclopaedias

A big set of encyclopaedias costs a lot and needs a whole shelf to itself. But you can get these and much more on a single multimedia DVD encyclopaedia for a fraction of the cost. And there is the bonus that you can see how things work and listen to sounds and speeches, hear the words pronounced and look up what you want in a matter of seconds. Then you can go to other related information. Some encyclopaedias such as Encarta and Britannica offer online subscriptions to their web sites which included most of their printed or DVD collections.

Art for art's sake

Want to find out what makes great art? Encyclopaedias such as Encarta are like interactive art catalogues that explain in detail the story behind the pictures and the secret references often hidden inside them.

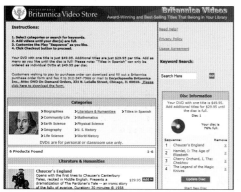

Make your own DVD

On the Encyclopaedia Britannica site you can pick and choose videos from a variety of topics to add to your own DVD, which will be burnt to disc and sent to you.

Call of the wild

Get the latest wildlife news and watch it on screen as well as videos on the National Geographic web site. There are also several multimedia nature encyclopaedias with which you can make a virtual wildlife trip. For keen bird watchers, some collections contain hundreds of bird songs.

Travel and learn the lingo

Planning a trip? You can experience the sights and sounds of the country you are going to from your PC. Interactive travel guides give you the lowdown on places to stay, as well as restaurants and sites to see. For local news, access the site online and use BabelFish to translate it. It's not perfect, but it's a start.

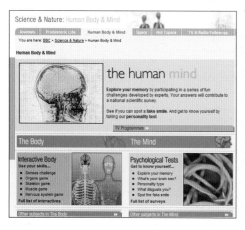

Your specialised topic

Some multimedia programs focus on specific topics and go into the subject in great detail. For instance, there are several multimedia CDs, that take a virtual tour of the human body, showing what's beneath all that skin and bone with 3D models of body parts, articles, video lectures and lines to on-line sites. There are useful reference sites, with the latest scientific research freely available online, such as the Human Body & Mind section of the BBC's web site.

Glossary

A Jargon-Buster's Guide

Active window
The section of a screen that is currently being used. To make a window active in Microsoft Windows, click on it and it will appear in front of any other window you have open.

Align
To make text appear with a straight margin. When text is left-aligned, for example, all the characters line up on the left-hand side, but don't on the right-hand side. *(See also Justify.)*

Alt key
A key on a PC's keyboard used in combination with other keys to open menus or to close windows or programs. For example, many programs allow you to press Alt-F to open the File menu. Exceptions include some Microsoft Office 2007 programs, such as Word and Excel, where the Menu bar and File menu have been replaced by the Office button and new-look Ribbon bar. *(See also Ribbon bar.)*

America On-line (AOL)
The world's largest on-line service that provides access to the Internet as well as a range of their own content and services, including newsgroups, chat forums and e-mail.

Anti-aliasing
A technique used to reduce the jagged edges that appear when circles or curves are displayed or printed out. Anti-aliasing masks the jagged edges with a shade of the relevant colour to give the impression of a smooth curve.

Applet
Mini programs which are embedded in a web page and may be downloaded to your machine to carry out a certain function – such as playing some animation, or an audio clip.

Application program/software
An application program/ software, is a program, such as a word processor or a spreadsheet, that makes the computer do useful work.

Archive
To transfer completed files on to a separate storage system, such as a CD or USB drive. *(See also Backup.)*

Arrow keys
The set of four keys on a keyboard that move the pointer up, down, left and right.

ASCII
Stands for American Standard Code for Information Interchange and is pronounced 'askey'. This standard set of numbers used to represent characters on a keyboard is used by almost all computers and software.

Attachment
A file that you transfer with an e-mail message. For example, you might send a spreadsheet file, ACCOUNTS.XLS, to your accountant as an attachment to an e-mail message.

Audio file
A file containing a digital recording of a sound. In Windows, audio files usually have a .WAV extension.

Backup
A second, safety copy of a file. You should back up your important files regularly in case of accidental loss. Keep the backup disks away from the computer.

Bad sector
A fault in a hard disk. If you have a bad sector, it means the disk surface has been damaged at this point and that the disk drive cannot read the data there. To fix it, use the disk tools in Windows or use a special program like Norton's SystemWorks.

Binary
In the binary system, the smallest unit is a bit (short for binary digit). This can have one of just two values: 0 or 1. PCs count using the binary system, since the values are easy to represent electronically.

BIOS
Basic Input/Output System. This is a series of instructions to manage the basic functions in your PC. It is stored in read-only memory (ROM) so that it starts when the computer is turned on. It checks the hardware at startup, launches the operating system and manages the keyboard, disk drives and the monitor.

Bitmap
A bitmap image is made up of tiny dots or pixels. If you zoom in, the dots grow larger.

Bits per second (bps)
The number of single bits of data that can be sent every second over a network or a communications system such as the Internet. For example, a 56K modem can receive information at up to 56,000 bits per second.

Bluetooth
Named after an ancient Viking monarch, Bluetooth is a standard for setting up a short-range wireless link between devices – such as laptops, mobile phones and digital cameras, or between a PC and a wireless mouse or keyboard.

Boot, boot up
To start up a computer. When your PC boots up, a sequence of instructions permanently stored on the BIOS chip searches for the main operating system, and instructs it to start loading.

Broadband
A way of transmitting large amounts of data, sound and video. A broadband connection can be made through the telephone line or via a television cable, and offers connection speeds up to 400 times faster than a conventional dial-up modem can provide.

Browser
A program used for viewing pages on the World Wide Web. Microsoft Internet Explorer and Mozilla Firefox are the most popular browsers. As well as being able to read text, most browsers can display graphics, play sound and video files, and run small programs (although you may need a helper application or plug-in to carry out some tasks). Most browsers also let you use e-mail, take part in newsgroups and send or receive files.

Buffer
An area in memory that's used for temporarily storing information. For example, if you send a file to print before you have switched the printer on, the data is stored in a print buffer until the printer is ready.

Burn
The term used for recording files to a CD or DVD disc. When you burn files in Windows Vista you have a choice of two formats, Live File System and Mastered Files. Using Live File System enables you to burn files on to the same disc and overwrite them again and again, but the disc will only play on computers with a similar type of CD or DVD rewriter. With Mastered Files, however, the file can only be burned to disc once, but the resulting disc will play on any computer's CD or DVD drive.

Button
A button-like image displayed on screen. You move the pointer over a button on the screen and click on the mouse to make something happen.

Byte
A group of eight bits – that's eight binary digits – which is the usual form in which data is manipulated within a computer. For example, each letter of the alphabet has a special numerical code that describes it *(see ASCII)*, and this code is stored within one byte. One byte can hold numbers between 0 and 255, so your computer can identify 256 different characters. *(See also Kilobyte, Megabyte.)*

Cache
A section of very high-speed memory that temporarily stores data before it is used by the PC's processor, increasing the speed at which data is read from a hard disk.

Cancel
A button usually displayed on a screen next to an OK button to allow you to stop the task you were about to do.

Capture
If you want to store the image that is currently displayed on the screen in a file, you can 'capture' it. In Windows, you can save the current screen as a graphics image by pressing the Print Screen (Prt Sc) key on the keyboard.

Case-sensitive
Software that can detect the difference between lower-case (small) and upper-case (capital) letters. You're likely to find this in the Find and Replace function in a word processor.

CD-R/CD-RW
CD-R drives can be used to make copies of existing CD-ROMs or to create totally new CDs. CD-R drives can be used for playback (reading) as well as for recording, but CD-R discs can be written to once only. If you want to re-record over the same CD disc several times, you will need a CD-RW drive and disc. CD-RW drives can read conventional CD-ROMs and CD-R discs, but write to the new discs more slowly. Because they can re-record over the same discs, CD-RW drives are good for making backups.

CD-ROM

A type of compact disc that contains up to 650MB of data. The name stands for Compact Disc-Read Only Memory. Many multimedia programs and software programs come on CD-ROMs. A normal music CD can also be played on your CD-ROM drive, using the Windows MediaPlayer and either speakers or headphones. You cannot save data on to a CD-ROM. *(See also Read-only.)*

Chat

Using the computer to have a written conversation in real-time. When you chat with someone you write what you want to say and then press the Enter key. Your words appear on the screens of the other people in the conversation. They can then reply to you. A Chat Room is a program that allows several people to chat at the same time.

Check box

Small boxes that are displayed to give you a set of options. To select an option, move the pointer on to the check box and click once; the box will now have a cross in it. If you don't want the option, click a second time and the cross will be deleted.

Chip

A small thin piece of silicon crystal onto which is etched a tiny circuit with hundreds of thousands of components. These components will do simple mathematical operations, such as adding and subtracting numbers (in a processor chip) or storing numbers (in a memory chip).

Click

To move the arrow pointer over an icon, button or menu option and press on a mouse button. Traditionally, one click selects, two clicks open. But it is now possible to set your desktop applications to open with a single click – just as you do with links on the Web. Windows uses a click on the right-hand button to display a menu of options that apply to an icon, such as its name and properties. *(See also Double-click, Drag and drop.)*

Clip art

A collection of ready-made images, borders and icons for use in your own presentations or desktop published documents, sometimes supplied with a software program.

Clipboard

An area of memory that is used for temporary storage of data, for example when you cut some text to paste it elsewhere. In Windows, the Clipboard can store any type of data, including text, audio and images.

Close

A menu option, usually found under the File menu – or the Office button in some Office 2007 programs – that will close an open document but will not quit the application. If you have not saved the document, the application will give you the chance to save any changes before closing it.

Colour

Any colour displayed on a monitor is made up of three tiny dots. The colours from these three dots combine to create millions of different colours, according to the capability of the graphics adapter that controls the monitor.

Communications software

A software program that works with a modem to send and receive information over a phone line to and from other computers and on-line services.

Compatible

One version of hardware or software that will work with another type or version of hardware or software.

Compression

To reduce the size of a file by encoding the data. Compression software programs can reduce the size of files but the software has to decompress the files again before they can be used.

Computer

The icon usually in the top left of the screen on a PC running Windows. It contains an overview of your PC. If you double-click on it, you'll see a graphic display of the drives and peripherals linked to your PC.

Configure

To set the functions of software or hardware so that it works the way you want it to. For example, you can configure Windows so that it displays a different colour background on the desktop.

Context-sensitive help

Usually accessed by pressing the F1 key, this will display helpful information about the particular thing you are trying to do.

Control key (Ctrl)

A key on the keyboard that is used for special functions, usually when pressed in combination with another key. For example, Ctrl-S will save the current document, Ctrl-N will create a new document, and Ctrl-P will print the document out.

Control Panel

A collection of icons that allow you to configure the basic functions of Windows and your PC. Within the Control Panel there are icons that give you access to the areas where you can change the fonts that are installed on your computer, the colour of the background to Windows, the type of printer that's installed, and a range of other options.

Cookie

Cookies are small files sent to your machine when you access home web pages. Your log-on information can be stored on them so you don't have to re-enter passwords each time you visit the site. It also allows the server to keep track of the pages you visit and then to give you further information that may be of interest. For example, if you buy a book from an on-line site, the information stored in the cookie can prompt recommendations of similar titles you may wish to buy on subsequent visits.

Copy

To make a duplicate version of a file or section of text (using the Copy command). If you want to copy a section of text, highlight it, choose Ctrl-C, move your cursor to where you want to add the copied text and choose Ctrl-V. The copied selection will appear in the new location.

CPU or central processing unit

An electronic device that contains millions of tiny electronic components that carry out basic arithmetic and control functions. Each of the actions of a CPU is controlled by machine-code instructions used in software programs. The computing power of a CPU is usually defined by its speed in MHz (Megahertz), which roughly defines the number of instructions that it can process each second. A 750MHz CPU can process around 750 million instructions per second, for example. There are two main manufacturers of processors for the PC – Intel with its range of Core, Pentium and lower spec Celeron processors, and AMD with their high-end Athlon or Turion processors and the lower cost Sempron chips.

Crash

This is what happens when your computer freezes up and won't respond. The only way to get out of this is to switch off or reset (using the reset button or by pressing Ctrl-Alt-Del at the same time). Unfortunately, you will lose anything you've input since you last saved your work, so make sure that you save your work regularly.

Database

Software that lets you enter information into a file so that it can be organised and searched. For example, a database could contain names and addresses or details of your recipe collection. Each separate entry is called a record, and each individual part of a record is called a field.

Default

The options that are used if no others are specified. For example, if you run a word processor and start typing a letter, it will use the default typeface and the default paper size and margins. You can change the default settings.

Defragmentation

A program that will reorganise your hard disk so that all the files are stored in continuous areas. When a file is saved to disk, the operating system does not necessarily save it all in the same place. If the disk is full, it can split files and save them in chunks in different places, making it slower to retrieve them. A defragmentation program will solve this problem.

Delete

To select text or other data and remove it from a file; to remove a file from your disk. If you delete a section of text, you can immediately undelete (using the Undo function). If you delete a file from your disk, you can sometimes undelete it, depending on your PC's setup. *(See also Undelete.)*

Desktop

What you see on your screen when Windows first starts up. The icons, Taskbar, Start button and the Recycle Bin sit together on the Desktop. In Vista, the Sidebar also sits on the Desktop, on the right. The Sidebar has various Gadgets, or mini-tools, such as a Clock, Slide Show or Calendar.

Desktop publishing (DTP)

The design, layout and printing of documents, books and magazines using desktop publishing software.

Dial-up connection

The process of connecting to another computer via a telephone line. A dial-up connection was the original method of accessing the Internet via an Internet Service Provider.

Dialogue/dialog box

A small box that appears on screen in Windows, usually to display a message from the computer's operating system or software. Sometimes it is a warning. At the bottom of many dialogue boxes are buttons. OK and Cancel are the two standard buttons, but there may be others depending on the message that's displayed.

Digital

Numbers and signals that can be processed by a computer. (*See also Digitise.*)

Digitise

To convert an analogue signal, such as speech, sound or light, into a numeric form that can be processed by a computer. For example, if you digitise an image using a scanner, you convert the reflected light into an array of dots, each one a number that represents the brightness at that point.

Directory

An organised list of files on a disk. A good way to think about directories is to imagine a filing cabinet: the cabinet is the disk, each drawer a directory. If you open a Directory, you'll see lots of folders that are sub-directories. Look in a folder and you will see documents or files.

DirectX

A must for gamers, DirectX-enabled applications have direct access to the computer's sound and graphics hardware in order to improve performance.

Disk

A flat, circular piece of plastic coated with a substance that stores digital information in a magnetic form. A hard disk consists of several rigid plastic disks arranged in parallel.

Disk tools

A set of software programs that help you monitor the performance of your hard disk, maintain it, and ensure that it's storing data efficiently and is in good condition. (*See also Defragmentation.*)

DLL (dynamic-link library)

A DLL is a program file that's stored on disk and loaded as and when an application needs it. That means it doesn't use up any memory until it is needed.

Large applications, such as a complex word processor, might use several DLLs: one to carry out the spell check; one to manage printing a letter; and a third for formatting the text. DLL files have a .DLL three-letter extension and so are easy to spot using Windows Explorer. The same DLL might be used by several programs so be careful before deleting any!

Domain/Domain name

In Windows, users on a network are grouped together by sharing the same domain name. A Domain is also used to identify sections of the Internet, each of which has a domain name. The domain name is part of the site name (or URL), and names you'll encounter frequently are .com (commercial), .co.uk (UK commercial), and .org (organisation).

Dots per inch (dpi)

The number of individual dots that a printer can print on an inch of paper. More dots per inch give a more detailed printout. Most laser printers can print at 600 dots per inch, the better ones print at a higher resolution of 1200 dots per inch.

Double-click

To click twice in rapid succession on a mouse button. For example, you run an application by double-clicking the left-hand button with the pointer over the application's icon. (*See also Click, Drag and drop.*)

Download

To copy a file from a remote computer to your own computer. If you use e-mail, you collect it from your Internet Service Provider by downloading it. Many web sites allow you to download images, videos and even software.

Drag and drop

A feature of Windows that lets you move a highlighted icon or piece of text from one place to another. For example, you can highlight a section of text in a word-processing document and then click and hold down the left-hand mouse button to move that section of text to another place in the document.

Drive

A mechanical unit that holds a disk, which could be a CD, a DVD or a hard disk, and responds to the instructions of a controller card. The drive has a motor that spins the disk and an access head that is positioned over the disk.

Drive letters

A PC can have a number of disk drives. Typically, there's a CD or DVD player and either a CD or a DVD rewriter drive, as well as a hard disk, which might be partitioned. Drives are named by letter, and are followed by a colon (e.g. the main hard drive is usually C:). If your PC is part of a network, additional letters are used to map shared drives on the network.

Driver

A special piece of software that translates the instructions from Windows into a form that can be understood by a peripheral piece of equipment, such as a printer.

DVD

An optical disc format called Digital Versatile Disc. In its basic form it can store seven times as much data as an ordinary CD-ROM (4.7GB), while some versions can store 17GB. Its main attraction is to distribute movies and advanced multimedia titles. DVD drives can also be used to read the other types of CDs, including CD-ROMs, CD-R and CD-RW discs. There are also DVD-recordable discs (DVD-R) that you can write over once and DVD-rewritable discs (DVD-RW) that can be recorded over many times.

E-mail

A way of sending and receiving messages on a network. If you are connected to the Internet, you can send messages to any other user who is also connected to the Internet.

Embedding

A feature of Windows that lets you drag a document, picture or sound into another document. For example, if you type a letter in WordPad and then want to add your signature, you start the Paint program, draw your signature and drag it into the WordPad document.

Error box or message

A small window that pops up to tell you an error has occurred – for example, if you have tried to do something that the program does not understand or if an error has occurred in the program.

Esc key

A key on a PC keyboard that is sometimes used to cancel an action. In Windows, pressing the Esc key is the same as selecting the Cancel button.

.EXE file

The three-letter filename extension – short for executable – that indicates that a file is a program that can be run by double-clicking it.

Expansion card

A set of electronic components on a plastic board that clips in to expand the functions of your PC. For example, you will need an expansion card if you want to fit an internal modem. If you want to connect your PC to a network, you will need to add a network expansion card.

Explorer

The way to manage all the files stored on a disk. With Explorer (officially called Windows Explorer) you can copy files, move files from one folder to another, create new folders, and rename or delete files and folders. Explorer can also view folders on other PCs in a network. To start Explorer, right click on the Start button and select Explore.

Export

To convert a file so that it can be read by a different program. For example, if you have written a letter in Microsoft Word and want to give it to a friend who uses a different word processor, you need to export the Word document to a format file that they can use.

Extension

The three-letter code at the end of a file name that generally indicates the type or format of the file. For example, a file name might be Letter1 with the extension .doc. The three-letter extension, .doc, shows the file is a document. Similarly, .bmp means a bitmap file, .exe means an executable program file, and so on.

FAQ

Stands for Frequently Asked Questions. A FAQ (pronounced fak) is a document that has the answers to the questions that are most often asked by users. They are usually posted on the vendor's support web site as a first-step guide to help you, if you're having problems.

Favorites/Favorites Folder

Favorites are a collection of shortcuts – or links – to web sites that you want to save and go back to later. In Internet Explorer, all these links are kept together in the Favorites Folder. In other browsers, these collections of shortcuts have different names – such as hotlists or bookmarks.

Field
An individual box in a database that can hold a particular type of information. For example, in a database of names and addresses, there would be separate fields for the name, address, phone number and other data.

File format
The way data is stored in a file. Each program stores information in its own format, which means it can be difficult to read a file that's been created by a different program from the one you are using. To get around this, you can either use the Import function or one of the standard file formats that lets you exchange data between programs.

Find
A feature of Windows that will search any disk – on your PC or, if you are on a network, on any other PC – for a particular file.

Find and replace
A function in a word processor or database that lets you search for a word or phrase and replace it with something else. In some word processors you can find and replace formatting or text.

Font
A set of characters in the same typeface. Windows has TrueType fonts that can be printed and displayed in almost any size and printer fonts that can be printed in predefined sizes.

Format
To arrange text, define margins and columns, and include special fonts in a word processor or desktop publishing program.

FTP
This stands for File Transfer Protocol and is the way of moving files backwards and forwards across the Web. Using an FTP program – such as Terrapin or CuteFTP – you can take the files, pictures and text for your web pages and 'upload' them, via an FTP server, to your web space.

Function keys
Twelve or more keys that run along the top of the keyboard. These have different uses according to different applications. However, most use the F1 key to display help information.

GB or Gigabyte
A measure of the data capacity of a storage device, such as a hard drive, equal to 1024 Megabytes (MB). Most of the newest computers have hard disks with a capacity of 60GB or more.

.GIF file
Stands for Graphics Interface Format. This is a commonly used format for storing images and bitmapped colour graphics, now one of the most popular formats for images stored on the Internet.

Graphical user interface (GUI)
A method of representing files, functions and folders with little images called icons. With a GUI, such as Windows, you can point and click on an icon using the mouse rather than typing in the name. This makes a PC easier to use.

Hacker
A person who is trying to break into a computer system for illegal purposes.

Hand-held scanner
A small scanner that contains a row of light-sensitive cells along its bottom surface. When you drag the scanner over an image, it reads the amount of light reflected from the image or photograph and converts this into a digital form that can be displayed on your PC.

Hard copy
A printed document or copy of a picture that's stored on the computer.

Hard disk
A rigid magnetic disk inside your computer that stores your software, operating system and files. In most PCs, the hard disk drive is called drive C: and can store anything from 60GB to 250GB of information, or more.

Header
The line of text that appears at the top of each page in a document, such as the page number. In Microsoft Word, look in the Header and Footer section under the Insert tab.

Help key
The key used to access a window that will display text to help you do what you are trying to do. Most Windows applications on a PC have standardised the F1 key as the Help key.

Highlight
To select a word or section of text in a document by moving the mouse pointer over the word and double-clicking on the mouse button. In Microsoft Word, a double-click will highlight the word you are over, and a triple-click will highlight the paragraph.

To highlight a line of text, move the pointer to the left margin until it turns into an arrow and then click.

Home page
The home page can be the first page you see when you log on to the Internet or the start page on any web site.

Hot key
A way of selecting a menu option or command by pressing two or more keys at the same time. For example, instead of selecting the File/Save menu option, many Windows programs use a hot key shortcut of Ctrl-S to do the same thing.

HTML
HyperText Markup Language, or HTML, is the special markup code used for creating web pages and saying how they should look. It's also used to create the links (called hypertextlinks, hyperlinks or hotlinks) that you can click to jump to different parts of the page or to other related pages. The link is usually underlined or in a different colour to make it stand out from the text around it.

Icon
A small picture displayed on screen to identify a command or file. In Windows, each application you install has its own icon. Its associated data files often use the same icon.

Import
The function in a program that allows you to use a file produced by another program.

Inkjet printer
A light, quiet and relatively cheap printer that produces pages by squirting a stream of tiny drops of ink on the surface of the paper. This is the most popular printer for home use.

Input
To put information into a computer. When you type text on your keyboard, you are inputting data into the computer. Other examples are using a scanner or using a mouse to draw on screen.

Install
To copy and set up an application program on your hard disk. The steps include downloading the files or copying them from the CD or DVD (on which the application may be sold) on to your hard disk, then configuring the options for your requirements.

Internet
An international network that links millions of computers using telephone and cable links. Users connect via a modem to the computers of an Internet Service Provider, which are like local phone exchanges. You can send e-mails and transfer files over the Internet around the world for the price of a local phone call. To get on to the Internet, you'll need a modem and an account with an Internet Service Provider.

ISP
Internet Service Providers are the companies that link users to the Internet. You will need to connect to them by either a dial-up or a broadband connection, using your modem. ISPs provide high-speed connection to the Internet as well as mail servers that store and deliver e-mail messages for their customers.

JPEG
Stands for Joint Photographic Experts Group. This is a standard you may come across if you use graphic images. JPEG is a complex way of storing images in a compressed format so they take up less disk space.

Justify
To align text so that both the left and right margins are even. This is usually an option on your word processor and is done automatically by inserting tiny spaces between words.

Keyboard layout
Different countries have different keyboard layouts. Britain and America use a standard Qwerty layout, which refers to the sequence of the first keys on the top left corner of the keyboard. Other countries have key layouts according to their need for accents and other local requirements. If you want to change the keyboard layout of your computer, you can plug in a different keyboard and configure Windows to support this.

Kilobyte (KB)
A measure of the capacity of a storage device that is usually written as KB. A KB is equal to 1024 bytes. If you want to check the size of a file, highlight the file name in Windows Explorer. The size of the file is displayed after the file name. Although 1KB is actually equal to 1024 bytes, many people use it to mean 1000 bytes. The reason that 1KB has 1024 bytes is that it is equal to 2 to the power of 10 – remember that PCs work in binary, base two. (See also Binary and Megabyte.)

Label
To identify a removable disk, such as a CD or DVD disc, by sticking a label on it. You can also identify it by giving it an electronic label, called its volume name. For example, if you want to give a short description to a CD disc (which will appear in the Computer window), highlight the disc icon, select its Properties window, and type in the new name on the General tab.

Laptop
A small portable computer. A laptop usually has a 'clam shell' construction with a fold-down lid that houses the screen, a keyboard (some are slightly smaller than full-size) and a CD or DVD and hard disk drive. An internal rechargeable battery pack provides power for a few hours.

Laser printer
A printer that produces very high-quality text using a laser beam. The beam draws the characters as tiny dots – normally 600 or 1200dpi – on to a special drum. The drum then attracts a fine powder (called toner) to these dots that is transferred to a sheet of paper. The final stage is to heat the toner, which melts on to the paper forming a permanent image. Laser printers are more expensive than inkjet printers, but are faster and provide superior text print quality. (*See also Inkjet printer*.)

Line spacing
The number of blank lines that are printed between each line of text. The text in this book is printed with single-line spacing. If you print with double-line spacing, each line of text is separated by a blank line.

Local area network
A communications network linking several computers within an office or building so that you can exchange files or messages with other users or send files to a printer.

Mail merge
To incorporate address details automatically from a database in any document, such as a standard letter, labels or envelopes. Almost all word processor programs let you carry out a mail merge with a database program.

Maximise
To increase the size of a window so that it fills the entire screen. To maximise any window, click on the Maximise button – the square box with thick lines in the top right-hand corner of the window.

Megabyte (MB)
A measure of the data capacity of a storage device that is equal to 1,048,576 bytes (which is equal to 2 to the power of 20 or 220). Megabytes are used to measure the storage capacity of files or drives, such as CD or DVD drives, or main memory (RAM). (*See also Kilobyte*.)

Memory
Electronic components that store data and make up the RAM (Random Access Memory) in your PC. Electronic memory chips remember data only for as long as electricity is supplied. This is not the same as disk storage, which is long-term data storage on magnetic media.

Menu bar
A line of options available that runs along the top of a window in many programs. An exception is Microsoft Office 2007 where, in some applications, such as Word and Excel, it has been replaced by the Ribbon bar. When one of the words in the Menu bar is selected, a further list of options is displayed beneath the word (this is called a dropdown menu). For example, many Windows programs have a Menu bar that starts with the word File. If you select File, it displays the options that include Open, Save and Close.

MIDI
Stands for Musical Instrument Digital Interface. This is a way of connecting electronic instruments to your computer. You tell the instruments what notes to play through the computer.

Minimise
To shrink an application or document window down to the size of an icon. To do this, select the button with the single line in the top right-hand corner of the window.

Modem
A device to convert electronic signals from your PC into sound signals that can be transmitted by phone. When receiving information, the modem works in reverse and converts the sound signals back into digital electronic signals. Modems are used to connect to the Internet and for sending and receiving faxes.

Monitor
A device that displays the text and graphics from your PC. Images are displayed as tiny dots on the screen (the smaller and closer the dots, the sharper the image).

Mouse
A small, hand-held device that is moved over a flat surface to control the position of a pointer on screen. A mouse usually has two buttons. In Windows, the left-hand button selects text or starts an application. The right-hand button displays options for the item.

Multi-tasking
The ability of Windows to run several programs at once. The trick is that Windows switches very rapidly between tasks, giving you the impression that they are running in parallel.

Network
A way of connecting several computers and printers so that they can share data. To set up a network, each PC needs a network interface card and a cable. If you are linked to a network, you'll be able to send files and messages to other users. (*See also E-mail*.)

Object Linking and Embedding (OLE)
A system that lets you cut and paste data from one application to another, retaining the formatting and controls. You can select part of a spreadsheet, switch to a word processor and paste the spreadsheet data in. To insert other objects, select the special Paste options and you'll see a list of the types of objects that you can include.

OCR
Optical Character Recognition software can convert text stored in an image file – such as from a fax or a document that has been scanned into a PC – into characters that can then be edited with a word processor. The 'translation' is not always that accurate so keep the original to check it.

On-line
(1) A modem that is currently transferring information to another modem via a telephone line.
(2) A printer that is ready and waiting to print.

Open
(1) To access a file and read its contents using an application. Most Windows applications will read a file via the File/Open menu option. In Office 2007 programs, where the Ribbon has replaced the Menu bar, it's reached via the Office button.
(2) To look inside a folder to view the list of files or sub-folders stored in it. Open a folder by clicking on it.

Operating system
The software that controls the actions of the different parts of your PC. For instance, Windows manages the screen, keyboard, disks and printers.

Page break
The point at which one page of text stops and the next starts. In Microsoft Word, you can force the start of a new page by going to the Insert tab and clicking the Page Break icon in the Pages group.

Paste
To insert a section of text or other information. To move a section of text in a document, select the text, choose Ctrl-X, move to its new location and choose Ctrl-V.

Path
The series of directories or folders that locate a particular file. If a file is in a sub-folder named Letters within a parent folder named Simon, on drive D:, its full path is D:\Simon\Letters.

PC
Stands for Personal Computer. Usually refers to an IBM-compatible computer that uses an Intel or equivalent processor and runs the Windows operating system.

PC-compatible
Software or hardware that will work on a standard PC that uses an Intel or equivalent processor and has standard ports and expansion slots.

Peripheral
Any add-on item, such as a printer or modem, that connects to your computer.

Phono connector or RCA connector
A plug and socket standard used to connect audio and video devices. If you have a sound card inside your PC, you'll see two phono connectors on the back plate. They let you connect your sound card directly to your sound system.

PhotoCD
A standard for storing 35mm photos in digital format on a CD-ROM. The PhotoCD is usually created at the same time as the photographic film is developed by digitising each frame. One PhotoCD can hold 100 photographs.

Pixel
The smallest single unit, or dot, on a monitor, or printer, the colour or brightness of which can be controlled.

Platform
The type of hardware or the combination of hardware and system software that make up a particular range of computers. For example, the platform might be an Intel Core processor running Windows Vista, or an Apple Macintosh running Mac OS X.

Pointer
A graphical symbol – usually a small arrow – used to show the position of a cursor on a monitor. If you are using Windows, the pointer changes shape according to what you are doing. For example, it is usually an arrow, but changes to an I-beam pointer (or cursor) when you are typing or editing.

POP
Stands for Point of Presence. A telephone access number for a service provider that you can use for a dial-up connection to the Internet. Most of the major service providers have dozens of POPs scattered across the country so that you can connect to the Internet with a local-rate telephone call.

Pop-up window
A window that is displayed on the screen at any time on top of anything that is already there. When the window is removed, the original screen display is restored. These are most often used to display warning messages or to confirm a choice.

Port
Communications channel that allows a computer to exchange data with a peripheral. On the back of your computer, you'll see a range of connectors. They are all ports between your computer and peripherals. (See also USB port.)

Preview
To display text or graphics on a screen as it will appear when it is printed out.

Print queue
A list of files waiting to be printed. If you are using Windows, the printing is usually controlled by the Print Manager, which temporarily stores documents on disk until the printer has finished the previous document.

Printer driver
A special file that tells Windows how to control a printer. Windows comes with hundreds of printer drivers which cover most printers. If you buy a new printer, make sure that it comes with the latest Windows printer driver.

Program
A self-contained set of software codes that is used to accomplish a particular task, such as word processing.

Properties
In Windows, the attributes of a file or object. To view or edit all the properties of a file, select the file with a single click to highlight the name, and click once on the right-hand mouse button. This displays a small menu of options. Select the Properties menu option and you will see the various properties for the object.

Protocol
Protocols form the common language that allows computers to communicate with each other. For instance, one protocol makes sure that data is correctly transferred from a PC to a printer along a printer cable. Other protocols ensure that a PC can communicate via the Internet or over a network. If you are having trouble getting two PCs to exchange information it's likely that they are using different protocols.

Prt Sc
Stands for Print Screen on an IBM PC keyboard. It is the key that sends the contents of the current screen to the printer or copies a Windows screen to the Clipboard.

Query window
(1) Window that appears when an error has occurred, asking you what action you would like to take.
(2) Window that is displayed with fields you can fill in to search a database.

Radio button
A circle displayed beside an option that has a dark centre when selected. Radio buttons are a method of selecting one of a number of options. Only one radio button in a group can be selected at any one time. If you select another in the group, the first is deselected.

RAM
Stands for Random Access Memory. The main memory chips in a PC are RAM chips, which hold the data that is being processed by the computer. The data remains in the RAM while the power is on, but is cleared once the PC is turned off. The chips are called Random because any part of the data they hold can be accessed randomly, without touching the rest of the information.

Read-only
A file or memory device whose stored data cannot be changed. A CD-ROM disc is read-only; you cannot save data on to it as you can with a hard drive.

Recycle Bin
An icon displayed on the Windows Desktop that looks like a wastepaper bin. If you want to delete a file or folder, drag it on to the Recycle Bin or press the Delete key. The contents of the Bin are not deleted from the disk until you clear it. To do this, right-click on the bin and select Empty Recycle Bin.

Red, green, blue (RGB)
High-definition monitor system that uses three separate input signals controlling red, green and blue colour picture beams.

Rename
This signifies changing the name of a file or folder. In Windows, click once on the file or folder that you want to rename and keep the pointer over the icon. After a few seconds, the description will be surrounded by a box and you can edit the name.

Resolution
This is the fineness of detail displayed on screen or printed on your printer. For printers, where characters are formed by small, tightly spaced dots, resolution is measured in dots per inch (dpi). The higher the figure the better the resolution. For monitors, the resolution is a measure of the number of pixels that are displayed on your screen. The more pixels, per given area, the sharper the image and the higher the resolution.

Ribbon bar
The Ribbon bar replaces the Menus and Toolbars in some Microsoft Office 2007 programs, including Word and Excel. The common commands you need to carry out a particular task are grouped together under separate tabs on the Ribbon bar. For example, under the Home tab, the Styles group has many of the commands for formatting text for headlines. Not all tabs are visible all of the time. The Picture Tools tab, for example, appears only when a picture is selected.

Rich text format (RTF)
A way of storing a document that includes all the commands that describe the page, type, font and formatting. RTF allows formatted pages to be exchanged between different word processors.

Run command
A command in Windows that lets you type in the name of a program that you want to run. To enter a command, click on the Start button, then All Programs, Accessories and Run.

Save
To store a document on a disk. Windows applications have a Ctrl-S shortcut for this function or you can choose the File/Save menu option. In some Office 2007 programs, including Word and Excel, click on the Office button for the Save option.

Save As
A way to save a named document to disk under a different name or in a different format. If you have written a message in Microsoft Word and want to save it in plain text format, you would click on the Office button, Save As and then Other Formats.

Scanner
A device that uses photo-electric cells to convert a drawing, photograph or document into data that can be manipulated by a PC. A flat-bed scanner has a flat sheet of glass on which the image is placed. The scan head moves below the glass. (See also Hand-held scanner.)

Screen resolutions
The original VGA standards for graphics display systems allowed screen resolutions of only 640 x 480 pixels with 16 colours. Now a 21-inch monitor will display 1600 x 1200 pixels, with the average 17 to 19-inch flat-screen monitor having 1280 x 1024 pixels. Most modern monitors can show up to 16 million colours, but the number of colours that can be shown simultaneously will also depend on the amount of memory you have on your system.

Screen saver
Software which, after a short period of inactivity, replaces the existing image on screen and displays a moving picture. Initially this was to protect against screen burn but in the case of modern monitors this is not necessary and is just for entertainment.

Scroll
To move displayed text vertically up or down a screen, one line or pixel at a time.

Search engine
The databases on the World Wide Web, which you can use to locate the information you are seeking. The main search engines include Google, Yahoo and Alta Vista. You simply

enter a keyword or two (e.g. Winston Churchill) and it will return a list of pages where those keywords were found.

Selection tool
In photo-editing and painting and drawing programs, the selection tool is an icon in a Toolbar that allows you to select an area of an image that can then be cut, copied or processed in some other way.

Server
On a network, the server is a computer that provides certain services – such as controlling who can access the network, managing print queues and printers, or enabling access to shared files or programs. On the Internet the server is responding to demands from users on their 'client' computers – so when they ask for a certain file from the server a copy is transferred to their machine.

Shareware
Software that is available free for you to sample. But if you want to keep it, you are expected to pay a fee to the writer. Often confused with public-domain software that is completely free.

Shortcut
An icon placed on the Desktop in Windows that links to a file, folder or program stored on the disk. The shortcut has the same icon as the original file except for a tiny arrow in the bottom left-hand corner. The shortcut is not a duplicate of the original – it is a pointer to the original.

Shut down
To switch off your PC. First exit Windows. This ensures that all the files are closed and that Windows sorts itself out internally before being switched off. To exit Windows Vista, select the Start button, then hover over the arrow beside the padlock and select Shut Down. With some new PCs, exiting Windows will automatically switch off the PC. With older PCs you need to wait until the screen tells you it's safe to switch off the PC.

Software
Any program or group of programs that tells the hardware how it should perform, including operating systems, word processors and applications.

Sound card
An add-on device that plugs into an expansion slot inside your PC. The sound card generates analogue sound from digital data, using either a digital to analogue converter or an FM synthesis chip. It also provides functions to record digital sound (using an analogue to digital converter) and control MIDI instruments.

Sound file
A file stored on disk that contains sound data. This can either be a digitised analogue sound signal or notes for a musical instrument digital interface (MIDI) instrument.

Spell check
A function of word processors and desktop publishing programs that checks the spelling of words by comparing them with words in a dictionary file.

Sub-directory
A directory of disk contents contained within another directory.

System software
The software that makes everything work correctly. The system software controls the hardware and manages programs. It looks after and controls all aspects of the computer. Windows is a form of system software, since it operates everything itself and does not rely on other software.

Tab key
A key on a keyboard – usually positioned on the far left, beside the Q key, with two arrows pointing in opposite horizontal directions – used to align the text at a preset tab stop. You can also use this key to cycle between any program windows that are open by pressing Alt and the Tab key.

Taskbar
A bar that usually runs along the bottom of the screen in Windows and displays the Start button and a list of other programs or windows that are currently active. You can move the entire Taskbar to any of the four sides of the screen by clicking on the bar and dragging it to another edge.

Template
A file containing a standard layout or format, such as a memo or invoice, which can be easily customised with your own details, such as company address, logo, terms and conditions, and so on.

Thesaurus
A file that contains a collection of synonyms that are displayed as alternatives. It is also a useful vocabulary guide when composing letters or any other type of document.

Tile
To arrange a group of windows so that they are displayed side by side without overlapping.

Toolbar
A window containing a variety of icons that allows you to access different tools. For example, paint programs usually have a Toolbar that includes different icons for colour, brush, circle, text and eraser tools.

ToolTips
A feature of Windows that displays a line of descriptive text under an icon when you move the pointer over that particular icon.

Undelete
A function of Windows that lets you restore deleted information or a deleted file. Unless you have set up your files to be deleted immediately, you can retrieve the file from the Recycle Bin.

Undo
A function of some applications that lets you undo the task that you've just carried out. For example, it can undo a paste or a delete operation.

Upgrade
To improve the performance or specification of your computer by adding more RAM, a larger hard disk or another kind of improvement. Software can also be upgraded from an old version to a more recent one.

URL
Stands for Uniform Resource Locator. It is the Internet system for standardising the way in which World Wide Web addresses are written. For example, the URL of the Microsoft home page is http://www.microsoft.com

USB
The Universal Serial Bus port is rapidly becoming the standard way to connect peripherals, such as scanners, printers etc, or even to set up networks. It has the advantage that as well as being fast you don't have to tinker around inside the PC to add new adapter cards. Using external hubs you can add up to 127 devices through a single port. USB also supports hot plugging, that is devices can be connected, or disconnected, without switching off the PC. The current version is USB 2.0, also known as hi-speed USB.

Video memory (VRAM)
A section of memory fitted on a video adapter that is used to store temporarily image data sent from the PC's main memory, or to store an image as it is built up and before it is displayed on the screen.

Virus
A software program created by a rogue programmer that can infiltrate your computer and cause serious damage. Some viruses are pranks, others are maliciously designed to destroy data and programs. They can get on to your hard disk from a CD-ROM or by being downloaded from the Internet. Effective anti-virus software is widely available.

Wallpaper
In Windows, an image or pattern used as a background in a window. You can change the wallpaper from within the Appearance and Personalization section of the Control Panel.

WAP
The Wireless Application Protocol is a standard that enables you to surf the Web using mobile devices, such as mobile phones or PDAs. WAP-enabled devices can view simple web pages to look at e-mail, check share prices, or get the latest traffic or weather reports.

WAVE or WAV file
A standard Windows sound file that stores an analogue signal in digital form.

Window
In programs, a portion of the screen that can contain its own document or message. Using Windows, the screen can be divided into several windows, each of which can contain a different document (or another view into the same document).

World Wide Web
Abbreviated as www. Within the Internet, millions of pages of formatted text and graphics allow a user to have a window to the Internet rather than a less user-friendly command-line. (See also Internet.)

WYSIWYG
Stands for What You See Is What You Get. A word-processing or desktop publishing program where what you see on the screen is exactly the same as the image or text that will be printed, including graphics and special fonts.

Zoom
To enlarge an area of text or graphics to make it easier to see or work on.

Index